The Gigantic Book
of Horse Wisdom

Also available from Skyhorse Publishing:

The Gigantic Book of Golf Quotations
The Gigantic Book of Baseball Quotations
The Gigantic Book of Fishing Stories
The Gigantic Book of Teachers' Wisdom

The Gigantic Book of Horse Wisdom

EDITED BY THOMAS MEAGHER

INTRODUCED BY BUCK BRANNAMAN

Skyhorse Publishing

www.skyhorsepublishing.com

Library of Congress Cataloging-in-Publication Data
The gigantic book of horse wisdom / edited by Thomas Meagher.
        p. cm.
    ISBN-13: 978-1-60239-096-6 (hardcover : alk. paper)
    ISBN-10: 1-60239-096-7 (hardcover : alk. paper)
1. Horses—Miscellanea. 2. Horses—Quotations, maxims, etc.
I. Meagher, Thomas.

SF285.G49 2007
636.1—dc22

                                        2007028968

10 9 8 7 6 5 4 3 2 1

Printed in the United States of America

With special thanks to Jeremy Selengut.

Contents

FOREWORD

People often say the American West was tamed by brave pioneers. That's partly true, but without their horses, those pioneers might still be "on their way"!

As the only available form of transportation on land in America for hundreds of years, the horse formed an ancient bond and a fragile alliance with the human, and the human with the horse.

That human was often the "Cowboy." His role developed out of the need for skilled horsemen and stockmen to tend the vast herds of cattle in North America. There have been Cowboys all around the world who have honed their skills despite great danger to themselves. Nowadays, "Cowboy" is a term that's often used derisively. But it's a shame everyone doesn't have a chance to experience the thrill of a newborn calf taking its first breath because a Cowboy had the skill to pen the cow and pull the calf—or even do a caesarean in a pasture with only a horse, a saddle, a rope, and some primitive operating instruments, managing to save two lives at the risk of his own.

Anyway, I hope you see how ignorant it is to use the term "Cowboy" with contempt.

Looking around today, we see that the horse is used for many purposes, including ranch work, dressage, jumping, reining, cutting, pleasure riding, and driving. Work with horses is therapeutic to kids who come from troubled homes. When you care for a horse and work with a horse, it can you help you find yourself and make progress as a person.

There is so much diversity in the horse world today that it often seems as though there are a multitude of cliques to be a member of! My dear departed friend Ray Harmon once said, "I hate those cliques … unless, of course, I'm included in one!" But all these groups, whether they are from the city or the country, the desert or the mountains, are attracted to the noble creature, the horse. He can make you feel secure or insecure, safe or worried, confident or doubtful, cared about … or not! All depending on how the horse feels about you and how you work with him.

In this book you will enjoy quips and quotes from many people you've heard of and many you haven't. You may find yourself thinking, "I wish I'd said that!"

The wisdom, humor, and wit in these pages will entertain, and as you read, I bet you will hope, as I do, that the bond between people and horses will always be a part of the human condition.

Buck Brannaman
July 2007

INTRODUCTION

I'm pretty certain that you love horses if you're having a peek at *The Gigantic Book of Horse Wisdom*.

But at the same time I would bet that you're wondering: "What exactly is the 'horse wisdom' this is a gigantic book of?"

Well, you might say that there are basically two types of horse wisdom, and both of them are in abundant supply throughout the hundreds of pages that follow.

On the one hand, there's wisdom about actually working with horses. In other words, useful practical advice about horsemanship and training and so on. Learning "why a horse does what he does" is absolutely crucial, and so it's usually worth listening to anyone who has given that subject the time and the study it requires. In this volume, then, you'll hear from masters who earned their hard-won knowledge through countless hours of hands-on experience. It all starts, pretty much, with Xenophon, an ancient Greek writer whose surprisingly modern advice on horses dates from around 350 BC. It then ranges through the centuries right up to today and to such respected figures as George Morris, Buck Brannaman, William Steinkraus, Pat Parelli, Jane Savoie, John Lyons, Klaus Ferdinand Hempfling, Craig Cameron, and Alois Podhajsky.

As for the second general type of horse wisdom to be found in this Gigantic Book, it also comes from working with and being around horses, but it ends up being less about them than about us. It's wisdom about ourselves, I mean. For example, to borrow one of Buck Brannaman's especially insightful observations, "Working with [horses] can be a very revealing time for the owner—any fear that was there to start with is greatly magnified. And I don't know anyone who wants the things below the surface of their psyches to be revealed publicly. Surprise! Around horses, it all comes to the surface."

It sure does.

So I think you're going to find that this book's treasure-trove of quotations will increase your own supply of both kinds of horse wisdom, and be of real use to you, as inspiration or instruction, when you're out there with your own horse sometime.

Before I turn things over to the hundreds of others who are itching to talk here, there's one last thing I've got to point out. Perhaps as you're holding this book in your hands you're worrying that maybe you haven't got the time or energy to devote to a Gigantic helping of horse wisdom.

Don't worry.

First of all, this is one book that's meant to be read in short stretches, picked up and put down, dipped into when you've got a spare moment or two.

("And when would that be, Tom?" I hear you asking. Right—I'll have to get back to you on that. But you know what I mean.)

Second, it's a book that truly has something for everyone who has a passion for horses. I mean, what a variety of people get to have their say! From Ring Lardner to Olivia Newton-John, Winston Churchill to GaWaNi Pony Boy, Joan Sutherland to Monty Roberts, Ernest Hemingway to

George Carlin, Anna Sewell to Dick Francis—folks you know, folks you don't, all of them talkin' horses.

And finally—well, I've got to admit that we've used a pretty elastic definition of "wisdom." I'm thinking especially of the stuff that'll make you laugh, such as the quip that "One way to stop a runaway horse is to bet on him." Or Bill Bryson's hilariously astute observation about one vintage television series that all of us baby boomers grew up with: "I watched a rerun on television of a 1960s comedy program called *Mr. Ed*, which was about a talking horse. Judging by the quality of the jokes, I would guess that Mr. Ed wrote his own material."

That's about it then—time to let *The Gigantic Book of Horse Wisdom* speak for itself. Hope you find it the biggest and best compilation of horse-related observations and insights ever assembled.

Thomas Meagher
July 2007

The Gigantic Book of Horse Wisdom

CHAPTER ONE

We Turn to Horses: Some Opening Observations

"Even in the twenty-first century, we turn to horses."

Simon Barnes's words came to mind the other day when I happened to be in a riding arena in Pennsylvania.

There were ten or so men and women on horseback. They were waiting at one end of the large arena. Milling around at the opposite end, having just entered from the sunny fields outside, were about a dozen cows. It was going to be interesting. Most of the riders had never worked cattle before; same for their mounts. Same, for that matter, for me. And though I was only seated in the wooden bleachers rather than on a horse, I looked on rapt, enthralled that I, raised an East Coast suburban boy, was able, even in the year 2007, to witness for the first time the unfolding of a timeless encounter that was full of such powerful historical echoes.

Then, in the space of a couple of seconds, two of the riders answered their cell phones.

Now, I try not to get annoyed when I see motorists using these infernal devices while driving. But riders in the saddle?! I don't know, it practically seemed sacrilegious, like somebody loudly yakking it up in the middle of services at church.

As I'll explain to you more fully later on, I'm still pretty "green" when it comes to horses. I fell in love with one a couple of years ago and haven't looked back: in middle age my life changed utterly. Everything about horses awes and intrigues me. I can get choked up just grooming one. Why, I even treat mucking their stalls as if it were a sacred rite. In short, in the presence of horses I feel humbled and, strange to say, called upon to be a better person than I've ever previously felt called upon to be. (More about *that* later, too.)

So my reaction to the cell-phoning cowboys—I really was shocked, you see—was obviously a newcomer's *over*reaction to the simple reality of the modern-day horse world. Sure, these amazing creatures connect us to our past and remind us that, through the course of many centuries and right up until the arrival of the automobile, we had a defining partnership with horses unlike any we enjoyed with our other domesticated animals. At the same time, however, here horses *still are,* accompanying us into a brand-new high-tech epoch. Indeed, to quote Simon Barnes at greater length this time:

"Even in the twenty-first century, we turn to horses. No, let me rephrase that. Especially in the twenty-first century, we turn to horses. Our world is too tame, too comfortable. But when we associate with horses, we claim back something of our lost wildness, our lost wilderness."

So yes, *especially* in this century . . .

Thus we turn to the start of *The Gigantic Book of Horse Wisdom,* and turn to horses.

Who would have thought that the horse, long ago replaced at its original jobs by machines, would return as one of the country's most important sport and recreational interests? . . . A century ago, people had horses in order to live; today many people live to have horses.

—ROBERT M. MILLER, D.V.M., AND RICK LAMB

———⊰◆⊱———

Working with [horses] can be a very revealing time for the owner— any fear that was there to start with is greatly magnified. And I don't know anyone who wants the things below the surface of their psyches to be revealed publicly. Surprise! Around horses, it all comes to the surface.

—BUCK BRANNAMAN

———⊰◆⊱———

A good horse has justice in his heart. I've seen it.

—CORMAC MCCARTHY

———⊰◆⊱———

Despite our best efforts, horses and accidents are, unfortunately, related subjects. . . . According to one source, "[horseback] riding, motorcycling, and automobile racing are the three most dangerous sports."

—JAMES CLARK-DAWE, ESQ.

The extraordinary and thrilling affinity between the radically different minds of humans and horses has rewarded both humans and horses for thousands of years.

—SIMON BARNES

Nothing brings such innocent joy or such profound awareness that I am not invincible as the horseback experience.

—MELISSA SOVEY-NELSON, *IF I HAD A HORSE*

Of course horses can be wrong in their truthfulness—they may report a tiger in the laundry basket or a brace of dragons flying overhead—but this wrongness isn't deception. Horses do not lie.

—HELEN HUSHER, *CONVERSATIONS WITH A PRINCE*

My mom used to say, "Winnie Willis, in the beginning God created heaven and earth and horses. And sometimes I have to wonder if the good Lord shouldn't have quit while he was ahead."

—DANDI DALEY MACKALL

Like human beings, horses are all individuals with singular personalities, their own virtues and their own faults. We become bound to them for their beauty, their eccentricities, their heart and the love they so often return to us.

—LANA SLATON

The horse—the noblest, bravest, proudest, most courageous, and certainly the most perverse and infuriating animal that humans ever domesticated.

—ANNE MCCAFFREY

Think of the horse as a pure survivor. He's an animal other animals eat; therefore, by nature, he's afraid. This instinct has kept him alive for fifty million years.

—CRAIG CAMERON

[My mother] told me the better I behaved, the better I should be treated . . . "But," said she, "there are a great many kinds of men . . . I hope you will fall into good hands; but a horse never knows who may buy him, or who may drive him; it is all a chance for us."

—ANNA SEWELL, *BLACK BEAUTY: THE AUTOBIOGRAPHY OF A HORSE*

You cannot remain unmoved by the gentleness and conformation of a well-bred and well-trained horse—more than a thousand pounds of big-boned, well-muscled animal, slick coat and sweet of smell, obedient and mannerly, and yet forever a menace . . .

—ALBERT BORGMANN, *CROSSING THE POSTMODERN DIVIDE*

The grace and beauty of the horse enthralls us today in the same way it enthralled caveman artists if many millennia ago. Horses are living works of art.

—ROBERT M. MILLER, D.V.M., *UNDERSTANDING THE ANCIENT SECRETS OF THE HORSE'S MIND*

It is not the duty of the horse to be a biofeedback mechanism for yearning humans; yet it is remarkable how consistently people with horses claim to have learned much about themselves through them.

—TOM MCGUANE

You're not working on your horse, you're working on yourself.

—RAY HUNT

Even in the twenty-first century, we turn to horses. No, let me rephrase that. Especially in the twenty-first century, we turn to horses.

—SIMON BARNES

CHAPTER TWO

Hoofprints on the Heart:
For the Love of Horses

So let me tell you about Koda.

He's a five-year-old quarter horse paint, a gelding, with, most of the time, a little bit of mischief in his eyes. (Okay, a lotta bit.) Two springs ago I looked into those eyes for the first time, and before I knew it we were a team.

Now, understand just how amazing this was. I was a few months shy of my fiftieth birthday. I had never been interested in horses—*had* no interest in them: I was merely at the stable because Alix, my wife, kept one of *her* horses there. In fact, not only was I completely *un*interested in horses, I was more than a little spooked by the two that Alix had. Not that Sasha and Tadik were bad or ornery—far from it. But look: it's a fact of life, if you reach middle age and your only contacts with horses have been betting on them at the track or going for a single brief trail ride decades earlier at a dude ranch while on a family vacation, well, you're simply not going to feel comfortable around thousand-pound animals you can't order to sit!

And I didn't feel comfortable around Koda right away, either. Ask anyone who was there at the stable during those first couple of months. I'd drive over every day, and though I would take him for walks on lead, feed him carrots, brush and curry him, or simply hang out, the whole time I was with him I was as unmistakably awkward as a kid with a crush, because I didn't have any idea what to *do* about what I was feeling.

(Other, of course, than talk about my infatuation. I was doing *that* from real early on. Indeed, it's been fair to say about me what Shakespeare's Portia declares exasperatedly about one of her maddening suitors in *The Merchant of Venice*: "He doth nothing but talk of his horse.")

But then I got lucky: an excellent teacher took me in hand and guided me into the world of natural horsemanship. Those lessons gave meaningful shape and direction to the burgeoning affection I felt for Koda. I began to learn a vocabulary of relationship and slowly began transforming myself into a horseman. Don't get me wrong: I don't pretend I'm *much* of a horseman. But listen: anyone whose life has genuinely changed because of his or her love for a horse, that person's going to do what it takes to be a good partner to that horse, and it's that striving for genuine partnership that is, so far as I'm concerned, the essence of true horsemanship.

There, anyway, is *my* horse love story. Hope it's got you in the mood for some memorable quotes about what it's like to feel "hoofprints on the heart."

He has a slight sag to his back, a short cropped mane, a nose that is scarred from too much sun exposure, and eyes that are somewhat glazed over from old eye injuries, one of them blind. But to me he is the most beautiful horse that I have ever seen.

—LYNNE M. CAULKETT, *SECOND CHANCES*

———◆———

Planes, automobiles, trains—they are great, but when it comes to getting the audience's heart going, they can't touch a horse.

—JOHN WAYNE (1907–1979)

———◆———

I feel fortunate to have the kind of love in my heart that I have for horses, because I think they've made me a better person … I've always been able to get on a horse and go for a trail ride and come back a better person, come back with a clearer mind.

—MEL BLOUNT

———◆———

Sometimes, when I'm lying in bed at night, … I play a game in my head, trying to recall the names of all the horses I've known since moving west from Illinois … They carried me from paycheck to paycheck, from Colorado to the Canadian line.

—TOM GRONEBERG, *ONE GOOD HORSE*

There is something about a horse that is good for the heart of a child.

—CHERRY HILL

You don't sell family members, and you don't sell your dream.

—KELLI KAMINSKI, ON TURNING DOWN A $150,000 OFFER FOR HER CHAMPION BARREL RACER ROCKEM SOCKEM GO

The horses remained my one real source of relief. When I was in their presence, nothing else mattered. Horses neither disapproved nor approved of what I looked like. All that counted was how I treated them.

—LUCY GREALY

Through the days of love and celebration and joy, and through the dark days of mourning—the faithful horse has been with us always.

—Elizabeth Cotton

How can anyone bear to put a horse—a horse that he loves—at risk? … Horses themselves seek excitement. I have put a horse at risk, many times, and it has brought me great joy. If the horse had died, I would never have forgiven myself …

—Simon Barnes

The essential joy of being with horses is that it brings us in contact with the rare elements of grace, beauty, spirit, and fire.

—Sharon Ralls Lemon

I like to visit my horse, have a walk with my dog.

—Cornelia Funke

When it comes to horses, there is no such thing as a passing fancy. They're a constant in life.

—VICKY MOON, *THE PRIVATE PASSION OF JACKIE KENNEDY ONASSIS*

———

A job and a place to train a colt. This is such a gift, out of the blue on a cold, gray day … The pieces of my life will fall into place again and everything will make sense.

—TOM GRONEBERG

———

The love of horses which they had, alive, and care of chariots, after death survive.

—VIRGIL

———

Courage, wisdom born of insight and humility, empathy born of compassion and love, all can be bequeathed by a horse to his rider.

—CHARLES DE KUNFFY

———

We horsemen live in a little world by ourselves. We live, breathe, and dream horses. We become so wrapped up in horses that we do not understand why everyone cannot understand us.

—P. T. ALBERT

A horse is a thing of such beauty … none will tire of looking at him as long as he displays himself in his splendor.

—XENOPHON

As a young girl I think I wanted to be a horsewoman. I loved horses.

—KAREN HUGHES

The path of learning, experiences, and challenges offered to us by horses is never-ending.

—PERRY WOOD, *REAL RIDING: HOW TO RIDE IN HARMONY WITH HORSES*

God forbid that I should go to any Heaven in which there are no horses.

—R. B. CUNNINGHAME-GRAHAM, IN A 1917 LETTER TO THEODORE
ROOSEVELT

Horses leave hoofprints on your heart.

—ANONYMOUS

Everything depends upon myself and my horse.

—MAMIE FRANCIS

There are many wonderful places in the world, but one of my favorite places is on the back of my horse.

—ATTRIBUTED TO VARIOUS

If a poet knows more about a horse than he does about heaven, he might better stick to the horse, and some day the horse may carry him into heaven.

—CHARLES IVES

The horse loves the hound, and I loves both.

—R. S. SURTEES

In the steady gaze of the horse shines a silent eloquence that speaks of love, loyalty, strength and courage. It is the window that reveals to us how willing is his spirit, how generous his heart.

—L. MCGUIRE

To see the wind's power, the rain's cleansing and the sun's radiant life, one need only to look at the horse.

—UNKNOWN AUTHOR

Whenever I was upset by something in the papers, Jack always told me to be more tolerant, like a horse flicking away flies in the summer.

—JACKIE KENNEDY ONASSIS

A stubborn horse walks behind you, an impatient horse walks in front of you, but a noble companion walks beside you.

—ANONYMOUS

When you are buying a horse, take care not to fall in love with him, for when this passion hath once seized you, you are no longer in a condition to judge his imperfections.

—ANONYMOUS

Some people have animal eyes—bears' eyes, cats' eyes, pigs' eyes—but horses have human eyes and I love horses better than people.

—JOSÉ GARCÍA VILLA

Closeness, friendship, affection—keeping your own horse means all these things.

—BERTRAND LECLAIR

I would much rather … look at one horse—his eyes, his nature, his suffering or, even better, his good fortune …

—KLAUS FERDINAND HEMPFLING

Nowadays, since my horse died of a stroke, I don't ride anymore, though I miss it.

—ANNE MCCAFFREY

I really like his character. If he was a person now, he'd be my best friend.

—IAN MILLER, ON HIS HORSE BIG BEN

Horses aren't my whole life, but they make my life whole.

—LINDSEY STEWART

I'm going to live in the country with my horse and I'll get a nine-to-five; I don't need this.

—STELLA MCCARTNEY

A lovely horse is always an experience … It is an emotional experience of the kind that is spoiled by words.

—BERYL MARKHAM

Suburban housewives sandwich an hour's hacking between carpools and shopping trips, and when dinner talk turns to riding, they and their children persuade Daddy to try. He does, likes it in spite of stiff muscles, and joins several commuter pals in an evening instruction class at the stable.

—STEVEN D. PRICE, *PANORAMA OF AMERICAN HORSES*

I am sure you have a dream horse. What do you see in this dream creature? You probably see beauty and balance, rhythm, lightness, and power, and you probably see all of these qualities demonstrated with confidence, attentiveness, and delight.

—SALLY SWIFT

But a horse is a labor of love as well as a responsibility, an aesthetic as well as a dynamic pleasure, something to contemplate as well as ride.

—SARAH MONTAGUE

I go about looking at horses and cattle. They eat grass, make love, work when they have to, bear their young. I am sick with envy of them.

—SHERWOOD ANDERSON (1876–1941)

A man that don't love a horse, there is something the matter with him.

—WILL ROGERS (1879–1935)

I would travel only by horse, if I had the choice.

—LINDA MCCARTNEY

———✦◆✦———

Is it the smell of their body as I hug their long neck,
Or the scent only a horse has that I can't forget?
Is it the depth of their eyes as they contentedly rest?
No, it's just being around them that I like the best.

—TERESA BECKER

———✦◆✦———

Whose laughs are hearty, tho' his jests are coarse,
And loves you best of all things—but his horse.

—ALEXANDER POPE (1688–1744)

———✦◆✦———

Horses are my family—sisters and brothers.

—TERESA TSIMMU MARTINO, *HORSE NATION: TRUE STORIES ABOUT HORSES AND PEOPLE*

———✦◆✦———

He doth nothing but talk of his horse.

—WILLIAM SHAKESPEARE

———◆———

I think the greatest experience that I've ever had with horses, I mean
the absolute greatest, is during foaling time, during foaling season in the
spring … When the babies are born on the ranch, it is absolute joy.

—CLAY WALKER

———◆———

It all dates from those summers alone in the high desert, my lying on my
belly and watching wild horses with my binoculars for hours at a time.
Straining to see in the moonlight, striving to fathom mustang ways, I
knew instinctively I had chanced upon something important. …

—MONTY ROBERTS

———◆———

Called my Roland his pet name, my horse without peer.

—ROBERT BROWNING (1812–1889)

———◆———

After seeing kids play polo against big guys, it only shows that horses are the greatest equalizer in the world. No matter what you weigh, the little fellow is your equal on a horse.

—WILL ROGERS

Hardly any feeling is more distressing than the certain knowledge that you and your horse are about to part company.

—MICHAEL KORDA, *Horse People*

My own horse fever I trace to my conviction that to write of horses I had to ride horses. … Long after it made practical sense, I kept hanging around horses.

—LAWRENCE SCANLAN, *Wild About Horses*

There comes a point in every rider's life when he wonders if it's all worth it. Then look at the horse, and he realizes—it is.

—KELLY STEWART

If a man sweats while doing a job horseback, that's somehow romantic; if the same man soils his hands afoot, he's nothing more than a common laborer.

—KURT MARKUS

Blind with love, my daughter
has cried nightly for horses,
those long-necked marchers and churners
that she has mastered, any and all,
reining them in like a circus hand.

—ANNE SEXTON, *PAIN FOR A DAUGHTER*

I can look a whole day with delight upon a handsome picture, though it be but of an horse.

—SIR THOMAS BROWNE (1605–1682)

Horses are something to dream about … and to wish for; fun to watch … and to make friends with; nice to pat … and great to hug: and, oh, what a joy to ride!

—DOROTHY HENDERSON PINCH, *HAPPY HORSEMANSHIP*

Don't let me take any horses home with me. It doesn't matter so much about stray dogs and kittens, but elevator boys get awfully stuffy when you try to bring in a horse.

—DOROTHY PARKER (1893–1967)

So many young girls collect statues of horses and decorate their bedroom walls with photos of horses. … [S]ome, when they have had the opportunity to stroke a real, live horse are reluctant to wash their hand so they can keep that heavenly scent around for as long as possible.

—CHERRY HILL

When I looked at life from the saddle, it was as near to heaven as it was possible to be.

—DAISY GREVILLE, COUNTESS OF WARWICK (1861–1938)

We attended stables, as we attended church, in our best clothes, no doubt showing the degree of respect due to horses, no less than the deity.

—SIR OSBERT SITWELL (1892–1969)

A true horseman does not look at the horse with his eyes, he looks at his horse with his heart.

—ANONYMOUS

I had every reason to give up on the human race for good, it was the horses that rescued my soul and renewed my passion for living.

—CHRIS IRWIN AND BOB WEBER, *DANCING WITH YOUR DARK HORSE*

———

Dog lovers hate to clean out kennels. Horse lovers like cleaning stables.

—MONICA DICKENS

———

If you have seen nothing but the beauty of their markings and limbs, their true beauty is hidden from you.

—AL-MUTANABBI, (C. 915–965)

———

Horses show people that there are other wills and other consciences.

—KLAUS BALKENHOL

———

Of all creature God made at the Creation, there is none more excellent, or so much to be respected as a horse.

—BEDOUIN LEGEND

————◆————

A man, a horse, and a dog never get weary of each other's company.

—ANONYMOUS

————◆————

People, then, are not friend to horses unless their horses love them in return.

—PLATO (C. 428–348 BC)

————◆————

Nothing is more sacred as the bond between horse and rider … no other creature can ever become so emotionally close to a human as a horse.

—STEPHANIE M. THORN

————◆————

My beautiful! My beautiful! That standest meekly by,
With thy proudly arch'd and glossy neck, and dark and fiery eye.
Fret not to roam the desert now, with all thy winged speed;
I may not mount on thee again—thou'rt sold, my Arab steed!

—CAROLINE NORTON (1808–1877)

Most important is love of the horse.

—WALDEMAR SEUNIG

When a horse is right for the owner, a precious bond ... a very real form
of love ... emerges from the response of one to the other.

—BETSY TALCOTT KELLEHER, *SOMETIMES A WOMAN NEEDS A HORSE*

The horses are blessed, chosen by God.

—TERESA TSIMMU MARTINO, *DANCER ON THE GRASS*

When a horse dies, the memory lives on because an enormous part of his owner's heart, soul, very existence dies also … but that can never be laid to rest, it is not meant to be.

—STEPHANIE M. THORN

The eternal and wonderful sight of horses at liberty is magical to watch.

—BERTRAND LECLAIR

I discovered a love for horses—the sound of them eating, how neat it is to come across a horse that's sweet and friendly and willing to spend a little time with you.

—CHRIS IRWIN, *HORSES DON'T LIE*

Machinery may make for efficiency and a standardization of life, but horse love is a bond of freemasonry, which unites the entire race.

—WILLIAM FAWCETT (1894–1974)

My obsession with horses was so great that I kept sugar cubes in my jacket pocket on the miraculous chance that I would somehow run into a horse I could befriend.

—SUSAN FARR FAHNCKE, *THE GIFT OF A DREAM*

The delicate and exquisite horse is itself a work of art.

—BERTRAND LECLAIR

The hooves of a horse! Oh! Witching and sweet
Is the music earth steals from the iron-shod feet;
No whisper of love, no trilling of bird,
Can stir me as hooves of the horse have stirred.

—WILL H. OGILVIE

This most noble beast is the most beautiful, the swiftest and of the highest courage of domesticated animals. His long mane and tail adorn and beautify him. He is of a fiery temperament, but good temperament, obedient, docile and well-mannered.

—PEDRO GARCIA-CONDE

Another reason why horses are so amazing: they can keep it interesting for a whole lifetime, and then some!

—PERRY WOOD, *REAL RIDING: HOW TO RIDE IN HARMONY WITH HORSES*

The warmest feeling arrives when you know the horse you love is all cozy and snug, and it's all because of you.

—FIONA-LOUISE MILLER

I can't help it, Father. I'd sooner have that horse happy than go to heaven.

—ENID BAGNOLD

And when you find yourself sleeping in the barn, waiting for your favorite mare to give birth to her first foal … you will admit, yes, you are a horse maniac; yes, it is incurable and yes, you wouldn't trade it for anything else in the world.

—JACKLYN LEE LINDSTROM

Visions of horses … make the moment brighter, inspire respect, and make the heart beat faster.

—THE FOUNDERS OF THE SUNSHINE HORSE LOVERS CLUB

She lifted the drooping muzzle with both hands. … It was a special embrace saved for special occasions.

—JEAN M. AUEL

Stars on faces, pearly socks on legs, whorls in hair—all are signs of wisdom or luck. Special horses carry birthmarks on their necks or shoulders, like thumbprints.

—TERESA TSIMMU MARTINO, *DANCER ON THE GRASS*

A gorgeous creature, born to live and run free and wild, but kind enough to share his abilities with us.

—SALLY SWIFT

Any halfway lonesome child who currycombs some rows in the dust caked on a horse's broad neck, or takes a minute to rub the white star on his forehead, is prompted by this look to feel that the horse loves and understands her as no one else.

—MARY KARR

He's the kind of horse with a faraway look. He'll sure take a man through some awful places and sometimes only one comes out.

—WILL JAMES

No matter how hungry he may be, [the cowman] takes care of his horse before looking after his own comfort.

—RAMON ADAMS

What a wonderful treat I had been given! To observe these beautiful animals, running free, was the greatest adventure I could have asked for.

—KAREN BUMGARNER

I have seen things so beautiful they have brought tears to my eyes. Yet none of them can match the gracefulness and beauty of a horse running free.

—ANONYMOUS

I ate, lived, and slept horses. I used to love even the smell of the tack—cleaned, oiled, and shined to an old burnished shimmer.

—CHRISTILOT HANSON BOYLEN

A horse certainly can't offer wise counsel to help solve a woman's problems, but a listening ear is always supportive, even a long, hairy one!

—BETSY TALCOTT KELLEHER, *SOMETIMES A WOMAN NEEDS A HORSE*

I inhaled her horse scent, that delicious sweetness that I would come to love.

—INGRID SOREN

It is wonderful when one is out with these animals, how attached they become. There were times when I would walk up to my horse, that he would nicker in a low tone and rub his nose against me in a very knowing manner.

—H. S. YOUNG

I rejoice in the union with a spirit who speaks to me with his heart. ...
And I understand.

—CAROLE HUDGENS

To learn all that a horse could teach, was a world of knowledge, but only
a beginning ... Look into a horse's eye and you instantly know if you can
trust him.

—MARY O'HARA

All horses deserve, at least once in their lives, to be loved by a little girl.

—ANONYMOUS

Humans experience unique forms of companionship with horses.

—ALLEN ANDERSON, *ANGEL HORSES*

A good soldier, like a good horse, cannot be of a bad color.

—OLIVER WENDELL HOLMES (1809–1894)

Names are important to horse people.

—SUSAN RICHARDS, *CHOSEN BY A HORSE: A MEMOIR*

Never let his fire die out, but kindle it with words. Let him know that you are honored to be carried along on his strong shoulders and swift feet.

—CARL RASWAN

When I am grown, I will have one hundred horses if I want.

—NATALIE KINSEY-WARNOCK, *IF WISHES WERE HORSES*

A fine little smooth horse colt
Should move a man as much as doth a son.

—THOMAS KYD (1558–1594)

The officer who never looks after his ponies, after a game, to see that they are properly put away, or who at the end of a long march or hard drill says, "Sergeant, fix up the horses. …" is without pride and lazy, and the men know it and despise him..

—GEORGE S. PATTON, JR.

The older I get the more I enjoy watching my daughter riding around the ring with no hands, jumping her pony and having fun.

—JAN WESTMARK, *KIDS BOUNCE, ADULTS DON'T!*

After fourteen years of struggling and hoping for more, I got a horse!

—BETSY TALCOTT KELLEHER, *SOMETIMES A WOMAN NEEDS A HORSE*

Horses are very forgiving of the people who truly love them.

—GINCY SELF BUCKLIN

———◆———

Beauty, delicacy, and position—these were the foundations of courtly equestrianism.

—HENNING EICHBERG

———◆———

Go anywhere in England where there are natural, wholesome, contented, and really nice English people; and what do you find? That the stables are the real center of the household.

—GEORGE BERNARD SHAW (1856–1950)

———◆———

To be loved by a horse, or by any animal, should fill us with awe—for we have not deserved it.

—MARION GARRETTY

———◆———

My horse has a hoof of striped agate. His fetlock is like fine eagle plume. His legs are like quick lightning. My horse has a tail like a trailing black cloud. His mane is made of short rainbows. My horse's eyes are made of big stars.

—NAVAJO WAR GODS HORSE SONG

Where in this wide world can a person find nobility without pride, friendship without envy, or beauty without vanity? Here, where grace is laced with muscle and strength by gentleness confined.

—RONALD DUNCAN

A horse will overcome its inborn shyness and gain confidence, the fundamental condition for mutual understanding, with a man whose love it feels. Subsequently, when strictness or punishment becomes necessary, the horse will know that it was deserved, for it has never suffered injustice or arbitrariness.

—WALDEMAR SEUNIG

All the centuries that men went to war on well-trained steeds seem trivial compared to a single moment of understanding between a teenage girl and her first bay mare.

—LINDA KOHANOV, *THE TAO OF EQUUS*

When I was a young girl, I thought of being a mounted policewoman, because I figured I could ride horses and be paid for it—what a job!

—OLIVIA NEWTON-JOHN

Love means attention, which means looking after the things we love. We call this stable management.

—GEORGE H. MORRIS, *THE AMERICAN JUMPING STYLE*

Dear to me is my bonnie white steed;
oft has he helped me at pinch of need.

—SIR WALTER SCOTT (1771–1832)

It may be broadly stated that . . . of all animals kept for the recreation of mankind the horse is alone capable of exciting a passion that shall be absolutely hopeless.

—BRET HARTE

I stopped by a former riding buddy's place. The first thing she asked when I walked up to the door was "You wanna buy a horse?" I chuckled but throughout our visit her question stuck in my mind like a dream that you can't quite shake. *Do* I want to buy a horse?

—CHERYL KIMBALL, FROM *HORSE WISE*

A family photo shows me . . . in favored costume: cowboy hat, western dress, steer horn round my neck. I look doe-eyed and awestruck, for beside me are my heroes of the day, Gene Autry and his famous horse Champion—replete with tiny guns on his bit shanks and tack embossed with shining silver.

—CAROLE FLETCHER AND LAWRENCE SCANLAN, *HEALED BY HORSES: A MEMOIR*

But it took a horse … the training, in fact, of a headstrong young mare … to open the door to a new world that began to nourish my lonely spirit.

—BETSY TALCOTT KELLEHER, *SOMETIMES A WOMAN NEEDS A HORSE*

An instinct sympathy which makes the horse and master one heart, one pulse, one understanding love—is never made, but born.

—GEORGE AGNEW CHAMBERLAIN

When they lay me down to rest,
Put my spurs and rope upon my chest,
Get my friends to carry me and then go turn my horses free.

—EPITAPH FOR CLYDE KENNEDY

Many professional horsemen scoff at anything that resembles a sentimental relationship between horse and rider. Yet, I have heard these same men admit countless times that horses perform better for some people than others. They're apt to attribute it to anything but what I think it is—love.

—WALTER FARLEY

Soon I shall go to sleep, in hopes of seeing him again. His intelligent soft eyes, his elegant head. His soft heart, and his four legs. For my horse is a dream, a dream of the making.

—LINDSAY TURCOTTE

I should like to be a horse.

—ELIZABETH II, WHEN ASKED ABOUT HER AMBITIONS AS A CHILD

Little Bay has been in horse heaven for many years now. When I get there I plan to have oats in my pocket for the best friend a girl ever had.

—CINDY JOHNSON HARPER, *OATS IN MY POCKET*

Children are naturally attracted to horses, and children have a knack for finding out about horses and falling in love with them. They don't need to be in the presence of a real horse for the magic to occur.

—JESSICA JAHIEL, *THE PARENT'S GUIDE TO HORSEBACK RIDING*

Our horses are our friends, companions, partners, teammates, and soul mates. They give us so much, so willingly—their strength, stamina, agility, and beauty—to give us the chance to vicariously experience freedom and power that comes so naturally to them.

—JESSIE SHIERS, *101 HORSEKEEPING TIPS*

Your horse loves you; not for your looks, but for your love!

—ANONYMOUS

———◆———

I ask more of each horse than is fair … Companionship, a listening ear, a soft neck to bury my face in … a friend. They stand ready, puzzled by the human woman, but willing to be with her. They are strong medicine for me.

—SHELLEY R. ROSENBERG, *MY HORSES, MY HEALERS*

———◆———

Horses must be loved at a distance until they let you into their hearts with the acknowledgement that you are a nice person after all, maybe even a friend.

—ALLEN ANDERSON, *ANGEL HORSES*

———◆———

I heard … the pounding of hooves—a herd of wild horses swept through the forest before us. An old bay mare led the way, followed by several mares heavy with foal … copper coats gleaming in the sun. They were as beautiful as any horses I had ever seen.

—DAYTON O. HYDE, *ALL THE WILD HORSES*

The barn smelled of horses, leather, hay, and creosote, a scent that was as familiar to Cassie as the smell of her own home. As familiar and as loved.

—LAURA MOORE

I cannot remember when I did not love horses.

—CAROLE FLETCHER AND LAWRENCE SCANLAN, *HEALED BY HORSES: A MEMOIR*

A horse is wonderful by definition.

—PIERS ANTHONY

There on the tips of fair fresh flowers feedeth he;
How joyous is his neigh, …
There in the midst of sacred pollen hidden all hidden he;
How joyous is his neigh.

—NAVAJO SONG

As a boy in a prairie town I learned early to revere the workhorse. To me, as to all boys, a dog was a slave, but a horse was a hero. And the men who handled him were heroes too.

—JAMES STEVENS

Go into a stall; close the door. Wait a moment. Something will occur to you, something that seems to shift in the air between the two of you. It is the weight of power … The horse is there looking at you … He cannot escape you, or whatever it is you mean to do with him.

—MELISSA PIERSON

What is a horse? It is freedom so indomitable that it becomes useless to imprison it to serve man: it lets itself be domesticated, but with a simple, rebellious toss of the head … it shows that its inner nature is always wild, translucent and free.

—CLARICE LISPECTOR, *DRY POINT OF HORSES*

As parents, when our child loves horses, we are first taken aback and then pleased on some deep subliminal level that our child has dragged us into this world where time has stopped and the language becomes one of smells and whinnies and warmth.

—SUSAN DANIELS, *THE HORSE SHOW MOM'S SURVIVAL GUIDE*

When I dream, I hear hoofbeats. The sound is so pure. A rapid thunder on a hard packed dirt track.

—JESSE COLT, *WHEN I DREAM I HEAR HOOFBEATS*

Silence takes on a new quality when the only sound is that of regular and smooth hoof beats.

—BERTRAND LECLAIR

People offered fabulous prices for the steed, but the old man ... refused. "This horse is not a horse to me. ... It is a person ... He is a friend, not a possession. How could you sell a friend?" The man was poor ... the temptation ... great. But he never sold the horse.

—MAX LUCADO, *THE OLD MAN AND THE WHITE HORSE*

I thought I'd gone to heaven: Never having seen the countryside from the back of a horse before ... I was in my element.

—INGRID SOREN, *ZEN AND HORSES*

Throughout my life, there have been several occasions in which I found myself in awe of that which exists between women and horses.

—GAWANI PONY BOY, *OF WOMEN AND HORSES*

I know I am a woman kept by horses.

—SHELLEY R. ROSENBERG, *MY HORSES, MY HEALERS*

———◆———

My horse, he spurs with sharp desire my heart.

—SIR PHILIP SIDNEY (1554–1586)

———◆———

The horse-crazy child will find horses everywhere.

—JESSICA JAHIEL, *THE PARENT'S GUIDE TO HORSEBACK RIDING*

———◆———

I've come to realize that women and horses are fully capable of weaving new myths into the future, perspectives based not on conquest and domination, but on harmony and collaboration.

—LINDA KOHANOV, *THE TAO OF EQUUS*

———◆———

But whether you regard the horse with awe or love, it is impossible to escape the sheer power of his presence, the phenomenal influence he exerts on the lives of all of us who decided at some stage that we wanted to become riders.

—MARY WANLESS, *THE NATURAL RIDER*

You know you love your horse when your mouth waters at the sight of a wagon-full of hay.

—ANONYMOUS

She was the embodiment of all that I love about horses—their nobility, their strength, their beauty and gentleness, and their amazing generosity of spirit.

—JENNIFER FORSBERG MEYER, *A FRIEND LIKE NO OTHER*

The horse. Man's noblest companion.

—Anonymous

I love horses with all that is in me. Some people think of them as animals—I think of them as my friends, my greatest friends.

—Steve Donoghue

The nature of the horse remains unchanged, whether it carries the saddle of the prince, or whether it draws the cart of the wagoner. The noble ones accept the yoke, they serve, but will never be slaves, for to themselves they can never be traitors.

—H. H. Isenbart

The horses were all so incredibly beautiful. Most of these wondrous creatures were mares and young fillies. ... My heart was bursting with love for all these graceful and beautiful creatures.

—JESSE COLT, *WHEN I DREAM I HEAR HOOFBEATS*

Kissed by sunlight, embraced by open fields. The horse is the center of all beautiful things.

—ANONYMOUS

I don't have a clue about this horse stuff other than I really want one.

—MARLENE MCRAE

They are more beautiful than anything in the world, kinetic sculptures, perfect form in motion.

—KATE MILLET

Fierce as the fire and fleet as the wind …

—A. L. GORDON

❖

Despite the unique all-around athleticism of the horse, "keeping on keeping on" is what most horses do best.

—MATTHEW MACKAY-SMITH

❖

The word *Chivalry* is derived from the French *cheval*, a horse.

—THOMAS BULFINCH (1796–1867)

❖

Horse people may be heads of state or professionally unemployed in their private lives, but horses are their passion, as Jerusalem was the passion of a soldier in some ancient crusade.

—JUDITH KRANTZ

❖

Enthusiasm for horses cuts across generations.

—STEVEN D. PRICE

Billy was a boy who loved horses more than anything in the world.

—C. W. ANDERSON, *BILLY AND BLAZE*

Honor lies in the mane of a horse.

—HERMAN MELVILLE (1819–1891)

In those border days every rider loved his horse as a part of himself.
If there was a difference between any rider of the sage and Bostil, it was,
as Bostil had more horses, so had he more love.

—ZANE GREY (1872–1939)

The horse is a creature who sacrifices his own being to exist through the will of another … he is the noblest conquest of man.

—GEORGES-LOUIS LECLERC, COMTE DE BUFFON (1707–1788)

There is a touch of divinity even in brutes, and a special halo about a horse that should forever exempt him from indignities.

—HERMAN MELVILLE

He had a horse—he dam' well had a horse!

—JOHN GALSWORTHY (1867–1933)

One of the sayings in the horse world is that a clean horse is a happy horse, but in my experience this is not really true. Horses like dirt, and go to considerable trouble to burrow around in as much of it as they can find.

—HELEN HUSHER, *CONVERSATIONS WITH A PRINCE*

Every evening at five o'clock when she got off work, we would go out to the barn and work with the horses. That was our entire pastime early in our relationship. It was nothing but horses.

—CLAY WALKER

Horse, you are truly a creature without equal, for you fly without wings and conquer without sword.

—THE KORAN

He was a terrific horse, my Black. He wasn't afraid of anything. He could climb the steepest hills, gallop to my heart's content and neigh on command. Always obedient and happy to be with me, he was my companion and friend on endless outings.

—CHRISTA IACONO, *THE PERFECT HORSE*

I remember feeling—no, I remember knowing, even then—that I was misplaced. *You belong with the horses,* my mind whispered. My eager heart could only whicker a soft response.

—DIANE LEE WILSON, *I RODE A HORSE OF MILK WHITE JADE*

And if he was going to lose a finger or a chunk of his backside, let it be a horse that bit him.

—JOHN O'HARA

Yes, I've just bought a new horse, named Jedi.

—BRUCE BOXLEITNER

She was his wife … He and she got along well … though sometimes he wished he had someone to talk to about horses.

—WILLIAM FAIN, *HARMONY*

I met my first horse when I could barely walk. … I stumbled into a pasture, drawn to the wonder of a tall, yellow stallion. He stood patiently as I gripped his legs and pulled myself upright. That was my first gift from a horse—support.

—TERESA TSIMMU MARTINO, *HORSE NATION: TRUE STORIES ABOUT HORSES AND PEOPLE*

Horses are very intelligent creatures, and emotional sensitivity is something that all intelligent, thinking creatures possess.

—BUCK BRANNAMAN

I love horses. If I could, I would ride the whole day. When I get married, I'll live in the countryside, ride on horses and live among cows, chickens, and dogs.

—GISELE BÜNDCHEN

This is really a lovely horse and I speak from personal experience since I once mounted her mother.

—TED WALSH

If a car passes me when I'm on a horse, I always think: "If I were in that car and saw me, I would wish I was me." Wistful children's faces, staring out of the back window, agree.

—MONICA DICKENS

She was the most beautiful horse in the world.

—ALISON HART

There are friends and faces that may be forgotten, but there are horses that never will be.

—CINDY ADAMS

I love the horse as I have said,
From head to hoof and back again.

—James Whitcomb Riley

I am fortunate that I can look out my back door and see my beautiful
horses looking back at me. I am so grateful that I get to watch them
run in their mountain pastures every day. I hope I never stop learning
from them.

—Kim Morton

My horse's feet are as swift as rolling thunder … His mane is there
to wipe away my tears.

—Bonnie Lewis

It is quite right what they say: the three most beautiful sights in the world
are a ship in full sail, a galloping horse, and a woman dancing.

—Honoré de Balzac (1799–1850)

The most beautiful, the most spirited and the most inspiring creature ever to print foot on the grasses of America.

—J. FRANK DOBIE, ON MUSTANGS

A four-legged friend,
a four-legged friend,
He'll never let you down.

—JACK BROOKS, *A FOUR LEGGED FRIEND*

I could proudly say I had made this horse all that he was—with my imagination, my black crayons and a scrap piece of plywood. Black was the best make-believe horse a little girl ever straddled.

—CHRISTA IACONO, *THE PERFECT HORSE*

And then I bought my own horse, which I had until it died.

—ERIC ROBERTS

My horse a thing of wings, myself a god.

—Wilfrid Scawen Blunt (1840–1922)

Before I loved horses, I had nothing to live for. Now I love horses and can't stop seeing things to live for.

—Anonymous

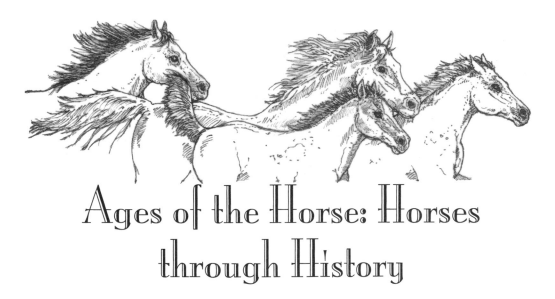

CHAPTER THREE

Ages of the Horse: Horses through History

Since my office is only a couple miles from home, I occasionally daydream about riding my horse to work.

I know: it's a completely crazy idea.

But wait—the fantasy starts out plausibly enough: we leave my farm and amble across the open fields.

So far, so good. A lovely picture…

Reality, though, soon barges in. Koda and I have to leave the fields and—some of those pickups *roar* by, don't they?—cautiously edge along the paved road as we follow the winding downhill into town. And when, having arrived at the ramshackle building (I'm upstairs over a grocery store), I prepare to leave Koda tied to some makeshift hitching post—well, the idyll falls right to pieces. I mean, even in this down-at-heel, formerly agricultural community you just can't leave a horse like they do in old Westerns.

Utter madness!

Still, I mention my daydream because I think it reflects the way that many of us horse lovers occasionally find ourselves feeling envious of the good old days, back when horses played a much bigger part in everyday life. Horses used to be everywhere, doing everything! Indeed, as John Trotwood Moore reminds us, "wherever man has left his footprint in the long ascent from barbarism to civilization, we will find the hoofprint of the horse beside it."

Yes, it was a glorious partnership, once upon a time.

And that's why I was puzzled, early in my horseman's education, to find people saying that this is actually a *good* era for horses, and maybe even a *better* one than any other. How, I wondered, could that be? After all, there are hardly any of those side-by-side foot- and hoofprints any more; our paths, it seems, diverged for good, as Margaret and Michael Korda point out: "the knowledge of how to care for horses went from common-place and normal to rare and esoteric in one generation. ... The generation that preceded the First World War was raised in the Age of the Horse; the generation that followed was raised in the Age of the Automobile."

What I came to realize, however, is that the Age of the Horse was in fact pretty damn rough on the horses themselves. Were you aware, for example, that many millions of them died in World War I? Or have you ever contemplated the stark truth that Lawrence Scanlan puts before us when he notes that "the history of horsemanship is less about sugar than pepper, less about light than dark, less about mindful kindness than thoughtless cruelty"?

No wonder, then, if the Age of the Auto turns out to be a better deal for horses, since a greater percentage of them now spend their lives with people who *want* to have them, rather than *need* to have them.

Worth pondering, at any rate, as you read the following quotations having to do with horses and history—their own, and the one they've shared with us.

Once tamed, horses changed human history.

—PATRICIA LAUBER, *THE TRUE-OR-FALSE BOOK OF HORSES*

———◆———

Horseshoes were common by the eleventh century, and by the twelfth century were being mass produced.

—DEBORAH EVE RUBIN, *HORSE TRIVIA: A HIPPOFILE'S DELIGHT*

———◆———

In the late 1920s, man-versus-horse races became popular across the country. [In 1927] Paul "Hardrock" Simpson ... took on a Texas pony named Maude in 500-mile race with a $500 prize. Exhausted, they both called it quits after two days. Simpson had covered 145 miles; Maude, 150.

—JOANNA SAYAGO, *RUNNER'S WORLD*

———◆———

The horse was acquired by the Sioux in 1770. By 1890 we were all confined to reservations. We still had horses, but we were no longer the great horse culture living that life.

—LINDA LITTLE WOLF

They had metal sandals for the Roman draft horses that they tied on to the horse's foot with a thong, but those could go no faster than a walk, so they were not used for the cavalry horses.

—SABINE KELLS

The largest horse in history was a Shire horse named Sampson, later renamed Mammoth, foaled in 1846 in Bedfordshire, England. He stood 21.2 $^1/_2$ hands high (i.e., 7 ft. 2 $^1/_2$ in. or 2.20m), and his peak weight was estimated at over 3,300 pounds.

—WIKIPEDIA

The knowledge of how to care for horses went from commonplace and normal to rare and esoteric in one generation. … The generation that preceded the First World War was raised in the Age of the Horse; the generation that followed was raised in the Age of the Automobile.

—Margaret Korda and Michael Korda, *Horse Housekeeping*

For at least fourteen thousand years before the arrival of the horse, Native Americans used dogs in everyday life. … When horses came along, it was only natural … to view them as big dogs. The horse was called big dog, medicine dog, elk dog, spirit dog, and mysterious dog.

—GaWaNi Pony Boy

The Bedouin people customarily congratulated each other on three occasions: The birth of a son, the emergence of a poet within a tribe, and when a foal was born.

—Bachir Bserani

In backwoods justice horse stealing was worse than manslaughter and a frequent occasion for lynching. To call a man a horse thief was the ultimate insult.

— DEBORAH EVE RUBIN, *HORSE TRIVIA: A HIPPOFILE'S DELIGHT*

The difference between people who own horses and horsemen is that horsemen are people who appreciate the sacrifice a horse has made to have a relationship with a predator—a human being.

—E. W. "BUFF" HILDRETH

May you always ride a good horse!

—RICHARD SHRAKE

People who have never lived horseback and are not familiar with the big pastures in rough country would not understand the feeling that is developed among all members of a ranch family for certain individual horses.

—BEN K. GREEN

A prince is never surrounded by as much majesty on his throne as he is on a beautiful horse.

—WILLIAM CAVENDISH (1592–1676)

Men on horseback have created most of the world's history.

—ANONYMOUS

Horses are humanity's best friends. They have done everything for us, their friends. Think about war. Think about bad weather. Think about the Wild West in America. What would they have done without the horse?

—GEORGE THEODORESCU

A horse is a safer bet than the trains.

—BORIS JOHNSON

I saw the World Spirit seated on a horse.

—GEORG WILHELM FRIEDRICH HEGEL (1770–1831)

The big horse market was the Army. You could get $200 for a gelding while a cow and a calf only sold for $40 to $50 and a new car for $1,000 so you could purchase a new car for five geldings. One day alone, I sold 185 horses to the army remount service.

—HARRY WIESCAMP

In London's fashionable West End, the mews—where tiny houses and apartments now sell for a fortune—were merely cobbled alleyways behind the great houses, where the family's horse (or horses) were kept, and above whose stable the coachman and the groom were lodged.

—MARGARET KORDA AND MICHAEL KORDA, *HORSE HOUSEKEEPING*

Remember that the most important gait of the hunter is the halt.

—WILLIAM P. WADSWORTH

———◆———

The origin of the Arabian horse is a great zoological mystery. When we first encounter him, he is somewhat smaller than his counterpart today. Otherwise, he has remained unchanged through all the centuries. "As old as time itself and as fleet as its flying moments" perfectly describes him.

—JUDITH FORBIS, *THE CLASSIC ARABIAN HORSE*

———◆———

The North African mule talks always of his mother's brother, the horse, but never of his father, the donkey, in favor of others supposedly more reputable.

—CLIFFORD GEERTZ

———◆———

A good example of a simple technology with profound historical consequences is hay. Nobody knows who invented hay, the idea of cutting grass in the autumn and storing it in large enough quantities to keep horses and cows alive through the winter.

—FREEMAN DYSON, *INFINITE IN ALL DIRECTIONS*

The cowboys ... each have to undergo much hard toil ... on account of the extreme slowness with which everything must be done, as trail cattle should never be hurried.

—THEODORE ROOSEVELT (1858–1919)

Many a man who sticks constantly to the roads and lines of gates, who, from principle, never looks at a fence, is much attached to hunting. Some of those who have borne great names as Nimrods in our hunting annals would as life have led a forlorn hope as to put a horse in flight of hurdles.

—ANTHONY TROLLOPE

As long as wild horses are galloping free,
I'll dream of the west as I want it to be.

—RITA AND CHARLIE SUMMERS

It was quite customary as late as 1890 to see a countryman returning from the market, fast asleep, slumped forward over his saddle bar while his horse plodded his own way home.

—DOROTHY HARTLEY

Certainly the opening of the western frontiers of America was made possible by horses that were ridden and packed under saddle and those that worked in harness.

—ANDY RUSSELL, *HORSES AND HORSEMEN*

Traces of ancient horse manure have been found in a remote 5,600-year-old Kazakh village—a discovery that could be the earliest known evidence of horse domestication.

—NationalGeographic.com

Assault was content. Life was good here. It was probably even better for him, he thought, than it was for the mustang horses who used to run here wild and free nearly one hundred years ago.

The history of horsemanship is less about sugar than pepper, less about light than dark, less about mindful kindness than thoughtless cruelty.

—Lawrence Scanlan

Assault was content. Life was good here. It was probably even better for him, he thought, than it was for the mustang horses who used to run here wild and free nearly one hundred years ago.

—Marjorie Hodgson Parker

Though I am an old horse … I never yet could make out why men are so fond of this sport; they often hurt themselves, often spoil good horses, and tear up the fields, and all for a hare, or a fox, or a stag … but we are only horses, and don't know.

—ANNA SEWELL

I got a horse for my cowboy … best trade I ever made!

—ANONYMOUS

[I]f one squadron of horse cavalry … had been available to me at San Stefano … they would have enabled me to cut off and capture the entire German force opposing me along the north coast road and would have permitted my entry into Messina at least forty-eight hours earlier.

—LT. GEN. L. K. TRUSCOT, JR., DURING WORLD WAR II

Cowboys call skill with horses being "handy."

—CHRIS IRWIN, *HORSES DON'T LIE*

———◆———

In some ways American hunting in the early twentieth century, when it became officially organized with associations and "recognized hunts," was more English than the English, a way for nouveau riche northern plutocrats and faded-glory southern gentry to burnish their self-styled aristocratic images.

—STEPHEN BUDIANSKY, *TALLYHO AND TRIBULATION*

———◆———

The equine influence reaches far back, to where the first captive horse was likely found in a bog by hunters somewhere in Europe or Asia.

—ANDY RUSSELL, *HORSES AND HORSEMEN*

———◆———

Through our entire history we have become accustomed to pushing [animals] around in ways dictated by our own wants and needs without much regard for theirs.

—STANLEY SCHMIDT

Other times he could not afford to eat. But there was never a day when he wanted to trade his chaps for a job with a boss looking over his shoulder.

—DIRK JOHNSON, *A COWBOY'S LAST CHANCE*

The first Marchioness [of Salisbury] was painted by Sir Joshua Reynolds, and hunted till the day she died at eighty-five, when, half-blind and strapped to the saddle, she was accompanied by a groom who would shout, when her horse approached a fence, "Jump, dammit, my Lady, jump!"

—BARBARA TUCHMAN, *THE PROUD TOWER*

Of all the animals the horse is the best friend of the Indian, for without it he could not go on long journeys. A horse is the Indian's most valuable piece of property.

—BRAVE BUFFALO, A TETON SIOUX MEDICINE MAN

Western fieldwork conjures up images of struggle on horseback.

—STEPHEN JAY GOULD

Maybe early man, tired of wearing down his callused feet on hard trails, watched ... a wild horse herd thunder by. ... Covetous of the speed and freedom promised ... he may have woven a rope ... hung it on a limb over a trail leading to water and hid to wait.

—ANDY RUSSELL, *HORSES AND HORSEMEN*

About four o'clock in the afternoon … he turns up at the hunting stables … he says nothing of himself. … Why should he tell that he had been nearly an hour on foot trying to catch his horse, that he had sat himself down on a bank and almost cried, and that he had drained his flask … before one o'clock?

—ANTHONY TROLLOPE

⊰⊱

In Westerns you were permitted to kiss your horse but never your girl.

—GARY COOPER

⊰⊱

The story is told of a man who, seeing one of the thoroughbred stables for the first time, suddenly removed his hat and said in awed tones, "My Lord! The cathedral of the horse."

—KENTUCKY: A GUIDE TO THE BLUEGRASS STATE (THE WPA GUIDE TO KENTUCKY)

⊰⊱

Fox hunting is essentially an inner struggle against dashed hopes. It is an elemental experience for horse and human being alike.

—STEPHEN BUDIANSKY, *TALLYHO AND TRIBULATION*

Of the horse I will say nothing because I know the times.

—LEONARDO DA VINCI (1452–1519), ON A HUGE EQUESTRIAN STATUE THAT LEONARDO HAD BEEN COMMISSIONED TO DESIGN AND CREATE, BUT WHICH WAS NEVER CAST UNTIL MORE THAN FIVE HUNDRED YEARS LATER, IN 1999, WHEN TWO HUGE STATUES BASED UPON HIS DESIGN WERE FINALLY MADE.

Anyone who has ever experienced the thrill of the rodeo life wishes it could go on forever. … To keep going down the road never giving a thought as to when it all might end. But we are finite creatures, only given a short time in life to live our dreams.

—RALPH CLARK

You know a horse is really part of our culture, and you know I think when you lose your culture, you lose your soul.

—NICK ZITO

Wherever man has left his footprints in the long ascent from barbarism to civilization, we find the hoofprint of a horse beside it.

—JOHN TROTWOOD MOORE (1858–1929)

If I was a cowboy in a lynch mob, I think I'd try to stay near the back. That way, if somebody shamed us into disbanding, I could sort of slip off to the side and pretend I was window-shopping or something.

—JACK HANDEY, *DEEP THOUGHTS*

Wild horses are a cultural symbol of our pioneering past, but too often the public becomes so enamored by their mystique that they lose all perspective.

—PAULA MORIN, *HONEST HORSES*

A century ago the most common form of transportation in America was the horse. The highways and byways echoed with the clip-clop of hoofs. … Half a century later, the aroma of hay and horse manure was rapidly giving way to the stink of oil and gasoline.

—JACK COGGINS, *THE HORSEMAN'S BIBLE*

Mules are always boasting that their ancestors were horses.

—GERMAN PROVERB

They [cattle ranchers] had learned that having a good string of saddle horses was an added inducement towards keeping top cowboys on payroll.

—PHIL LIVINGSTON AND ED ROBERTS, *WAR HORSE: MOUNTING THE CAVALRY WITH AMERICA'S FINEST HORSES*

You can tell a true cowboy by the type of horse that he rides.

—COWBOY EXPRESSION

No one who longs for the "good old days" sighs for the passing of the working horse. Not if he or she loves horses.

—MARION C. GARRETY

The bucking started from the back door of hell on a hot day, and came out on the run.

—CHARLIE SIRINGO

Let the hunting lady, however, avoid any touch of this blemish, remembering that no man ever likes a woman to know as much about a horse as he thinks he knows himself.

—ANTHONY TROLLOPE

The Roman Empire did not need hay because in a Mediterranean climate the grass grows well enough in winter for animals to graze. North of the Alps, great cities dependent on horses and oxen for motive power could not exist without hay. So it was hay that allowed populations to grow.

—FREEMAN DYSON, *INFINITE IN ALL DIRECTIONS*

A cowboy's best friend is his pony.

—WILF CARTER

The animal shall not be measured by man. In a world older and more complete than ours they move finished and complete, gifted with extensions of the sense we have lost or never attained, living by voices we shall never hear.

—HARRY BESTON

There are only two classes of good society in England; the equestrian classes and the neurotic classes. It isn't mere convention; everybody can see that the people who hunt are the right people and the people who don't are the wrong ones.

—GEORGE BERNARD SHAW

Wherever man has left his footprint in the long ascent from barbarism to civilization, we will find the hoofprint of the horse beside it.

—JOHN TROTWOOD MOORE

One out of every three mustangs captured in southwest Texas was expected to die before they were tamed. The process often broke the spirits of the other two.

—J. FRANK DOBI

In time … warriors became merely soldiers, and the horses, those disguised bearers of hope and good fortune, became primarily symbols of war, vanity, gambling sports, superficial entertainment, and power.

—KLAUS FERDINAND HEMPFLING, *WHAT HORSES REVEAL: FROM FIRST ENCOUNTER TO FRIEND FOR LIFE*

———

Never trust a cowhand that doesn't know how to properly tie a horse.

—COWBOY SAYING

———

The typical cowboy was wolf wild and free as the wind.

—CHARLIE COWBOY

———

In a little while all interest was taken up in stretching our necks and watching for "pony-rider"—the fleet messenger who sped across the continent from St. Joe to Sacramento, carrying letters nineteen hundred miles in eight days! Think of that for perishable horse and human flesh and blood to do.

—MARK TWAIN (1835–1910)

"We'll ride horses on the beach, right in the surf. Now, but you'll have to do it like a real cowboy. None of that side saddle stuff."
"You mean, one leg on each side?"

—JACK DAWSON TO ROSE DEWITT BUKATER IN *TITANIC*

If we were to deduct from the hunting—crowd farmers, and others who hunt because hunting is brought to their door, of the remainder we should find that the "men who don't like it" have the preponderance ... Of all such men, the hunting men are perhaps the most to be pitied.

—ANTHONY TROLLOPE

If you're a cowboy and you're dragging a guy behind your horse, I bet it would really make you mad if you looked back and the guy was reading a magazine.

—JACK HANDEY

Be prepared to spend several months of your life in plaster of paris.

—LARRY MAHAN, ADVICE TO ASPIRING RODEO RIDERS

The sights and sounds of the countryside, as well as the color and action and excitement of the racecourse, are what turn me on.

—PAUL MELLON

Towering above ordinary mortals, the rider could survey the landscape and move through it at a speed … beyond his natural abilities. The horse was rapid enough to cover major distances in one day, so that any rider, with a bit of training, could arrive at his destination in good shape.

—FULVIO CINQUINI, MAN AND HORSE: AN ENDURING BOND

There was always a market for good saddle horses, including the army.

—PHIL LIVINGSTON AND ED ROBERTS, *WAR HORSE: MOUNTING THE CAVALRY WITH AMERICA'S FINEST HORSES*

———

After the Spaniards settled the Southwest, the Navajo began another burst of cultural borrowing—or, more actually, stealing. Spanish ranches and villages were so depleted of horses—not to mention sheep—that by 1775 the Spaniards had to send to Europe for 1,500 additional horses.

—PETER FARB

———

Many a cowboy owes his very life to his horse.

—ROYAL HASSRICK

———

Men's achievements have been enlarged by horses almost as if the animals' plangent silence implied what could never be merely said.

—TOM MCGUANE

———

It ain't the 'unting as 'urts 'un, it's the 'ammer, 'ammer, 'ammer along the 'ard, 'igh ground.

—FROM A CARTOON IN *PUNCH* MAGAZINE

Cowboys hate walking; they really know how to use their horses. They conserve the energy of the horse, treating it like a valuable piece of farm equipment.

—ROBERT REDFORD

Henry Kissinger may have wished I had presented him as a combination of Charles DeGaulle and Disraeli, but I didn't ... out of respect for DeGaulle and Disraeli. I described him as a cowboy because that is how he describes himself. If I were a cowboy I would be offended.

—ORIANA FALLACI

A good cowboy will make whatever he's riding better—and a poor cowboy will be afoot even on a good horse.

—RAY HUNT

Wild horses have become living symbols—of liberty and beauty and power.

—MONTY ROBERTS, *SHY BOY: THE HORSE THAT CAME IN FROM THE WILD*

He was a picture to make any cowboy miss a few heartbeats as he sometimes raced across the prairie sod and with head up showed off the qualities that struck out at his every move.

—WILL JAMES, *SMOKY THE COWHORSE*

We find that during sixty million years horse evolution went from the dog-like *Hyracotherium*, with four toes on the forelegs and three on the hind, to the genus *Equus,* with a single digit supporting each leg.

—GEORGE WARING

The Arabian horse was bred ... and raised as "a drinker of the wind, a dancer of fire."

—GERALD HAUSMAN AND LORETTA HAUSMAN, *THE MYTHOLOGY OF HORSES: HORSE LEGEND AND LORE THROUGHOUT THE AGES*

Occasionally I scared up a herd of buffaloes, or antelopes, or coyotes, or deer, which would frighten my horse for a moment.

—BUFFALO BILL (1846–1917)

We must not be misled to our own detriment to assume that the untried machine can displace the proved and tried horse.

—JOHN HERR

[M]en who hunt are not more iniquitous than men who go out fishing, or play dominoes, or dig in their gardens.

—ANTHONY TROLLOPE

Rather than depending upon horses captured from the wild herds, man began to raise his own. He learned that breeding the best to the best produced a superior mount.

—PHIL LIVINGSTON AND ED ROBERTS, *WAR HORSE: MOUNTING THE CAVALRY WITH AMERICA'S FINEST HORSES*

Perhaps I may be allowed to explain to embryo Dianas—to the growing huntresses of the present age—that she who rides and makes no demand receives attention as close as it ever given to her more imperious sister.

—ANTHONY TROLLOPE

The first movie star was a horse. *Equus Caballus*, that potent symbol of human aspiration, had been capturing the imaginations of painters, poets, songsmiths, and sculptors for centuries when he was finally captured in action by motion pictures on a fine June day in 1879.

—PETRINE DAY MITCHUM, *HOLLYWOOD HOOFBEATS*

It's been argued that of all the animals humans have domesticated, the horse is the most important to our history. For thousands of years, horses were our most reliable mode of transportation.

—ELTON GALLEGLY

Being a cowboy was the only job Joe knew. He had been riding horses, herding cattle and climbing on the backs of steers since he was a kid.

—DIRK JOHNSON, *A COWBOY'S LAST CHANCE*

The Arabian horse became a healer of nations … peace was achieved when a desert wanderer and his horse came into a strange camp and found a haven from the sun. In time, the pact was sealed by stallion, mare, and foal.

—GERALD HAUSMAN AND LORETTA HAUSMAN, *THE MYTHOLOGY OF HORSES: HORSE LEGEND AND LORE THROUGHOUT THE AGES*

I took to the life of a cowboy like a horse takes to oats.

—CLINTON MCCOY

"I'll be a cowboy and ride the range." He pulled the reins on an imaginary horse and galloped around the room.

—GERTRUDE CHANDLER WARNER, *THE MYSTERY HORSE*

In my event, at a rodeo like Houston, there might be 90 bareback riders that you're competin' with. You'll probably get three horses and you have to draw a good buckin' horse. That's mighty tough.

—CHRIS LEDOUX

My great forte in killing buffaloes was to get them circling by riding my horse at the head of the herd and shooting their leaders. Thus the brutes behind were crowded to the left, so that they were soon going round and round.

—WILLIAM DREW CODY

The rodeo ain't over till the bull riders ride.

—RALPH CARPENTER

I saw the hounds occasionally, sometimes pouring over a green bank, as the charging breaker lifts and flings itself, sometimes driving across a field, as the white tongues of foam slide racing over the sand; and always ahead of me was Flurry Knox …

—SOMERVILLE AND ROSS

The origin of the horses of Assateague is shrouded in mystery. … One romantic … theory has seventeenth-century pirates combing a … sandy island off the coast of Maryland looking for a place to bury their ill-gotten treasure, leaving behind … horses to use in an emergency … if they needed to return.

—RICH POMERANTZ, *WILD HORSES OF THE DUNES*

Horses changed the way men conquered territories. United with men, horses afforded the ability to travel across the earth in relative ease, as few other animals had done before.

—FULVIO CINQUINI, *MAN AND HORSE: AN ENDURING BOND*

Hot Bloods are those breeds descended from the Arab—most notably, the Thoroughbred. Their speed and their high-spirited temperament are legendary. The term *cold blood* refers to breeds that trace their ancestry to the medieval Great Horses that carried armored knights into battle.

—*THE WHOLE HORSE CATALOG*

One of those game old things, whether they are old colonels … or old horses … I say, he was one of those game old things that make a virtue of looking fit even when they might be excused drooping their heads and lying down to die.

—LIAM O'FLAHERTY, *THE OLD HUNTER*

I made over forty Westerns. I used to lie awake nights trying to think up new ways of getting on and off a horse.

—WILLIAM WYLER

For Grey Horse, there was only one way to travel, by horseback, and only one place to live, the prairie.

—TYLER TAFFORD, *THE STORY OF BLUE EYE*

Before Thomas Edison and D. W. Griffith began their careers as film pioneers, before the first cowboy actor on a trusty steed galloped across a silent screen … there were a revolutionary series of motion pictures starring a Standardbred harness racer with the unlikely name of Abe Edgington.

—PETRINE DAY MITCHUM, *HOLLYWOOD HOOFBEATS*

A good horse knows just when to turn a cow, just how to cut a steer from the bunch. A good cow pony knows, as if by instinct, when to walk slowly through the brush, how to miss the gopher hole at a high canter. … The cowpoke and the cow pony become not just a team working in unison, they become as one.

—ROYAL B. HASSRICK

Cowboying requires real knowledge of a horse and his capabilities. ... A horse can sense when a real horseman is in the saddle. He knows when the rider is going to tough it out.

—ROBERT REDFORD

People talk about size, shape, quarters, blood, bone, muscle, but for my part, give me a hunter with brains; he has to take care of the biggest fool of the two and think for both.

—G. J. WHYTE-MELVILLE

King Richard would have won the battle of Bosworth Field and lived—if he'd only had a horse.

—SALLY KEEHN, *THE FIRST HORSE I SEE*

Cowgirl: A better-looking cowboy with brains.

—ANONYMOUS

CHAPTER FOUR

Horse Power: Great Horses

In May 2006, at Pimlico Race Course in Baltimore, one of the horses who was running in the Preakness Stakes, the middle event of the "Triple Crown," suddenly pulled up short. While the rest of the field galloped furiously on—the race had only just begun—the injured colt, whose right hind leg was obviously badly damaged, staggered to an excruciating-to-watch halt.

Thus began the saga of Barbaro. For the next nine months his fate was a headline story across the nation. His shattered limb, broken in something like twenty places, required numerous surgeries, and hospital pictures of the Thoroughbred in a body-supporting sling became familiar to everyone. It was always acknowledged that the odds were against him, but for weeks at a time it seemed as if the three-year-old would make a miraculous recovery. After a series of heartbreaking ups and downs, however, there was one final setback, and in January 2007 Barbaro was euthanized. His owner, Gretchen Jackson, seemed to speak for everyone who was fighting back tears at the news that day when she said, "Grief is the price we all pay for love."

For millions of people, loving Barbaro and wondering how he was doing became a part of daily life during the latter half of 2006. Few of those millions would ever have otherwise been in the habit of giving a thought to horses, nor would more than a handful have been able to tell you the name of another active racer, such as the eventual winner of the Preakness itself: Bernardini. But that's just the way it is with horses and the general public nowadays—out of sight, out of mind.

Yet every year the Kentucky Derby, or the other two "jewels" in the Crown, manage to remind everybody about equine greatness. The big races bring a horse or two, in triumph or in tragedy, to our collective attention: from out of the pages of the *Daily Racing Form* comes this absolutely breathtaking creature, and it's as if there's a national "horse fix" that has to be satisfied. We can't get enough.

In recognition of this, it's the stakes-racing athletes who get the most space in this chapter devoted to equine greatness. Man o' War. Foolish Pleasure. Seabiscuit. Ruffian. Secretariat. You probably will recognize most of the names. But also on hand are a few other horses whose claim to greatness rests on something other than racetrack speed. To mention but one striking example: Black Jack, the riderless horse in the funeral cortege of President Kennedy. There indeed was a different kind of great horse.

Napoleon's famous horse Marengo, George Washington's gray Arab Magnolia, Grant's horse Cincinnati, Lee's horse Traveller, and Comanche, the one horse to survive the Battle of the Little Big Horn, were regarded with awe because horses, even the bones of horses, remember everything.

—TOM MCGUANE

Johnny Tivio, April 24, 1956 to April 24, 1981. Known to all as the greatest all-around working horse ever to enter an arena.

—EPITAPH ON THE GRAVESTONE OF MONTY ROBERTS'S JOHNNY TIVIO

Every so often, perhaps once every fifteen or twenty years, there comes to racing a horse so perfectly conformed, so talented and so tragic that it breaks the hearts of even the most hardened horsemen. Such a horse was the filly Ruffian.

—THE COMPLETE BOOK OF THOROUGHBRED RACING

Nothing focused the nation's mourning like the riderless black horse in the funeral cortege of John Kennedy.

> —Tom McGuane, on Black Jack, named in honor of General John J. "Black Jack" Pershing

Nothing can take away the horror of seeing a horse break down. It's like seeing a masterpiece destroyed.

> —Jack Whitaker, on the tragic 1975 match race between Foolish Pleasure and Ruffian

In 1938, near the end of a decade of monumental turmoil, the year's number-one newsmaker was not Franklin Delano Roosevelt, Hitler, or Mussolini. ... The subject of the most newspaper column inches in 1938 wasn't even a person. It was an undersized, crooked-legged racehorse named Seabiscuit.

> —Laura Hillenbrand, *Seabiscuit: An American Legend*

It is a curious fact that today, two centuries later, the name of the Godolphin Arabian is found in the pedigree of almost every superior Thoroughbred. His blood reigns. To him goes the title: Father of the Turf.

—MARGUERITE HENRY, *KING OF THE WIND: THE STORY OF THE GODOLPHIN ARABIAN*

The Arabian stallion is magnificent, and the mare quite glamorous, but the airy-fairy foal is so delicate and fawn-like, he steals your heart away!

—GLADYS BROWN EDWARDS, *KNOW THE ARABIAN HORSE*

There are various ways to talk about what could possibly motivate a horse, or any animal, to such an effort. Fear certainly does not do it. Courage, joy, exaltation are more like it, but beyond that horses have, some of the time, a strong sense of artistry.

—VICKI HEARNE

No two paint horses are marked alike, so to own one is to own one of
Mother Nature's original pieces of art.

—HARDY OELKE, *THE PAINT HORSE: AN AMERICAN TREASURE*

Silvery, shining, radiant, like something in a dream. Only she wasn't a
dream. She was real.

—JANE SCHWARTZ, *RUFFIAN: BURNING FROM THE START*

I know great horses live again.

—STANLEY HARRISON

Dad said I looked and moved a lot like his great-grandfather, the
legendary Secretariat. My mom knew she had something special …
In fact, if other horses came near me, she would run at them with ears
pinned back and give them a swift kick. Now that could smart!

—ROBERT L. MERZ, *QUIPS, QUOTES & OATS: SMARTY JONES TALKS*

From 1936 to 1940, Seabiscuit endured a remarkable run of bad fortune, conspiracy, and injury to establish himself as one of history's most extraordinary athletes. Graced with blistering speed, tactical versatility, and indomitable will, he … shattered more than a dozen track records.

—LAURA HILLENBRAND, *SEABISCUIT: AN AMERICAN LEGEND*

There is a notion that you get only one great horse in a lifetime, a persistent notion that I hope isn't true; because if that's the case, I've already had mine.

—THOMAS MCGUANE

If I was an artist like you, I would draw a true picture of Traveller … But I am no artist and can therefore only say he is a Confederate grey.

—ROBERT E. LEE, IN A NOTE TO HIS WIFE'S COUSIN WHO WISHED TO PAINT A PORTRAIT OF LEE'S HORSE, TRAVELLER

I like Cutter because he has the fabled "eye of the eagle" … I just didn't know he could fly.

—GREG BRASS

I could see he felt entitled to a compliment, and so I said I had never seen lightning go like that horse. And I never had.

—MARK TWAIN

Some people show evil as a great racehorse shows breeding. They have the dignity of a hard chancre.

—ERNEST HEMINGWAY (1899–1961)

Wherever Domino's blood has gone, speed and courage have followed.

—AVALYN HUNTER, *THE KINGMAKER*

Somebody … has said that a fine man on a fine horse is the noblest bodily object in the world.

—G. K. CHESTERTON, *THE EVERLASTING MAN*

———◆———

"Speed Miracle"

—THE *NEW YORK TIMES*, ON MAN O' WAR AFTER SETTING ASTONISHING SPEED RECORDS

———◆———

On the bright cold afternoon of November 12, 1973 … several hundred people gathered at Blue Grass Airport in Lexington to greet Secretariat after his flight from New York into retirement in Kentucky.

—WILLIAM NACK

———◆———

In the course of his sixteen-month racing career, Secretariat rose higher and faster and larger than any U.S. horse of modern times.

—WILLIAM NACK

———◆———

Even his name was un-regal. Funny Cide. It sounded like laughing yourself to death.

—SALLY JENKINS, *FUNNY CIDE*

Man o' War suffered his only defeat in the 1919 Sanford Stakes to a horse named Upset.

—BILL HELLER

Here lies the fleetest runner the American Turf has ever known, and one of the gamest and most generous of horses.

—INSCRIPTION ON THE GRAVE OF DOMINO

In the darkest days of depression and war, a horse named Seabiscuit elevated our country's spirit and embodied the qualities we cherish in our horses; heart, drive, loyalty, love, and playfulness.

—*CHICKEN SOUP FOR THE HORSE LOVER'S SOUL*

"You wanna see the best-lookin' two-year-old you've ever seen? … What do you think? … Don't forget the name: Secretariat. He can run. … Don't quote me, but this horse will make them all forget Riva Ridge."

—JIMMY GAFFNEY

His greatest performance was almost certainly his match race with the 1894 Belmont Stakes winner Henry of Navarre; over a distance of nine furlongs, at least an eighth of a mile farther than he cared to go, Domino absolutely refused to be defeated and ran Henry to a dead heat.

—AVALYN HUNTER, *THE KINGMAKER*

Magnanimous in defeat, he was a superb loser and did not waste time dwelling on what might have been.

—VINCENT O'BRIEN, ON SANGSTER

I'm a red, chestnut colt of average size. They say my best features are a fine head and lustrous red coat. I've been nicknamed "Little Red" after my ancestor Secretariat who of course was "Big Red." Although not a big horse, I have been referred to by my trainers as "A little piece of iron."

—ROBERT L. MERZ, *QUIPS, QUOTES & OATS: SMARTY JONES TALKS*

———

"There's more people out here to meet Secretariat than there was to greet the governor." "Well, he's won more races than the governor," pilot Dan Neff replied.

—WILLIAM NACK

———

De mostest hoss that ever wuz.

—WILL HARBUT, EULOGIZING MAN O' WAR

———

In more than three hundred years of New York racing, no filly or mare had ever lugged such a load on the flat. In a sense the voters were right. She isn't Horse of the Year. She's the Horse of Three Centuries.

—RED SMITH

Barbaro was euthanized Monday after complications from his gruesome breakdown at last year's Preakness, ending an eight-month ordeal that made him even more of a hero than he was as a champion on the track.

—ANONYMOUS

Based on looks and lineage, Seattle Slew at birth could not have been termed a horse destined for greatness. "He was ugly. … He had big ears, and they flopped all over the first week."

—DAN MEARNS

Here is living harmony in horseflesh; an embodiment of rhythm and modulation, of point and counterpoint, that sang to the eye and made music in the heart.

—JOHN HERVEY, ON EQUIPOISE

His trainer said that managing him was like holding a tiger by the tail. His owner compared him to "chain lightning." His jockeys found their lives transformed by him, in triumphant … ways.

—DOROTHY OURS, *MAN O' WAR: A LEGEND LIKE LIGHTNING*

A fine horse or a beautiful woman, I cannot look at them unmoved, even now when seventy winters have chilled my blood.

—SIR ARTHUR CONAN DOYLE

I am very pleased with Smarty's move. I wanted him to finish up strong, and he did.

—JOHN SERVIS, SMARTY JONES'S TRAINER

———◆———

As a physical specimen, Secretariat had a muscular build that belied his youth. As an athlete, he moved with breathtaking style, combining the raw power of a fullback with the agility of an Olympic gymnast.

—*THE 10 BEST KENTUCKY DERBIES*

———◆———

"If man breeds one genius to a decade it is enough. And so it goes with hawses … In those days ninety colts were foaled each spring at Sanfo'd Hall. … How many hawses—truly great hawses—did such brood mayehs as that produce? How many do you think?" "Not many," he murmured.

—JOHN TAINTOR FOOTE

———◆———

Most racehorses that amount to anything, which is to say they win stakes races, have pedigrees that on hindsight have a stakes winning tinge. The adage that all racehorses are well-bred of one goes far back enough is one of the glorious ironies of a tradition-rich sport.

—TIMOTHY T. CAPPS, *SPECTACULAR BID*

[He] was blessed to have forgotten his binoculars.

—TOM CALLAHAN, ON CHARLIE WHITTINGHAM WHEN HIS HORSE FERDINAND WON THE KENTUCKY DERBY

I was born with the perfect combination of athleticism and power. I weigh a little more than a half ton and can reach speeds of up to 45 miles per hour. I wear what are known as racing plates, or as you call them, horseshoes. ... I want all the sneaker companies to know I'm available as a spokeshorse.

—ROBERT L. MERZ, *QUIPS, QUOTES & OATS: SMARTY JONES TALKS*

Once he strengthened up, you could do whatever you wanted on him. It was like driving a Ferrari rather than a Cortina.

—COLIN BROWN, FORMER JOCKEY ON DESERT ORCHID

Ask anyone on the street for one name in horse racing and they will always say Secretariat. He is the definitive touchstone between racing and the American public.

—PENNY CHENERY, OWNER OF SECRETARIAT

My father hated selling horses, he was afraid the good one was going to get away.

—ROBERT LEHMAN

Funny Cide wasn't the product of money and breeding, but rather, of the vast middle class in horse racing. Had he belonged to a larger stable, or fallen into the hands of a less conscientious trainer, he might not have become what he did. But he was a fortunate horse.

—SALLY JENKINS, *FUNNY CIDE*

She stumbled coming out of the gate, and that will be part of the legacy of Rags to Riches—the sudden stabbing fear of danger. But she regained her equilibrium quickly and caught up with the colts, and now racing has a new champion, a new story, a new hope.

—GEORGE VECSEY ON RAGS TO RICHES, WHO IN 2007 BECAME ONLY THE THIRD FILLY TO WIN THE 139-YEAR-OLD BELMONT STAKES, AND THE FIRST TO DO SO SINCE 1905

"We just invested in a dream. … We didn't take a chance on Funny Cide … he took a chance on us. This little horse has helped us show the world that sometimes the dreams of the little guy *do* come true. … Funny Cide rewarded us all in far greater ways than we ever deserved."

—CHRIS RUSSELL-GRABB, *THE FUNNY CIDE OF LIFE*

On the turn I could see all the horses clearly at once, but the image I remember is that of the reddish brown colt going by three horses so fast it made me blink. Twice he changed gears to avoid further trouble. ... "A freak," I said to myself.

—STEVE DAVIDOWITZ, *BETTING THOROUGBREDS*

He's good enough for me. I won't say he's a superhorse because you're never a superhorse until you're retired. Any horse can be beaten on any given day.

—ANGEL CORDERO, JR.

"The Biscuit [Seabiscuit], he'd lay back and let them come right up, side-to-side, get them feeling like the match was theirs, then he'd look them in the eye and take off like a bullet." Floss laughed out loud at that.

—THERESA PELUSO, *AN UNLIKELY TRIO OF HOPE*

Man o' War … won twenty of his twenty-one races. … "Big Red," as he was known, lived to be thirty and became a symbol of American force and durability, so beloved that his birthday party was once broadcast to the nation on NBC Radio.

—ERIC RACHLIS, BLOSSOM LEFCOURT, AND BERT MORGAN, *HORSE RACING: THE GOLDEN AGE OF THE TRACK*

And it was not Foolish Pleasure whose importance—whose symbolic importance—had transcended the world of racing and even sports in general. It was the larger-than-life filly with the perfect record; the coal black daughter of Reviewer and Shenanigans; the speedball, the beauty, the female, the freak.

—JANE SCHWARTZ

On the long ride from Louisville, I would regale them with stories about the horse [Secretariat]. … Oh, I knew all the stories, knew them well. … Knew them as I knew the stories of my children. Knew them as I knew stories of my own life.

—WILLIAM NACK

Even the most forlorn thoroughbred, seen at a distance—like a woman outside the fence at an army camp—is flawlessly beautiful.

—Joe Flaherty

I really liked Lassie, but that horse, Flicka, was a nasty animal with a terrible disposition. All the Flickas—all six of them—were awful.

—Roddy McDowall

He's a proper horse. He's brilliant.

—Ruby Walsh, on Hedgehunter

Once trainer Louis Feustel unleashed Man o' War onto the … sports scene, the colt was quick about the business of ensuring that he would rank with such athletes as Babe Ruth, Jack Dempsey, and Red Grange among the hallowed sports figures produced by his era.

—The Blood-Horse Staff, *Thoroughbred Champions*

The average colt has a stride of 24.6 feet, according to Equix, a company in Lexington, Kentucky, that conducts biometrical analyses of Thoroughbreds. Secretariat's was 24.8. Bernardini, in the Preakness, checked in at 26.5 feet—"off the charts."

—TOMMY CRAGGS

A champion racehorse at the winning line, unattached, eats the blooms of his victory wreath.

—SAIOM SHRIVER

All our best horses have Arab blood, and once in a while it seems to have come out strong and show in every part of the creature, in his frame, his power, and his wild, free, roving spirit.

—ERNEST THOMPSON SETON

On rare occasions, a horse like Funny Cide … comes along … reminding people just how much a racehorse and this sport can affect a person, a town, a city, a state, a country.

—STEVE HAKSIN

⬥

[O]nly ten colts have won the Triple Crown since Sir Barton first did it in 1919 … a dynasty of equine royalty as distinguished as the aristocratic families.

—ERIC RACHLIS, BLOSSOM LEFCOURT, AND BERT MORGAN, *HORSE RACING: THE GOLDEN AGE OF THE TRACK*

⬥

Secretariat is blazing along! The first three-quarters of a mile in 1:09 … Secretariat is widening now. He is moving like a tremendous machine!

—ANNOUNCER CHIC ANDERSON, AT THE BELMONT STAKES IN 1973

⬥

A racehorse that consistently runs just a second faster than another horse is worth millions of dollars more. Be willing to give that extra effort that separates the winner from the one in second place.

—H. Jackson Brown Jr.

Twenty-nine lengths. Thirty. The colt took a final leap. Thirty-one. The timer froze: 2:24 … it is frozen there still.

—William Nack

He was as near living flame as horses ever get.

—Joe Palmer, on Man o' War

I am still under the impression that there is nothing alive quite so beautiful as a Thoroughbred horse.

—John Galsworthy

Black Ruby knows exactly where the finish line is, and she just refuses to lose … She always seems to find that extra gear, call it "mulepower" if you will.

—DEBRA GINSBURG, *THE FASTEST MULE IN THE WEST*

———◆———

He was a man of few words, but he had something to say to me that morning. He said, "Son, there is no way you can get this horse beat today … Believe me, boy, you are riding the greatest horse of all time and I have seen them all."

—RON TURCOTTE, SECRETARIAT'S JOCKEY, RECALLING WHAT HOLLIE HUGHES TOLD HIM BEFORE THE 1973 BELMONT STAKES

———◆———

If this isn't a Triple Crown horse, I don't know what one looks like.

—BARCLAY TAGG, ON A HORSE NAMED NOBIZ LIKE SHOBIZ

———◆———

The ultimate equipment change.

—D. WAYNE LUKAS, ON FUNNY CIDE

———◆———

[E]leven victories in eleven starts. The highlights included the Belmont Stakes by twenty lengths; the Dwyer over the audacious effort by John P. Grier to bring him [Man o' War] to a drive in the stretch; the Lawrence Realization by a recorded one hundred lengths.

—THE BLOOD-HORSE STAFF, *THOROUGHBRED CHAMPIONS*

———◆———

Arabians: A little bit of everything perfect.

—AMANDA FERBER

———◆———

I used to think the greatest thing I ever saw was the Ali-Frazier fight in Madison Square Garden. This was even better.

—PETE AXTHELM, ON SECRETARIAT'S THIRTY-ONE-LENGTH VICTORY IN THE BELMONT STAKES

———◆———

His [Funny Cide] run in the Preakness left everyone but the horses breathless, winning by an astounding nine and three-quarter lengths.

—CHRIS RUSSELL-GRABB, *THE FUNNY CIDE OF LIFE*

Horses have a way of getting inside you, and so it was that Secretariat became like a fifth child in our house.

—WILLIAM NACK

His nature just speaks to me. I didn't want him too far back to get dirt in his face, to get discouraged.

—JULIE KRONE, ON COLONIAL AFFAIR

[Thoroughbreds] are exuberant. They are sensitive. They have opinions. They in general have too much of every lively quality than too little.

—JANE SMILEY

Winner of twenty races in twenty-one starts, Man o' War had earned a record at the time, $249,465.

—THE BLOOD-HORSE STAFF, *THOROUGHBRED CHAMPIONS*

The most important thing I learned from Johnny ... was that when he had been abused and forced, he didn't reach his full potential. When there was a request rather than demand, and love instead of neglect, he was able to perform like no other horse before him.

—MONTY ROBERTS

Secretariat became the most expensive animal in history when he was sold to a breeding syndicate for the then shocking sum of $6.08 million.

—WILLIAM NACK

Other than being castrated, things have gone quite well for Funny Cide.

—KENNY MAYNE, BEFORE THE RUNNING OF THE BELMONT STAKES

CHAPTER FIVE

Horselaughs: The Humorous Horse

A horse walks into a bar. The bartender says, "Why the long face?"

Bahrumbump!

Then this pony walks in. In a scratchy voice he says, "Let (*coughs*) me (*clears his throat*) have a (*coughs*) beer." The barman says, "You sick?" The pony says, "No, just a little hoarse."

Bahrumbump!

I know several *humans* who love those jokes, but the question remains: do *horses* have a sense of humor? Mine certainly does. Here, for instance, is the joke that Koda likes:

A man walks into a stall. He begins to groom the horse. He starts with what they call a shedding blade, applying it first to the horse's back and then to his flank and belly. The man bends over to groom the horse's belly. The horse nips the deerskin work gloves out of the man's back pocket and drops them in the shavings.

Bahrumbump!

(While I do actually find Koda's joke, which he regularly plays on me, quite amusing, I also recognize that Pam Brown is right to warn us to "be wary of the horse with a sense of humor.")

Now, it should be pointed out that the jokes I've related here are not, in fact, truly representative of the kind of "horselaughs" you're going to find in the present chapter. Indeed, most of the quotes in the following pages can't be classified as jokes at all. Instead, what we've put together is a collection of witty observations inspired, in one way or another, by horses. They range from Will Rogers's persuasive contention that our four-legged friends *must* be smarter than we are because "you never heard of a horse going broke betting on people," to a traditional bit of British cavalry advice about how to catch a loose horse; it's tremendously effective, if you can manage it: "Make a noise like a carrot."

My own personal favorite among these quotations comes from Roy Rogers. Funny to think of ol' Roy, after a lifetime in the saddle, putting into words exactly what we middle-aged, weekend riders try not to think about when we mount up: "When you're young and you fall off a horse, you may break something. When you're my age and you fall off, you splatter."

And *that* is no joke, I assure you.

Most of our horses … are … named from some feat or peculiarity. Wire Fence … ran into one of the abominations after which he is now called. … Fall Back would never get to the front. … Water Skip always jumps mud puddles; and there are dozens others with names as purely descriptive.

—THEODORE ROOSEVELT

Feed 'em and lead 'em.

—CONFORMATION CLASSES IN A NUTSHELL

I watched a rerun on television of a 1960s comedy program called *Mr. Ed*, which was about a talking horse. Judging by the quality of the jokes, I would guess that Mr. Ed wrote his own material.

—BILL BRYSON, *THE LOST CONTINENT: TRAVELS IN SMALL-TOWN AMERICA*

If you can lead it to water and force it to drink, it isn't a horse.

—ANONYMOUS

Gordon Wright was showing a jumper at the National Horse Show. He had just had one of his books published, and when his horse stopped at a fence, Joe Green, who has a voice that could carry, yelled in from the in gate, "Hey, Gordon, what chapter is that in?!"

—CLARENCE "HONEY" CRAVEN

And do you think Paul Revere even would have looked at a horse if all the taxis hadn't been engaged with the theater crowds that night?

—RING LARDNER, *TIPS ON HORSES*

A horse is not only good fun, it is also a beautiful-looking psychotherapist who lives on grass and doesn't charge by the hour!

—PERRY WOOD

In England I would rather be a man, a horse, a dog, or a woman, in that order. In America I think the order would be reversed.

—BRUCE GOULD

Honey Rider beat Film Maker by a nose for the win. Or as track announcer Durkin called it, "Honey Rider ... by a nostril!"

—C. N. RICHARDSON, *REMEMBERING FOREGO—THE HANDICAP HORSE OF THE DECADE*

When will they make a tractor that can furnish the manure for farm fields and produce a baby tractor every spring?

—GEORGE RUPP

Yesterday I moved a ton of manure. Actually, it was the horses who moved it; I merely pitched it into a wheelbarrow.

—MELISSA PIERSON

Horse sense is the thing a horse has which keeps it from betting on people.

—W. C. FIELDS (1880–1946)

Be wary of the horse with a sense of humor.

—PAM BROWN

When you're young and you fall off a horse, you may break something. When you're my age and you fall off, you splatter.

—ROY ROGERS

He knows when you are happy. He knows when you are proud. He also knows when you have a carrot.

—ANONYMOUS

You're better off betting on a horse than betting on a man. A horse may not be able to hold you tight, but he doesn't wanna wander from the stable at night.

—BETTY GRABLE (1916–1973)

Whoever said a horse was dumb, was dumb.

—WILL ROGERS

Found a smoldering cigarette left by a horse.

—DAVE BARRY

It's a lot like nuts and bolts—if the rider's nuts, the horse bolts!

—NICHOLAS EVANS

Whenever you observe a horse closely, you feel as if a human being sitting inside were making fun of you.

—ELIAS CANETTI

Defenders of le Horse will … point to the term "good, common horse sense," … as being proof of the beast's virtues, but if a horse has such good common sense, why do they always have to have a jockey show them the way round a … race track when you couldn't possibly go wrong unlest you was dumb.

—RING LARDNER, *TIPS ON HORSES*

The horse bit the pastor. How came this to pass? He heard the good pastor say, "All flesh is grass."

—EMMET GRIBBIN JR., IN A LETTER TO *LIVING CHURCH* MAGAZINE

All I pay my psychiatrist is the cost of feed and hay, and he'll listen to me any day.

—ANONYMOUS

If the world was truly a rational place, men would ride sidesaddle.

—RITA MAE BROWN

The mule was asked: "Who is your father?" It responded with: "The horse is my uncle."

—ARABIC PROVERB

I never play horseshoes 'cause Mother taught us not to throw our clothes around.

—MR. ED, THE TALKING HORSE OF THE 1960s TV SERIES

Even an E-type Jaguar looks merely flash beside a really smart pony and trap.

—MARION C. GARRETTY

How do you catch a loose horse? Make a noise like a carrot.

—BRITISH CAVALRY JOKE

I've fallen in love with my horse. It's a safer bet. We all know from my illustrious past that I should be sticking to men with four legs.

—SHARON STONE

We are ... a small army composed of slave masters who are in turn enslaved by our slaves. We are the ones who assiduously pick up their excrement ... We bathe, curry, brush, mane-pull, tail-detangle, hoof-pick and take off and put on blankets ... They stand there and loudly demand their food.

—MELISSA PIERSON

Few girls are as well-shaped as a good horse.

—HANNAH ARENDT

In horse vernacular, Roy has always "given me my head," and I have tried to do the same for him.

—DALE EVANS

You know horses are smarter than people. You never heard of a horse going broke betting on people.

—WILL ROGERS

The Budweiser Clydesdales! I'm so glad to see you. Now that John Wayne and Elvis are gone, you're all we have left!

—CB MESSAGE FROM A DRIVER WHO SAW THE VANS PULLING THE BUDWEISER CLYDESDALES

There has to be a woman, but not much of a one. A good horse is much more important.

—MAX BRAND (1892–1944), ON WRITING WESTERNS

Hundreds and hundreds of beautiful horses in the [Santa Barbara] parade, and a man without a silver saddle is a vagrant.

—WILL ROGERS

When any one of our relations was found to be a person of a very bad character ... or one we desired to get rid of, upon his leaving my house I ... lend him a riding-coat, or a pair of boots, or sometimes a horse of small value, and I always had the satisfaction of finding he never came back to return them.

—OLIVER GOLDSMITH

"Your wife is extremely pretty ... Does she ride?"

"I'm glad you like her looks," I replied, "as I fear you will find her thoroughly despicable otherwise. For one thing, she not only can't ride, but she believes that I can!"

—SOMERVILLE AND ROSS

"Later on, can I see Volponi?"

"Yeah, but ... don't try to pet him, unless you want to start typing with your toes."

—JOE MCGINNISS, *THE BIG HORSE*

In my opinion, a horse is the animal to have. Eleven-hundred pounds of raw muscle, power, grace, and sweat between your legs—it's something you just can't get from a pet hamster.

—ANONYMOUS

On horseback he seemed to require as many hands as a Hindu god, at least four for clutching the reins, and two more for patting the horse soothingly on the neck.

—Saki (H. H. Munro) (1870–1916)

They use the snaffle and the curb all right,
But where's the bloody horse?

—Roy Campbell

One of the earliest religious disappointments in a young girl's life devolves upon her unanswered prayer for a horse.

—Phillis Theroux

A woman needs two animals—the horse of her dreams and a jackass to pay for it.

—Anonymous

I prefer a bike to a horse. The brakes are more easily checked.

—LAMBERT JEFFRIES

Men are generally more careful of the Breed of their Horses and Dogs than of their Children.

—WILLIAM PENN (1644–1718)

The wildest broncos are those you rode some place else.

—KEN ALSTAD

You can lead a horse to water, and if you can train it to float on its back, you've got something.

—JOHNNY CARSON

You know you're a Horse Mom when: The equine feed bill is a bigger portion of your family budget than the human feed bill … ditto the medical bills … and shoes.

—BARBARA GREENSTREET, *ARE YOU A REAL HORSE MOM?*

Three things are men most likely to be cheated in, a horse, a wig, and a wife.

—BENJAMIN FRANKLIN (1706–1790)

I preferred a safe horse to a fast one—I would like to have an excessively gentle horse—a horse with no spirit whatever—a lame one, if he had such a thing. Inside of five minutes I was mounted, and perfectly satisfied with my outfit.

—MARK TWAIN

Computers are like horses—press the right button and they'll take you anywhere.

—ANONYMOUS

For the man … whose duty it is to sweep up manure, the supreme terror is the possibility of a world without horses. To tell him that it is disgusting to spend one's life shoveling up hot turds is a piece of imbecility. A man can get to love shit if his livelihood depends on it, if his happiness is involved.

—HENRY MILLER (1891–1980)

Changing horses in the middle of a stream, gets you wet and sometimes cold. … Changing faces in the middle of a dream gets you old … oh, gets you old.

—DAN FOGELBERG

Your horse has a reason to be vain. You don't.

—ANDREW GLASS, 14

———◆———

Proper scientific name for horses: Equus keepus brokeus.

—ANONYMOUS

———◆———

The grass is green where the horse has pooped.

—ANNAMARIA TADLOCK

———◆———

[Robert Frost] was like a horse you could get along with if you came up beside him on the okay side.

—ARCHIBALD MACLEISCH

———◆———

Why, I'd horse-whip you if I had a horse.

—GROUCHO MARX

＊

He was so learned that he could name a horse in nine languages; so ignorant that he bought a cow to ride on.

—BENJAMIN FRANKLIN

＊

For some young women, horses become a substitute for boys, who appear to be too much of a risk.

—GAWANI PONY BOY

＊

Ticket seller: "Wait a minute … your ass just sneezed. And horses can't talk. No, no … nothing here adds up at all."

—*FAMILY GUY*, FROM A SCENE IN WHICH BRIAN AND CHRIS TRY TO
SNEAK INTO A FAIR BY WEARING A HORSE SUIT

＊

Fight smog, buy a horse.

—CHARLOTTE MOORE

———◆———

Electronic transfer of funds.

—WALTER T. KEES, WHEN ASKED FOR THE BEST THING EVER SAID
ABOUT HORSES

———◆———

Whisky for my men, beer for my horses.

—WILLIE NELSON AND TOBY KEITH

———◆———

Trust in God, but tie your horse.

—ANONYMOUS

———◆———

I went to horseback riding camp. That's where I discovered Mötley Crüe and acid. My horse fantasies are combined with Mötley Crüe and hallucinogenics.

—MELISSA AUF DER MAUR

If you love horses you'll get horse-shit.

—ERNEST HEMINGWAY

There are no handles to a horse, but the 1910 model has a string to each side of its face for turning its head when there is something you want it to see.

—STEPHEN LEACOCK (1869–1944)

In what other sport do you put on leather boots, stretch-fabric breeches, a shirt and tie, a wool jacket, a velvet-covered cap, and leather gloves, and then go out and exercise?

—A. LONDON WOLF, ON HORSE-SHOWING IN NINETY-DEGREE WEATHER

Women, I never met one yet that was half as reliable as a horse.

—JOHN WAYNE IN *NORTH TO ALASKA*

Why is it that a woman will ignore homicidal tendencies in a horse, but will be furious at a man for leaving a toilet seat up?

—ANONYMOUS

He's definitely one of those horses that walks the fine line between genius and insanity.

—SUE BLINKS

"You know, Doctor," said the horse, "that vet over the hill knows nothing at all. He has been treating me six weeks now—for spavins. What I need is spectacles. I am going blind in one eye. There's no reason why horses shouldn't wear glasses, the same as people."

—HUGH LOFTING, *DOCTOR DOLITTLE*

You know you're a horse lover when you always keep carrots, apples, and sugar cubes in your refrigerator.

—*CHICKEN SOUP FOR THE HORSE LOVER'S SOUL*

You know you're a horse lover when your favorite outfit is made of leather and includes whips and spurs.

—*CHICKEN SOUP FOR THE HORSE LOVER'S SOUL*

I ride horses because it's the only sport where I can exercise while sitting down.

—JOAN HANSEN

A horse that can count to ten is a remarkable horse, not a remarkable mathematician.

—SAMUEL JOHNSON

When I was a kid, if a guy got killed in a Western movie I always wondered who got his horse.

—GEORGE CARLIN

UNDERSTANDING, n. A cerebral secretion that enables one having it to know a house from a horse by the roof on the house. Its nature and laws have been exhaustively expounded by Locke, who rode a house, and Kant, who lived in a horse.

—AMBROSE BIERCE (1842–1914?), *THE DEVIL'S DICTIONARY*

You know you're a horse lover when you talk to your horse more than your spouse.

—*CHICKEN SOUP FOR THE HORSE LOVER'S SOUL*

The one thing I do not want to be called is First Lady. It sounds like a saddle horse.

—JACKIE KENNEDY ONASSIS

❦

My brain is hung like a horse!

—SCOTT KURTZ

❦

To sentence a man of true genius, to the drudgery of a school is to put a racehorse on a treadmill.

—ATTRIBUTED TO VARIOUS

❦

You know you're a horse lover when you think a great vacation is spending a long weekend in front of a horse trailer by a dusty arena.

—CHICKEN SOUP FOR THE HORSE LOVER'S SOUL

❦

In truth, one of our company, the solemn warrior Ecthgow, was so demented from liquor that he was drunk while still upon his horse, and he fell attempting to dismount. Now the horse kicked him in the head, and I feared for his safety, but Ecthgow laughed and kicked the horse back.

—MICHAEL CRICHTON, *EATERS OF THE DEAD*

A horse with a horn is called a unicorn
A horse with stripes is called a zebra
A horse with wings is called Pegasus
And a horse with a broken leg is called glue.

—*THE RED GREEN SHOW*

The first buck, he bucked so hard, I lost my stirrups. Then he bucked so high his left hind foot got into the left stirrup. Well, sir, I figured if he's gettin' on, I'm gettin' off.

—A COWBOY ON WHY HE BAILED OFF A BRONCO HE WAS TRYING TO BREAK

Every horse thinks its own pack heaviest.

—THOMAS FULLER (1608–1661)

If a horse can be said to have a sense of humor, I think Snow Chief may have one.

—BILL BARICH, *DREAMING*

How did you feel feeding doughnuts to a horse? Had a kick out of it, huh? Got a big laugh. Did you ever think of feeding doughnuts to a human being? No!

—ROBERT RISKIN, *MR. DEEDS GOES TO TOWN*

It takes a good deal of physical courage to ride a horse. This, however, I have. I get it at about forty cents a flask, and take it as required.

—STEPHEN LEACOCK

Life ain't certain ... ride your best horse first.

—ANONYMOUS

English Bob: What I heard was that you fell off your horse, drunk, of course, and that you broke your bloody neck.
Little Bill Daggett: I heard that one myself, Bob. Hell, I even thought I was dead. 'Til I found out it was just that I was in Nebraska.

—DAVID WEBB PEOPLES, *UNFORGIVEN*

He who said he made a small fortune in the horse business probably started out with a large fortune!

—ANONYMOUS

Suppose by chance you do get picked up. What have you done? You shot a horse; that isn't first-degree murder; in fact, it isn't even murder; in fact, I don't know what it is.

—STERLING HAYDEN AS JOHNNY CLAY IN *THE KILLING*, ON HIRING A SHOOTER TO CREATE A DIVERSION DURING A ROBBERY

Some folks get credit for having horse sense that hain't ever had enough money to make fools of themselves.

—K. HUBBARD

Why is there always a secret singing when a lawyer cashes in? Why does a hearse horse snicker hauling a lawyer away?

—CARL SANDBURG (1878–1967)

Pat: He was an Anglo-Irishman.
Meg: In the blessed name of God, what's that?
Pat: A Protestant with a horse.

—BRENDAN BEHAN, *AN GIALL (THE HOSTAGE)*

I saw him out riding in the Row, clutching to his horse like a string of onions.

—MARGOT ASQUITH (1864–1945)

Stable thinking is the ability to say "neigh."

—ANONYMOUS

If I weren't reasonably placid, I don't think I could cope with this sort of life. To be a diva, you've got to be absolutely like a horse.

—JOAN SUTHERLAND

She who waits for her knight must remember—she will have to clean up after his horse.

—ANONYMOUS

I know if she falls off she will probably bounce and I know that I will never … try something so silly because if I … happened to fall off, I know adults don't bounce.

—JAN WESTMARK, *KIDS BOUNCE, ADULTS DON'T!*

I didn't say the meat was tough. I said I didn't see the horse that is usually outside.

—W. C. FIELDS

All I say is, nobody has any business to go around looking like a horse and behaving as if it were all right. You don't catch horses going around looking like people, do you?

—DOROTHY PARKER

Alimony is like buying oats for a dead horse.

—ARTHUR BAER

If you're a horse, and someone gets on you, and falls off, and then gets right back on you, I think you should buck him off right away.

—JACK HANDEY

An old horse finds its way best.

—NORWEGIAN PROVERB

I have the experience to be governor. I know how to play craps. I know how to play poker. I know how to go in and out of the Baptist Church and ride horses.

—GOVERNOR EARL LONG

All you need for happiness is a good gun, a good horse, and a good wife.

—DANIEL BOONE (1734–1820)

MUSTANG, n. An indocile horse of the Western plains. In English society, the American wife of an English nobleman.

—AMBROSE BIERCE, *THE DEVIL'S DICTIONARY*

Small children are convinced that ponies deserve to see the inside of the house.

—MAYA PATEL

SIXTY HORSES WEDGED IN A CHIMNEY
The story to fit this sensational headline has not turned up.

—J. B. MORTON

All King Edward's Horses Canter Many Big Fences.

—MNEMONIC FOR THE A-K-E-H-C-M-B-F LETTERS AROUND A
DRESSAGE ARENA

The famous capriole, in which the horse simultaneously leaps into the air while kicking its rear legs backward, was used to clear more space around the horse during armed engagement. It's the equine way of saying, "Get off my back!"

—HERBERT MUSCHAMP

Saddle your horse before sassin' the boss.

—KEN ALSTAD

England is a paradise for women, and hell for horses; Italy is a paradise for horses, hell for women.

—ROBERT BURTON (1577–1640)

You can tell a gelding, you can ask a mare, but you must discuss it with a stallion.

—ANONYMOUS

I voted for *Seabiscuit*. That's the most realistic horse costume I've ever seen.

—BILLY CRYSTAL, AT THE SEVENTY-SIXTH ANNUAL ACADEMY AWARDS

You can't lead a cavalry if you think that you look funny riding a horse.

—JOHN PEERS

My horse was so late getting home, he tiptoed into the stable.

—HENNY YOUNGMAN

They are unpredictable—horses are like women.

—JIMMY PIKE

I speak Spanish to God, Italian to women, French to men, and German to my horse.

—KING CHARLES V (1500–1558)

He don't need a cavalry, but that's just because he's too drunk to ride a horse!

—JERRY "THE KING" LAWLER, PROFESSIONAL WRESTLER, ON JIM FULLINGTON

Paying alimony is like feeding hay to a dead horse.

—GROUCHO MARX

One horse-laugh is worth ten thousand syllogisms. It is not only more effective; it is also vastly more intelligent.

—H. L. MENCKEN (1880–1956)

I know two things about the horse, and one of them is rather coarse.

—ANONYMOUS

The Trojans lost the war because they fell for a really dumb trick. Hey, there's a gigantic wooden horse outside and all the Greeks have left. Let's bring it inside! Not a formula for long-term survival.

—ADAM C. ENGST

A horse divided against itself cannot stand.

—REPORTEDLY, A "STUDENT BLOOPER"

My horse's jockey was hitting the horse. The horse turns around and says, "Why are you hitting me, there is nobody behind us!"

—HENNY YOUNGMAN

GNU, n. An animal of South Africa, which in its domesticated state resembles a horse, a buffalo, and a stag. In its wild condition it is something like a thunderbolt, an earthquake and a cyclone.

—AMBROSE BIERCE, *THE DEVIL'S DICTIONARY*

I believe in the horse; the car will not survive.

—WILHELM II (1859–1941)

Years ago, I saved up a million dollars from acting—a lot of money then—and I spent it all on a horse farm in Tucson. Now when I go down there, I look at the place and I realize my whole acting career adds up to a million dollars' worth of horseshit.

—ROBERT MITCHUM

You might be a redneck if you think a quarter horse is that ride in front of Kmart.

—JEFF FOXWORTHY

—⧫—

You've got to put the saddle on the right horse.

—NAVJOT SINGH SIDHU, INDIAN CRICKET COMMENTATOR. HE IS
FAMOUS FOR HIS WITTICISMS THAT HAVE COME TO BE KNOWN AS
SIDHUISMS.

—⧫—

Never let a gift horse in the house.

—ANONYMOUS

—⧫—

You can take a horse to water, but a pencil must be lead.

—STAN LAUREL

—⧫—

A loose horse will always be found at the barn.

—INDIAN PROVERB

Want to end up with a million bucks in the horse business? Start out with five million.

—ANONYMOUS

I don't mind when my horse is left at the post. I don't mind when my horse comes up to me in the stands and asks, "Which way do I go?" But when the horse I bet on is at the $2 window betting on another horse in the same race?

—HENNY YOUNGMAN

Horses just naturally have Mohawk haircuts.

—ANONYMOUS

My other car is a horse.

—ANONYMOUS

'Orses and dorgs is some men's fancy. They're wittles and drink to me.

—CHARLES DICKENS (1812–1870)

There are only two emotions that belong in the saddle; one is a sense of humor and the other is patience.

—JOHN LYONS

When a saboteur asked her why the horse was so hot and sweated up; "If I had you between my legs for two and a half hours you dear sir, you would be equally as hot and sweaty."

—LADY THORNICROFT, AFTER A HUNT

The horse stopped with a jerk, and the jerk fell off.

—JIM CULLETON

Suddenly it became a one-horse fight.

—STEVE BUNCE

A camel is a horse designed by a committee.

—ALEC ISSIGORIS, *THE GUARDIAN*

Some of my best leading men have been dogs and horses.

—ELIZABETH TAYLOR

They think they can make fuel from horse manure. ... Now, I don't know if your car will be able to get thirty miles to the gallon, but it's sure gonna put a stop to siphoning.

—BILLIE HOLIDAY

They say he rides as if he's part of the horse, but they don't say which part.

—ROBERT SHERWOOD, ON TOM MIX

It doesn't matter what you do in the bedroom as long as you don't do it in the street and frighten the horses.

—DAPHNE FIELDING, *DUCHESS OF JERMYN STREET: ROSA LEWIS*

When your horse bolts for ten minutes flat, you know to get off and give up. The question is, how?

—ANNAROSE ROBINSON

Heaven is the place where the donkey finally catches up with his carrot: hell is the eternity while he waits for it.

—RUSSELL GREEN

———⊰◈⊱———

Your horse probably won't go too far without you if there is some tasty grass around—remember to keep some handy if you anticipate falling off.

—*THE HORSE ILLUSTRATED GUIDE TO ENGLISH RIDING*

———⊰◈⊱———

[E]ither don't screw up your kids, or don't have any! It's a lot like owning a horse: If you can't keep it in a stall, feed it some hay, and brush it down once in a while, then don't have one! … Just don't have one and let it rot in the yard!

—ADAM CAROLLA

———⊰◈⊱———

To confess that you are totally ignorant about the horse is social suicide: You will be despised by everybody, especially the horse.

—W. C. SELLAR

———⊰◈⊱———

You can tell a horse owner by the interior of their car. Boots, mud, pony nuts, straw, items of tack, and a screwed-up waxed jacket of incredible antiquity. There is normally a top layer of children and dogs.

—HELEN THOMPSON

Whoever said money can't buy happiness didn't know where to buy a horse.

—ANONYMOUS

One white foot, buy 'em; Two white feet, try 'em; Three white feet, be on the sly; Four white feet, pass 'em by.

—COWBOY PROBERB

CENTAUR: One of a race of persons who lived before the division of labor had been carried to such a pitch of differentiation, and who followed the primitive economic maxim, "every man his own horse."

—AMBROSE BIERCE, *THE DEVIL'S DICTIONARY*

She will do everything and anything I ask her as long as she thinks
it is okay!

—MARY ANN HOLAN, OWNER OF APPALOOSA MARE

"We're wild horses. We're going to eat your food, knock down your tent,
and poop on your shoes. We're protected by federal law, just like
Richard Nixon."

—DAVE BARRY, ON WILD HORSES

Emily, I've a little confession to make. I really am a horse doctor.
But marry me, and I'll never look at any other horse!

—GROUCHO MARX

Hoof picks migrate.

—ANONYMOUS

I don't mind what Congress does, as long as they don't do it in the streets and frighten the horses.

—VICTOR HUGO (1802–1885)

There is just as much horse sense as ever, but the horses have most of it.

—ANONYMOUS

When I hear somebody talk about a horse or cow being stupid, I figure it's a sure sign that the animal has outfoxed them.

—ANONYMOUS

Trickle-down theory—-the less than elegant metaphor that if one feeds the horse enough oats, some will pass through to the road for the sparrows.

—J. K. GALBRAITH, *THE CULTURE OF CONTENTMENT*

Behind every great horse is a human cleaning up.

—ANONYMOUS

———————

To err is human. To forgive, equine.

—ANONYMOUS

———————

I've spent my whole life being told that I have a face like a horse.
You are just what you are, aren't you?

—JEREMY PAXMAN

———————

Rodeo, the only sport that gets you off in eight seconds or less.

—ANONYMOUS

———————

Certain comic effects can be achieved by a brand-new rider, especially a man who dresses like a fashion model and rides like a tailor.

—C. J. J. MULLEN

———◆———

They used to take your horse and if they were caught they got hung for it. Now if they take your car and if they are caught, it's a miracle.

—WILL ROGERS

———◆———

I don't understand anything about the ballet; all I know is that during the intervals the ballerinas stink like horses.

—ANTON PAVLOVICH CHEKHOV

———◆———

If I didn't own a horse, this would be a Ferrari!

—SEEN ON A BUMPER STICKER

———◆———

There are fools, damn fools, and those who remount in a steeplechase.

—BILL WHITBREAD

Having a jealous wife means if you come home with a hair on your coat, you'd better have the horse to match.

—KEN ALSTAD

All music is folk music, I ain't never heard no horse sing a song.

—LOUIS ARMSTRONG

If you ride a horse, sit close and tight; If you ride a man, sit easy and light.

—BENJAMIN FRANKLIN

Politicians are like the bones of a horse's foreshoulder—not a straight one in it.

—WENDELL PHILIPS (1811–1884)

I'd like to play a horse, many people think I already have. Either end of the horse would be fine.

—DAWN FRENCH

It's not his fault that he's the rear end of a pantomime horse.

—VINCENT MANIS

CIRCUS, n. A place where horses, ponies, and elephants are permitted to see men, women, and children acting the fool.

—AMBROSE BIERCE, *THE DEVIL'S DICTIONARY*

You can lead a horse to water … if he's thirsty.

—HANK KETCHUM, *DENNIS THE MENACE* COMIC STRIP

Motherhood is the strangest thing; it can be like being one's own Trojan horse.

—REBECCA WEST

The difference between playing the stock market and the horses is that one of the horses must win.

—JOEY ADAMS, *READER'S DIGEST*

CHAPTER SIX

"My Kingdom for a Horse!": The Horse in Literature (Including a Shakespearean Interlude)

There are many obvious disadvantages to waiting until middle age to discover horses. One came up in the introduction to Chapter Five: namely, that to fall off your horse when you're fifty-plus involves a worrisomely high probability that you won't just break, you'll splatter.

On the other hand, there are a couple of definite *advantages* to having waited, and perhaps the chief among them, if you're a booklover as well as a horselover, is that there are so many great horse books to finally get around to.

(I thought the same would be true about horse movies, by the way, but I've been sadly disappointed. Maybe I've just been unlucky in my choices down at our local Blockbuster: I ended up half-watching a herd of real stinkers, most of them of recent vintage and the worst of which didn't even offset the clichéd script and lousy human acting by giving lots of screen time to the couldn't-be-faulted equine cast.)

But back to reading. Take, for instance, *Black Beauty*. For many years now I have made my living in the world of books—editing, writing, publishing, bookselling—but until I went horse mad I'd never even peeked into Anna Sewell's poignant story of sweet Beauty's life in nineteenth-century England. You, I hope, by contrast have known and loved the tale since your own horse-happy childhood, and might even be able to recite from memory the excerpts from the book that you'll find in this and other chapters—excerpts like this simple yet movingly evocative one: "It was a great treat to us to be turned out into the home paddock or the old orchard. The grass was so cool and soft to our feet, the air so sweet, and the freedom to do as we liked was so pleasant—to gallop, to lie down, and roll over on our backs, or to nibble the sweet grass."

If, though, you haven't read *Black Beauty*, or other masterpieces sampled here such as Marguerite Henry's *King of the Wind*, perhaps you'll be inspired to *want* to read them. Indeed, if you haven't realized yet, this whole *Gigantic Book* ought to supply you with hundreds of leads to classic writing about horses.

Let me also note that we've turned several pages over to the writer who penned the famous line that we quote in this chapter's title. It's really no surprise that Shakespeare often referred to horses in his work: they were indispensable to and omnipresent throughout the Britain of his day, after all. But while there are some unforgettable horse-themed phrases and images in his plays, do they actually tell us anything about what kind of horseman the Bard of Avon was? Hard to say—although, as parodist James Agate has cleverly suggested, Hamlet probably *did* mean to soliloquize: "What a piece of work is a horse! ... In form and moving how express and admirable!"

With hearts pounding and breath quickening, the men … stared toward the silvered hills. Not four hundred yards away, they saw him coming! Fury—the ebony king of the range! He was moving at an easy gallop, his hoofs making hollow, drumlike sounds on the grass.

—ALBERT G. MILLER, *FURY: STALLION OF BROKEN WHEEL RANCH*

His son, Emile, had tried this foolish experiment of raising horses on the reef, and given his life under the stallion's hoofs.

—CHARLES TENNEY JACKSON, *THE HORSE OF HURRICANE REEF*

February's early morning chill filled the barn and steam billowed from the horse's heaving body and flared nostrils.

—EUGENE DAVIS, *FROM THE HORSE'S MOUTH*

Billy explained how to use a stick of licorice for a bit until Galiban was used to having something in his mouth. Billy explained, "Of course we could force-break him to everything, but he wouldn't be as good a horse if we did.

—JOHN STEINBECK (1902–1968)

For a hundred and fifty years,
In the pasture of dead horses,
Roots of pine trees pushed through the pale curves of your ribs,
Yellow blossoms flourished above you in autumn, and in winter
Frost heaved your bones in the ground—old toilers, soil makers:
O Roger, Mackerel, Riley, Ned, Nellie, Chester, Lady Ghost.

—DONALD HALL, *NAMES OF HORSES*

I went up to the table, snatched up a glass of brandy and filled my mouth with it, then went back to the pony, took him by the head, and sent a squirt of brandy up each nostril; I squirted the rest down his throat.

—SOMERVILLE AND ROSS, *THE BAGMAN'S PONY*

⬥

"Are horses smart or dumb?" I asked Buster.
"They are very smart," he said with conviction. "Very intelligent. And if you ask one to do something he was going to do anyway, you hurt his feelings, you insult his intelligence."

—THOMAS MCGUANE, *BUSTER*

⬥

Thou shall be for Man a source of happiness and wealth; thy back shall be a seat of honor, and thy belly of riches; every grain of barley given thee shall purchase indulgence for the sinner.

—THE KORAN

⬥

At its best, the poetry of the open range remains, not in the sacred, melodramatic antics of the stunt horses but in the precision of that minority singled out as "cow horses," sometimes lost in the artificial atmosphere of the big events.

—THOMAS MCGUANE

No horse ... can be courageous if it has no spirit.

—PLATO

He began to speak softly to the old horse but his voice was steady, almost conversational, as though he was chatting to a friend.

—JAMES HERRIOT, *ALL THINGS BRIGHT AND BEAUTIFUL*

Give a man a horse he can ride,
Give a man a boat he can sail;
And his rank and wealth, his strength and health,
On sea nor shore shall fail.

—JAMES THOMSON (1700–1748)

"Get up!" he shouted … And the great horse did so. First plunging up, but with his haunches squatted in the water … Then to all fours and standing and standing with his tail whipped about on his heaving flanks. He seemed watching that wall of water blow for the Gulf.

—CHARLES TENNEY JACKSON, *THE HORSE OF HURRICANE REEF*

Stronger than that was sense of partnership between these officers and their charges, the incredible bond between them created by so many shared experiences and so many hours spent together.

—TAD COFFIN

Man, encompassed by the elements which conspired to destroy him, would have been a slave had not the horse made him a king.

—ANONYMOUS

The horses swam ashore to the same mysterious island—Assateague—and for years afterward were seen by visitors from the nearby mainland wandering the pine forests like shadows.

—RICH POMERANTZ, *WILD HORSES OF THE DUNES*

Far back, far back in our dark soul the horse prances … The horse, the horse! The symbol of surging potency and power of movement.

—D. H. LAWRENCE (1885–1930)

As I was going by Charing Cross,
I saw a black man upon a black horse.
They told me it was King Charles the First.
Oh dear, my heart was ready to burst!

—ANONYMOUS

"Many's the thousand miles I've walked after you, awd lad, and many's the talk we've had together. But I didn't have to say much to tha, did I? I reckon you knew every move I made, everything I said. Just one little word and you always did what ah wanted you to do."

—JAMES HERRIOT, *ALL THINGS BRIGHT AND BEAUTIFUL*

She pulled his right ear, stroked it; then pressed her fingers against his poll. Duke's head came lower over her shoulder. His big lips twitched. He reached even lower and with his lips cleanly plucked a carrot from Pauline's jacket pocket.

—JOCELYN REEKIE, *THE WEEK OF THE HORSE*

She knew that the horse, born to serve nobly, had waited in vain for someone noble to serve. His spirit knew that nobility had gone out of men.

—D. H. LAWRENCE

Horse, thou art truly a creature without equal, for thou fliest without wings and conquerest without sword.

—THE KORAN

Children, dogs, and horses is regarded in this country as sacred items and it is considered pretty close to a felony to even make a face when any of the three is mentioned.

—RING LARDNER, *TIPS ON HORSES*

Look at the horse … that great animal that stands so close to man.

—FYODOR DOSTOEVSKY (1821–1881)

"Well, this horse, he's eager, he's willing. He's straightforward and honest, you know. You ask him something and he understands. He's willing to work with you."

—GENE SMITH, *THE CHAMPION*

And God took a handful of southerly wind, blew His breath over it and created the horse.

—BEDOUIN SAYING

He outran the colts his own age and the seasoned running horses as well. He seemed not to know that he was an earthly creature with four legs, like other horses. He acted as if he were an airy thing, traveling on the wings of the wind.

—MARGUERITE HENRY, *KING OF THE WIND: THE STORY OF THE GODOLPHIN ARABIAN*

Villain, a horse—
Villain, I say, give me a horse to fly,
To swim the river, villain, and to fly.

—GEORGE PEELE (1556–1596)

I turned away. I had dreamed great dreams. They were gone. There would never be another racehorse born in our barn.

—GENE SMITH, *THE CHAMPION*

He met her and fell in love and married her, and part of the wedding vows were "love me, love my horses." It was part and parcel of the whole relationship.

—COOKY MCCLUNG, *FROM SAILBOATS TO SNAFFLES IN ONE EASY MARRIAGE*

Suffering for the pleasure of others is nothing new to me. I have even begun to find a certain equine pleasure in it. Let him swagger, poor fellow! … thought the gelding, and stepping carefully on his crooked legs he went along the middle of the road.

—LEO TOLSTOY, *STRIDER—THE STORY OF A HORSE*

[T]he Lord looked down on a Sunday morning and saw that something was missing—something that represented His patience, His understanding, His love, His everything, indeed all that was good—and He created the horse.

—FRANZ MAIRINGER, *HORSES ARE MADE TO BE HORSES*

She could hardly wait for it to be morning. She was going to spend two whole weeks on a real farm with horses. What a perfect vacation!

—GERTRUDE CHANDLER WARNER

It was a great treat to us to be turned out into the home paddock or the old orchard. The grass was so cool and soft to our feet, the air so sweet, and the freedom to do as we liked was so pleasant—to gallop, to lie down, and roll over on our backs, or to nibble the sweet grass.

—ANNA SEWELL, *BLACK BEAUTY: THE AUTOBIOGRAPHY OF A HORSE*

The mares are for whoever is man enough to take them.

—CHARLES TENNEY JACKSON, *THE HORSE OF HURRICANE REEF*

Yet when books have been read and reread, it boils down to the horse, his human companion, and what goes on between them.

—WALTER FARLEY

Every single movement of Florian's revealed nobility, grace, significance, and distinction all in one; and in each of his poses he was the ideal model for a sculptor, the composite of all the equestrian statues in history.

—FELIX SALTEN (1869–1945)

He is white and clearly one of the most beautiful horses I have ever beheld. Seeing him reminds one that there is still a God, even though we are in the middle of some dismal war.

—ANN RINALDI, *A RIDE INTO MORNING: THE STORY OF TEMPE WICK*

The great majority of men, especially in France, both desire and possess a fashionable woman, much in the way one might own a fine horse—as a luxury befitting a young man.

—STENDHAL

Higher and higher receded the sky, wider and wider spread the streak of dawn … People began to get up, and in the owner's stable-yard the sounds of snorting, the rustling of litter, and even the shrill angry neighing of horses crowded together and at variance about something, grew more and more frequent.

—LEO TOLSTOY (1828–1910)

The farmer's horse is never lame, never unfit to go. Never throws out curbs, never breaks down before or behind. … He does not paw and prance, and arch his neck, and bid the world admire his beauties … and when he is wanted, he can always do his work.

—ANTHONY TROLLOPE (1815–1882)

My name is Sunka Wakan, the Great Spirit Horse. I guess you could say that I am a very unique animal. … I have lived all these years because I have become a legend. You see, legends never die. They live on forever in the hearts of those who love to hear them.

—LINDA LITTLE WOLF, *GREAT SPIRIT HORSE*

He was a horse of goodly countenance, rather expressive of vigilance than fire; though an unnatural appearance of fierceness was thrown into it by the loss of his ears, which had been cropped pretty close to his head.

—AUGUSTUS B. LONGSTREET (1790–1870)

The sight of him did something to me I've never quite been able to explain. He was more than tremendous strength and speed and beauty of motion. He set me dreaming.

—WALT MOREY

His make and shape were so nearly perfect that he looked smaller at first glance. His shoulders were strong and well placed. … But perhaps the thing which struck you most about him was his proud and honest outlook. He was a beautiful horse.

—RICHARD FINDLAY, *THE DREAM*

———⋙⋘———

The horse is a very gregarious creature.

—ARTHUR CONAN DOYLE (1859–1930)

———⋙⋘———

Every day I pray to God to give me horses—wonderful horses—to make me the best rider in England.

—ENID BAGNOLD (1880–1981)

———⋙⋘———

We be of one blood, ye and I.

—RUDYARD KIPLING (1865–1936)

The cult of the horse as their idol is as central to their lives as cocaine is to some and applause is to others.

—JUDITH KRANTZ

At least a half mile behind us was the Stable-Mart, the sorry excuse for a stable, where I had the royal job of mucking out stalls. Anything to be near horses.

—DANDI DALEY MACKALL

She could still hear Dad's words when he'd given Dove to her five years earlier. "I picked him because he looks like you, Jan. Both long-boned graceful. And you got the same look in your eyes, like you were wanting something."

—C. S. ADLER, *ONE UNHAPPY HORSE*

The ability and intelligence is remarkable … Prince was able to walk the length of the furrow, between the growing potatoes, and when he was done you might never guess that he passed that way, so sure and careful was every footfall.

—PAUL HEINEY

The eyes, circled by his sad and beautiful darkness, were so sorrowful, lonely, gentle, and nobly tragic, that they killed all other emotions except love.

—T. H. WHITE

The smell was a mixture of hay and leather and—OK, maybe the faint odor of horse poop. But nothing had ever smelled as good.

—NANCY RUE

The bay filly ... had more than beauty—she was so obviously the outcome of a splendid and selected ancestry. Even her manners were aristocratic.

—JOHN TAINTOR FOOTE

If Samantha had been born a horse, she would have been a plain bay.

—SUSAN NUSSER, *IN SERVICE TO THE HORSE*

I groomed the stallion until the desired change, because, comrades, I am a lover of white horses and have put into them that small quantity of strength that has remained to me.

—ISAAC BABEL (1894–1940)

My brother shall have a pair of horses with wings to fly among the clouds.

—RABINDRANATH TAGORE (1861–1941)

Whose only fit companion is his horse.

—WILLIAM COWPER

I saw a child who couldn't walk,
sit on a horse and laugh and talk; …
I saw a child who could only crawl,
mount a horse and sit up tall; …
I saw a child born into strife,
take up and hold the reins of life;
And the same child was heard to say,
'Thank you God for showing me the way.'

—JOHN ANTHONY DAVIS

Inside the archway I paused. I love stables and horses and grooms, the cheerful sound of buckets, the heady smell of straw, the orderly fussiness of a saddle-room; always the same and ever different. The mind halts … at the moment when one sets foots within a stable-yard.

—MOLLY KEANE

My horse Abramka I endow to the regiment, I endow my horse for the remembrance of my soul.

—ISAAC BABEL

Magic was stabled at the sort of yard which should have warned Angela to beware … caution was nowhere to be found. She looked trustingly at the nondescript bay gelding produced for her inspection and saw only her dreams.

—DICK FRANCIS, *SPRING FEVER*

A Woman never looks better than on horseback.

—JANE AUSTEN (1775–1817)

The two piebald horses, though they had shining coats and were obviously well cared-for, a fact Maria noticed at once because she adored horses, were old and stout and moved slowly.

—ELIZABETH GOUDGE, *THE LITTLE WHITE HORSE*

His neck is high and erect, his head replete with intelligence, his belly short, his back full, and his proud chest swells with hard muscles.

—VIRGIL (70–19 BC)

Buster began by breaking broncs, grubbing prickly pear, chopping firewood, wrangling horses, and held the cut when a big herd was being worked, a lowly job where much can be learned.

—THOMAS MCGUANE, *BUSTER*

I have never seen such a perfectly formed animal. Beautiful and graceful like a gazelle, he burned hot and wild with the deserts of Egypt in his soul.

—LYNN V. ANDREWS

Over the centuries the horse and his movement have been an inspiration to artists, poets, and writers.

—SUSAN E. HARRIS

And horses and mules and asses (hath He created) that ye may ride them, and for ornament. And he createth that which ye know not.

—THE KORAN

A fine horse or a beautiful woman, I cannot look at them unmoved, even now when seventy winters have chilled my blood.

—SIR ARTHUR CONAN DOYLE

The creator was glad. He had given habitations to his other creatures, forests to some, caves to others, but because of his enjoyment of the disinterested spirit of energy in the Horse, he gave him an open meadow under the eye of Heaven.

—RABINDRANATH TAGORE

The difference between an author and a horse is that the horse doesn't understand the horse dealer's language.

—MAX FRISCH

[H]is mind was for a time … of thoughts diverse and wayward. Jim. His brother, so suddenly and so violently gone. The stallion. That beast that had kicked him to death. With anger and hate and pitiless impatience of time he thought of the morrow, when they could catch him.

—WILBUR DANIEL STEELE, *BLUE MURDER*

[T]he man grew more familiar with horse terminology. When early on, one suggested he put a loafing shed in the big pasture, the man said, "That sounds nice; what's a loafing shed?"

—COOKY MCCLUNG, *FROM SAILBOATS TO SNAFFLES IN ONE EASY MARRIAGE*

And the hoofs of the horses shakes the crumbling field as they run.

—VIRGIL, *THE AENEID*

They had searched and searched to find the man a horse with a personality like his boat's, a horse that did pretty much what you told it to … the man often longed for an anchor to "throw overboard" when they got going a little too fast.

—COOKY MCCLUNG, *FROM SAILBOATS TO SNAFFLES IN ONE EASY MARRIAGE*

I will sing to the Lord, for he has triumphed gloriously; horse and rider he has thrown into the sea.

—EXODUS 15:1

The Iron Horse was coming … Thundering and panting and breathing black smoke, it was a fearsome thing.

—PAUL GOBLE, *DEATH OF THE IRON HORSE*

I think I learned this (not necessarily to follow the majority opinion) when, as a boy on horseback, my interest was not in the campus; it was beyond it; and I was dependent upon. Not the majority of boys, but myself and the small group that happened to have horses.

—LINCOLN STEFFANS (1866–1936)

Some evenings his wife would find him just sitting in the pasture among the daisies like Ferdinand among his flowers, watching his very own horse as it strolled about chomping grass.

—COOKY MCCLUNG, *FROM SAILBOATS TO SNAFFLES IN ONE EASY MARRIAGE*

If some beggar steals a bridle he'll be hung by a man who's stolen a horse. There's no surer justice in the world than that which makes the rich thief hang the poor one.

—PÈIRE CARDENAL (1180–1278)

The talisman was held by the People of the Horse. … They carved a great white horse to honor Equus.

—ANDREA SPALDING, *THE WHITE HORSE TALISMAN*

Nor was he in the fields or anywhere except the place where good horses go when they are dead.

—RUSSELL A. VASSALLO, *TEARS AND TALES*

Hobbs did something I have never seen any horse do before or since. As the child stood by the pony's shoulder, Hobbs reached around with his head and neck and pressed Adam into his body. The pony held him so tightly in the curve of his neck that he could not raise his arms.

—KIM MEEDER, *STORIES FROM THE RANCH OF RESCUED DREAMS*

The mare lies down in the grass where the next of the skylark is hidden. Her eyes drink the delicate horizon moving behind the song. Deep sink the skies, a well of voices. Her sleep is the vessel of Summer.

—VERNON WATKINS

I would lean against my father's warmth and never suspect there was any other thing to be but happy.

—CAREY WINFREY, *TIP ON A LOST RACE*

[A]ll the good horsemen … are good people, too. There is a correlation at the deepest level.

—MELISSA PIERSON

[H]orses have always been subtle symbols of wealth and power. The Bedouin tribesmen of the Arabian desert are quick to point out that "a man's treasure is carried in the bellies of his mares."

—ROBERT M. MILLER, *UNDERSTANDING THE ANCIENT SECRETS OF THE HORSE'S MIND*

———◆———

They swayed about upon a rocking horse,
And thought it Pegasus.

—JOHN KEATS

———◆———

[S]hould I ever be designated Creator for a Day, one of my first duties will be to see to it that horses live as long as parrots or turtles.

—PAUL ZARZYSKI, *GOOD HORSE KEEPING*

———◆———

Here lies the body of my good horse, The General. For years he bore me around the circuit of my practice and all that time he never made a blunder. Would that his master could say the same.

—EPITAPH FOR JOHN TYLER'S HORSE

When God wanted to create the horse, he said to the South Wind, "I want to make a creature of you. Condense." And the wind condensed.

—ABD AL-QADIR (1808–1883)

I have a horse in Ireland. … I've not bought her, but we all know she's my horse. … I do know that never have I had such telepathy with a horse. When I'm mounted, boundaries dissolve. Horse and rider—sisters, if you will—share one body, one mind and yes, one soul.

—ELLIE PHAYER

The day was as hot as the sun on a bay horse's back.

—VERLYN KLINKENBORG, *GRATITUDE: WHEN CONTENTEDNESS COMES HOME*

The great horse suddenly appeared with a neigh that was like the roar of a lion.

—CHARLES TENNEY JACKSON, *THE HORSE OF HURRICANE REEF*

The outside of a horse is good for the inside of a man.

—SIR WINSTON CHURCHILL

I am not irreverent if I ask this, my prayer, in the name of Him who was born in a stable.

— CAPTAIN DE CONDENBOVE, FRENCH ARMY, WORLD WAR I. THIS APPEARED IN *FIELD ARTILLERY MANUAL, VOL. 1*, BY ARTHUR R. WILSON, CAPT., FIELD ARTILLERY, U.S. ARMY, 1926

Sir, I'm not a horseman, but it didn't take a horseman to admire that horse. He was a seal-brown three-year-old with white on three of his legs, a white star on his forehead, and the largest, finest eye I ever saw on any horse.

—GORDON GRAND, *A NIGHT AT THE OLD BERGEN COUNTY RACE-TRACK*

So long as a man rides his Hobby-Horse peaceably and quietly along the King's highway, and neither compels you or me to get up behind him— pray, Sir, what have either you or I to do with it?

—LAURENCE STERNE (1713–1768)

At a tavern hereabouts the hostler greeted our horse as an old acquaintance, though he did not remember the driver. … Every man to his trade. I am not acquainted with a single horse in the world, not even the one that kicked me.

—HENRY DAVID THOREAU (1817–1862)

"In the beginning there was a wild horse, and that horse was man. ..." So goes the oldest of Babylonian myths.

—GERALD HAUSMAN AND LORETTA HAUSMAN, *THE MYTHOLOGY OF HORSES: HORSE LEGEND AND LORE THROUGHOUT THE AGES*

One reason why birds and horses are happy is because they are not trying to impress other birds and horses.

—DALE CARNEGIE, *HOW TO WIN FRIENDS AND INFLUENCE PEOPLE*

Antar drifted off to sleep. He dreamed of horses ... of manes flying in the wind like flags, of horses that drank the wind like water ... of bright hooves that were round and flat as beaten coins ... of stallion's eyes that were deeper than the deepest well.

—GERALD HAUSMAN, LORETTA HAUSMAN, AND ROBERT FLORCZAK, *HORSES OF MYTH*

The horse moved like a dancer, which is not surprising. A horse is a beautiful animal, but it is perhaps most remarkable because it moves as if it always hears music.

—MARK HELPRIN, *A WINTER'S TALE*

A man on a horse is spiritually, as well as physically, bigger than a man on foot.

—JOHN STEINBECK

Pegasus seemed hardly to be a creature of the earth. Whenever he was seen, up very high above people's heads, with the sunshine on his silvery wings, you would have thought that he belonged to the sky, and that … he had got astray … and was seeking his way back again.

—NATHANIEL HAWTHORNE (1804–1864),

If I had a horse, I'd ride off in the sunset, where dreams and shadows lie. To a life where pain and sorrow don't exist, and to where hopes and dreams become reality.

—LINDSAY TURCOTTE

The wind of heaven is that which blows between a horse's ears.

—ARABIAN PROVERB

Centuries of literature supply … confusion. One reads that horses are hysterically timid, yet courageous in war and sport. … We are told that the horse is … dim-witted. …We then learn that the horse finds its way home in the dark over many miles of the most difficult and unfamiliar terrain.

—TOM AINSLIE, *THE BODY LANGUAGE OF HORSES*

His hooves pound the beat, your heart sings the song.

—JERRY SHULMAN

God held a handful of ash, blew into it saying: "Let it be the purest of creatures." Out of His hand galloped the black horse.

—ROBERT FROTHINGHAM

The old grey horse … simply abandoned himself to his natural emotions. Rearing, plunging, backing steadily, in spite of all the Mole's efforts at his head, and all the Mole's lively language directed at his better feelings, he drove the cart backwards towards the deep ditch at the side of the road.

—KENNETH GRAHAME (1859–1932)

True to her noble spirit, Brenda had spared us from ever having to make the decision to end her life. Instead, she died out in he pasture as she had lived her life, with class and courage … no doubt just the way she would have wanted to go.

—EILEEN WATKINS, *CLASS AND COURAGE*

There's something in a flying horse,
There's something in a huge balloon.

—WILLIAM WORDSWORTH (1770–1850)

Creature with a pretty face,
wild spirit, gentle grace
walking in a golden lace
beneath the open sky.

—ANONYMOUS

Without the horse what would have become of man? It has served us for transport, in agriculture, industry since the dawn of time.

—BERTRAND LECLAIR

[T]he floss-silk manes tossed up like the crest of a breaking wave. … Light ran and glittered on them. They were obedient … you would have sworn … as the white horses of the wave crests are to pull of the moon.

—MARY STEWART

And indeed, a horse who bears himself proudly is a thing of such beauty and astonishment that he attracts the eyes of all beholders. No one will tire of looking at him as long as he will display himself in his splendor.

—XENOPHON

His neck is high and erect, his head replete with intelligence, his belly short, his back full, and his proud chest swells with hard muscles.

—VIRGIL

Old age is sometimes majestic, sometimes ugly, and sometimes pathetic. But old age can be both ugly and majestic, and the gelding's old age was just of that kind.

—LEO TOLSTOY

It's always been and always will be the same in the world: The horse does the work and the coachman is tipped.

—ANONYMOUS

Is there a sensitive ear, alert as a flame, in your every fiber? Hearing the familiar song from above, all in one accord you strain your bronze chests and, hooves barely touching the ground, turn into straight lines cleaving the air, and all inspired by God it rushes on!

—NIKOLAI GOGOL (1809–1852)

A horse loves freedom, and the weariest old workhorse will roll on the ground or break into a lumbering gallop when he is turned loose into the open.

—GERALD RAFERTY

I can always tell which is the front-end of a horse, but beyond that, my art is not above the ordinary.

—MARK TWAIN

I heard a neigh. Oh, such a brisk and melodious neigh as that was! My very heart leaped with delight at the sound.

—NATHANIEL HAWTHORNE

The ass will carry his load, but not a double load; ride not a free horse to death.

—MIGUEL DE CERVANTES (1547–1616)

The reckless expenditure of air and ether in his composition was amazing. And, in consequence, he perpetually struggled to outreach the wind, to outrun space itself. Other animals ran only when they had a reason, but the Horse would run for no reason whatever, as if to run out of his own skin.

—RABINDRANATH TAGORE

Four things greater than all things are
Women and Horses and Power and War.

—RUDYARD KIPLING

Papa's own daddy had been killed when a horse kicked him in the head,
so I guess he's got good reason to be cautious, but I still think it's not fair
… you can die from choking on a piece of bread or meat, but that doesn't
mean you're not gonna eat, does it?

—NATALIE KINSEY-WARNOCK, *IF WISHES WERE HORSES*

For want of a Nail the Shoe was lost;
for want of a Shoe the Horse was lost;
and for want of a Horse the Rider was lost …

—BENJAMIN FRANKLIN

All the sounds dear to a horseman were around me—the snort of the horses as they cleared their throats, the gentle swish of their tails, the tinkle of irons as we flung the saddles over their backs—little sounds of no importance, but they stay in the unconscious library of memory.

—WYNFORD VAUGHAN-THOMAS

———✦———

Only the stars of the desert are more numerous than the thoughts in my head," Antar whispered to himself. "Oh, how filled with longing am I, and how deeply I wish to ride on a mare's back and to feel the desert storm unfurl about my spurred heels."

—GERALD HAUSMAN, LORETTA HAUSMAN, AND ROBERT FLORCZAK, *HORSES OF MYTH*

———✦———

They say princes learn no art truly but the art of horsemanship. The reason is the brave beast is no flatterer. He will throw a prince as soon as his groom.

—BEN JONSON (1572–1637)

———✦———

Take most people, they're crazy about cars. I'd rather have a goddam horse. A horse is at least human, for God's sake.

—J. D. SALINGER, *THE CATCHER IN THE RYE*

His ears pricked forward and joined his nose and eyes in deep attention. … His posture was that of intense curiosity, a primary characteristic of horses.

—TOM AINSLIE, *THE BODY LANGUAGE OF HORSES*

Gipsy gold does not chink and glitter. It gleams in the sun and neighs in the dark.

—ATTRIBUTED TO THE CLADDAUGH GYPSIES OF GALWAY

The horse is flesh and blood on a noble scale.

—JEFF GRIEFFEN

I am a good horse to travel, but not from choice a roadster. The landscape-painter uses the figures of men to mark a road. He would not make that use of my figure.

—HENRY DAVID THOREAU, *WALKING*

Gamaun is a dainty steed,
Strong, black, and of a noble breed,
Full of fire, and full of bone,
With all his line of fathers known;
Fine his nose, his nostrils thin,
But blown abroad by the pride within;
His mane is like a river flowing,
And his eyes like embers glowing
In the darkness of the night,
And his pace as swift as light.

—BARRY CORNWALL (1787–1874)

Then, day sniffed with its blue nose through the open stable window, and found them—the foal nuzzling its mother, velvet fumbling for her milk.

—Ferenc Juhász

⟞⟝

I create you, Arabian, and you are the most Blessed of all the animals. Wealth will be carried on your back and kindness in your eyes. Bedouins, let your horses run freely.

—Bedouin legend

⟞⟝

At my door the Pale Horse stands to carry me to unknown lands.

—John Milton Hay (1838–1905)

⟞⟝

She lifted the drooping muzzle with both hands … It was a special embrace saved for special occasions.

—JEAN M. AUEL

———⟫•⟪———

Lived in his saddle, loved the chase, the course,
And always, ere he mounted, kiss'd his horse.

—WILLIAM COWPER (1731–1800)

———⟫•⟪———

There will never be a time when the old horse is not superior to any auto ever made.

—WILL ROGERS

———⟫•⟪———

The horses of Achilles stood apart from their battle weeping, because they had learned that their charioteer had fallen. ... When Zeus saw ... he took pity. ... "Poor creatures, why did I give you to King Peleus, a mortal destined to die—you who are immortal."

—HOMER (C. 800 BC), *THE ILIAD*

The hooves of the horses had been worn thin by steady marching.

—DIODORUS SICULUS (90–30 BC)

Take care to sell your horse before he dies. The art of life is passing losses on.

—ROBERT FROST (1874–1963)

One may lead a horse to water,
Twenty cannot make him drink.

—CHRISTINA ROSSETTI

The stranger was cloaked in black robes and sat upon a horse of iron gray. This was the most glorious equine Antar had ever seen. He had an arched neck, fine delicate nostrils, intelligent eyes, and smooth limbs that seemed to have been sculpted.

—GERALD HAUSMAN, LORETTA HAUSMAN, AND ROBERT FLORCZAK,
HORSES OF MYTH

An old horse knows the road.

—CHINESE PROVERB

I have seen flowers come in stony places …
And the gold cup won by the worst horse at the races …

—JOHN MASEFIELD

———⊰◈⊱———

I was the horse and the rider, and the leather I slapped to his rump spanked my own behind.

—MAY SWENSON

———⊰◈⊱———

A good seat on a horse steals away your opponent's courage and your onlooker's heart.

—FRIEDRICH NIETZSCHE (1844–1900)

———⊰◈⊱———

And I looked, and behold a pale horse: and his name that sat on him was Death.

—REVELATION 6:8

———⊰◈⊱———

Mother dear, we cannot stay!
The wild white horses foam and fret.

—MATTHEW ARNOLD (1822–1888)

⊰◆⊱

The chief part of the stories, however, turned upon the favorite spectre
of Sleepy Hollow, the Headless Horseman, who had been heard several
times of late, patrolling the country; and, it was said, tethered his horse
nightly among the graves in the churchyard.

—WASHINGTON IRVING (1783–1859)

⊰◆⊱

The sound of the horses' hooves pounded inside my chest. I made out a
blur of legs under the for cloud—hooves, pasterns, cannons … Like
a vision, a white mare, silky mane flying, burst through the fog in front
of me.

—DANDI DALEY MACKALL, *WILD THING (WINNIE THE HORSE GENTLER,
BOOK 1)*

⊰◆⊱

Her thick mane swung loosely to the rhythmic nod of her head as she walked, a fountain of coarse brown hair with auburn and straw-colored lights in it.

—INGRID SOREN, *ZEN AND HORSES*

Do not trust the horse, Trojans! Whatever it is, I fear the Greeks even bringing gifts.

—VIRGIL

The roan horse is young and will learn: the roan horse buckles into harness and feels the foam on the collar at the end of a haul: the roan horse points four legs to the sky and rolls in the red clover.

—CARL SANDBURG, *POTATO BLOSSOM SONGS AND JIGS*

Before you know it, horse and human look as comfortable with each other as two partners dancing a waltz.

—PAUL TRACHTMAN

⎯⎯◆⎯⎯

It didn't especially matter to me whether I rode or not; I was happy just to be in the presence of horses. I wanted to inhale them, and I wanted to take them in.

—MAXINE KUMIN, *WHY IS IT THAT GIRLS LOVE HORSES?*

⎯⎯◆⎯⎯

Horses live on dry land, eat grass, and drink water. When pleased, they rub necks together. When angry, they turn round and kick up their heels at each other.

—ZHUANGZI (C. 400 BC)

⎯⎯◆⎯⎯

"He's not going to look back if you don't," he said. "They're the most forgiving creatures God ever made."

—NICOLAS EVANS, *THE HORSE WHISPERER*

Their [the Tartars'] horses are so well broken-in to quick changes of movement, that upon the signal given, they instantly turn in every direction; and by these rapid manoeuvers many victories have been won.

—MARCO POLO (1254–1324)

Remember, a horse can tell you a lot of things, if you watch, and expect it to be sensible and intelligent.

—MARY O'HARA, *MY FRIEND FLICKA*

While I was young I lived upon my mother's milk, as I could not eat grass. In the daytime I ran by her side, and at night I lay down close by her.

—ANNA SEWELL, *BLACK BEAUTY: THE AUTOBIOGRAPHY OF A HORSE*

In his dreams he was a rider of the finest blooded horseflesh. However, when Antar awoke, there he was—just a barefoot boy who belonged to an arrogant prince, and whose first task of the morning was bathing his master's feet.

—GERALD HAUSMAN, LORETTA HAUSMAN, AND ROBERT FLORCZAK, *HORSES OF MYTH*

She felt the eyes of that horse; great glowing, fearsome eyes, arched with a question, and containing a white blade of light like a threat. What was his non-human question, and his uncanny threat? She didn't know. He was some splendid demon, and she must worship him.

—D. H. LAWRENCE

Love animals. God has given them the rudiments of thought and joy untroubled. Do not trouble their joy, do not harass them, do not deprive them of their happiness, do not work against God's intention.

—FYDOR DOSTOYEVSKY, *THE BROTHER KARAMAZOV*

———

I am Buffalo Bill's horse. I have spent my life under his saddle—with him in it, too, and he is good for two hundred pounds, without his clothes; and there is no telling how much he does weigh when he is out on the war-path.

—MARK TWAIN

———

Sometimes they paused … at the edge of a meadow and stared into the distance as though looking for the band of mares that had birthed them. Sometimes they … sniffed the ground hoping to pick up a scent of lost friends whose trails had long ago turned to dust.

—DAYTON O. HYDE, *ALL THE WILD HORSES*

———

I saw you when you came. I recognized your master. He is a bad sort.
Trap-robber, horse-thief, squaw-man, renegado—Hank Butters—I
know him very well. Stole you, didn't he?

—MARK TWAIN

I was holding a horse. *My* horse. The best thing that had ever happened
to me.

—SUSAN RICHARDS, *CHOSEN BY A HORSE: A MEMOIR*

I couldn't take my eyes off the ghostly mare. In the fog she appeared
pure white. Her dish jowls, big eyes, and finely carved head left no doubt
that she was Arabian. Arabians have black skin, but hers barely showed
through her … white coat … casting a gray shadow near her leg joints.

—DANDI DALEY MACKALL

While inside … the blood pulsed and the bowels shifted in their massive blue convolutions of who's will and the stout thighbones and knee and cannon and the tendons like flaxen hawsers that drew and flexed and drew and flexed at their articulations …

—CORMAC McCARTHY, *ALL THE PRETTY HORSES*

A promise is a promise, and before she died, Willo's mother made her father promise Willo could finally have a horse. Her grandfather … warns her: don't pick the first horse you see. But Willo falls in love with that first horse … and convinces her grandfather to buy her.

—SALLY KEEHN, *THE FIRST HORSE I SEE*

Because, my horses are so alive they might leap right off the paper.

—HAN GAN (C. 706–783), ON WHY HE WILL ONLY PAINT HORSES ON SILK CANVASES, AND THE ANIMALS ARE ALWAYS TETHERED

At the beginning of June, I took him over to the track, a half-mile oval. As soon as we entered the gate, he picked up a huge, even, ground-covering trot on very light contact. He trotted happily, his ears pricked, for two miles.

—JANE SMILEY, *MR. T'S HEART*

I can feel the rush of power beneath me. I can feel him, responding to my every command, surging forward towards the head of the thundering pack, every ounce of muscle striving to please me … Damn! There I go, daydreaming again.

—JESSE COLT, *WHEN I DREAM I HEAR HOOFBEATS*

I have never forgotten my mother's advice; I knew she was a wise old horse, and our master thought a great deal of her. Her name was Duchess, but he often called her Pet.

—ANNA SEWELL, *BLACK BEAUTY: THE AUTOBIOGRAPHY OF A HORSE*

I was not in control, but he was, and I never doubted that he knew exactly where each foot was at every stride.

—JANE SMILEY, *MR. T'S HEART*

———⊰•⊱———

[S]he was all I could see. Warm gusts from her giant nostrils blew across my face. Silky black hide, stretched over bony sun and shadow, framed liquid eyes. I stared into their depths. Like black water in a moonless night, they hid what lay beneath, yet drew me in, breathless.

—DIANE LEE WILSON, *I RODE A HORSE OF MILK WHITE JADE*

———⊰•⊱———

[H]undreds of horses are wandering around, gathering into herds and into twos and threes, lost, exhausted, bony, but still alive where they have been able to wrench themselves free from a team whose other horses have been killed.

—ALEXANDER SOLZHENITSYN

———⊰•⊱———

Hurrah, hurrah for Sheridan!
Hurrah, hurrah for horse and man!
And when their statues are placed on high,
Under the dome of the Union sky,
The American soldier's Temple of Fame,
There with the glorious General's name
Be it said in letters both bold and bright:
"Here is the steed that saved the day
By carrying Sheridan into the fight,
From Winchester,—twenty miles away!"

—OLIVER WENDELL HOLMES, *ELSIE VENNER*

———⊰◆⊱———

[W]hen a foal dies, you always leave it with the mare for a while—long enough for her to realize that it is not going to get up again, and to come to terms with that. I thought then that this is true to people, too. We have to experience the absence of life in order to accept it.

—JANE SMILEY, *MR. T'S HEART*

———⊰◆⊱———

The horse claimed you as its own and invited you upon its back to travel with the mind.

—DIANE LEE WILSON, *I RODE A HORSE OF MILK WHITE JADE*

He was never unkind and never unwilling—those were his special qualities.

—JANE SMILEY, *MR. T'S HEART*

I have now before my eyes one who was pretty, brave, and a good horse-woman; but how men did hate her!

—ANTHONY TROLLOPE, *THE LADY WHO RIDES TO HOUNDS*

[B]ut at Apollo's pleading,
If that my Pegasus should not be founder'd,
I think to canter gently through a hundred.

—LORD BYRON (1788–1824), *DON JUAN*

Then the bay horse spoke to me again and said: "See how your horses all come dancing!" I looked, and there were horses, horses everywhere—a whole skyfull of horses dancing around me.

—BLACK ELK (1863–1950)

Only mugs ... would be putting in a nine-to-five stint in the sort of July heat wave that would have done justice to the Sahara. Sensible guys like himself sat around ... with the windows open and their shirts off, letting their beards grow while the sticky afternoon waned toward opening time.

—DICK FRANCIS, *A ROYAL RIP-OFF AT KINGDOM HILL*

In grateful and reverent memory of the Empire's horses (some 375,000) who fell in the Great War (1914–1918). Most obediently, and often most painfully, they died.

—MEMORIAL AT CHURCH OF ST. JUDE IN LONDON

This ... horse has marched forever through time with humans.

—ADELE MCCORMICK AND MARLENA MCCORMICK, *HORSE SENSE AND THE HUMAN HEART*

It makes men imperious to sit a horse.

—OLIVER WENDELL HOLMES, SR., *THE AUTOCRAT OF THE BREAKFAST TABLE*

A man in passion rides a mad horse.

—BENJAMIN FRANKLIN

Racecrowds are not hooligans, my dear Bellamy.

—DICK FRANCIS

"Good riding day, eh?"
"Great."
"Well, Geth, don't break your neck."
"You bet not."
"I'll put a P.S. on the prayer for you," said the wag.

—ESTHER FORBES, *BREAKNECK HILL*

Hast thou given the horse strength? hast thou clothed his neck with thunder? Canst thou make him afraid as a grasshopper? the glory of his nostrils is terrible. He paweth in the valley, and rejoiceth in his strength; he goeth on to meet the armed men.

—JOB 39:19–22

For the wonderful brain of man,
However mighty its force,
Had never achieved its lordly plan
Without the aid of a horse.

—ELLA WHEELER WILCOX (1850–1919)

So hurry to see your lady,
like a stallion on the track.

—LOVE SONG OF THE NEW KINGDOM OF ANCIENT EGYPT

He knelt down beside his horse. He put out his hand and touched
the soft muzzle. October Miracle neighed feebly, and his muzzle stirred
faintly in Bobby's hand. Suddenly he quivered, stretched his limbs,
and was still. Bobby … knelt beside his dead horse, in the rain.

—RICHARD FINDLAY, *THE DREAM*

All in green went my love riding
on a great horse of gold
into the silver dawn.

—E. E. CUMMINGS (1894–1962)

[A]ll his father's stable of great Thoroughbreds needed something except Cuddy, who waited only for the bullet.

—ESTHER FORBES, *BREAKNECK HILL*

Everything is good … as long as it is unpossessed. Satiety and possession are Death's horses; they run in span.

—JACK LONDON (1876–1916)

You could see the warm, moist breath—the radiant and peaceful breath
that came from the tremulous, life-filled, flaring nostrils of stallions
and mares in the cold of certain dawns.

—CLARICE LISPECTOR, *DRY POINT OF HORSES*

Above each stall was hung the brass plate giving the name and pedigree
and above that up to the roof the hay was piled sweet and dusty-smelling.

—ESTHER FORBES, *BREAKNECK HILL*

The horseman on the pale horse is Pestilence. He follows the wars.

—BORIS KARLOFF AS GENERAL NIKOLAS PHERIDES IN *ISLE OF THE DEAD*

A short life in the saddles, Lord! Not long life by the fire.

—LOUISE IMOGEN GUINEY (1861–1920)

I hear the Shadowy Horses, their long manes a-shake,
Their hoofs heavy with tumult, their eyes glimmering white …

—WILLIAM BUTLER YEATS (1865–1939)

The mare soon after my entrance rose from her mat, and coming up close, after having nicely observed my hands and face, gave me the most contemptuous look, and turning to the horse, I heard the word *Yahoo* often repeated twixt them; the meaning of which I could not comprehend.

—JONATHAN SWIFT, *GULLIVER'S TRAVELS*

Cicero said loud-bawling orators were driven by their weakness to noise, as lame men to take horse.

—PLUTARCH (C. 46–127)

It was a day of such abounding life one could pity the worm the robin pulled. For on such a day everything seemed to have the right to live and be happy ... Suddenly he realized that Cuddy, too, was pleased and contented, for he was going quietly now.

—ESTHER FORBES, *BREAKNECK HILL*

As I spoke a powerful bay horse swept out from the weighing enclosure and cantered past us, bearing on its back the well-known black and red of the Colonel.

—ARTHUR CONAN DOYLE, *SILVER BLAZE*

And the hoofs of the horses as they run shake the crumbling field ...

—VIRGIL

The colt flinches a little, its muscles quivering. Buck rubs its mane, and the colt settles down, chewing things over and deciding the cowboy's not a predator after all.

—PAUL TRACHTMAN

A small, select aristocracy, born booted and spurred to ride, and a large dim mass born saddled and bridled to be ridden.

—A. G. GARDINER, *PROPHETS, PRIESTS AND KINGS,* ABOUT
    GREAT BRITAIN BEFORE WORLD WAR I

Wind Spirit … may you dance with the wind; may your majestic call find loving response from our other friends resting on The Hill. I shall think of your loud whinny, shining black body and deep, loving eyes as you rear and paw at the sky of infinity. Adieu for now.

—KATRINA L. WOOD, *WIND SPIRIT*

The cart before the horse is neither beautiful nor useful.

—HENRY DAVID THOREAU

That mare that lives by Divine orders as a mute and obedient companion of man, has an insight into the mind of her master whom she may even prefer to her own kind.

—CARL RASWAN, *DRINKERS OF THE WIND*

[N]ews of Mary White's death declared that it came as a result from the fall from a horse. … She never fell from a horse in her life! Horses have fallen on her and with her—"I'm always trying to hold 'em in my lap," she used to say. … She could ride anything that had four legs and hair.

—WILLIAM ALLEN WHITE (1868–1944), IN *MARY WHITE*, HIS FAMOUS EULOGY FOR HIS DAUGHTER

The regularity of the horses' strides, and the horsemanship of the four riders aroused the spectators to a gay pitch, no one could have said why; it was sheer rapture evoked by the beautiful, blooded animals and their artistry.

—FELIX SALTEN

Under his spurning feet, the road like an arrowly alpine river flowed and the landscape sped away behind like an ocean flying before the wind.

—THOMAS BUCHANAN READ (1822–1872)

[A] chieftain was ... killed, and when his adversary came ... his horse kicked him and bit him till he died; another horse, when his blinkers were removed and it found out that the mare he had covered was his dam, made for a precipice and committed suicide.

—PLINY THE ELDER (C. 23–79)

What a creature he was! Never have I felt such a horse between my knees. His great haunches gathered under him with every stride, and he shot forward ever faster and faster, stretched like a greyhound, while the wind beat in my face and whistled past my ears.

—SIR ARTHUR CONAN DOYLE

They were as fed horse in the morning: every one neighed after his neighbor's wife.

—JEREMIAH 5:8

The first place that I can well remember was a large pleasant meadow with a pond of clear water in it.

—ANNA SEWELL, *BLACK BEAUTY: THE AUTOBIOGRAPHY OF A HORSE*

Florian stood in the center. … In a row of white steeds he stood out as the only *pure* white one. … His liquid dark eyes, from whose depths his very soul shone forth, sparkled with inner fire and energy and health.

—FELIX SALTEN

I smell her still, I see her still, I hear that way she used to move about at night. What horse is ever so old as to forget his dam?

—JOHN HAWKES, *SWEET WILLIAM*

Noblest of the train that wait on man, the flight-performing horse.

—WILLIAM COWPER

With his brown frock-coat, his chiseled, reddish brown features, and his fixed mane, he seemed to have been poured in metal.

—FELIX SALTEN

Onc of the beauties of the Tennessee walking horse was that its gait spared you from having to post, to pump up and down at the knees when the horse trotted. He wasn't sure he could take posting on this chilly February morning.

—TOM WOLFE, *A MAN IN FULL*

What the horses o' Kansas think today, the horses of America will think tomorrow; and I tell you that when the horses of America rise in their might, the day o' the Oppressor is ended.

—RUDYARD KIPLING, *THE DAY'S WORK*

We've had a stirring life, old woman!
You, and I, and the old grey horse.

—GEORGE MEREDITH (1828–1909), *JUGGLING JERRY*

Their tails were braided with gold, with gold also their waving manes.
Pair by pair they were led through the steps of the High School;
approached from the far side toward the middle, and went into their
syncopated, cadenced stride.

—FELIX SALTEN

When I dream about horses, as I sometimes do, I often dream about
my own horse, a large and touchy palomino, on the one day in ten years
of fox hunting when everything went right.

—STEPHEN BUDIANSKY, *TALLYHO AND TRIBULATION*

I thought it the saddest ending in the history of literature.

> —MAXINE KUMIN, COMMENTING ON HER FAVORITE BOOK AS A CHILD,
> *SILVER SNAFFLES*

The book was real, after all! Then I carried it up to the Poetry Room that overlooks the Capitol and the Mall and read the story all over again, savoring the parts I had remembered verbatim, and wept.

> —MAXINE KUMIN, WHEN SHE LOCATED HER FAVORITE BOOK
> AS A CHILD, *SILVER SNAFFLES*, FORTY YEARS AFTER SHE LAST SAW IT,
> IN THE LIBRARY OF CONGRESS

Nothing made the horse so fat as the king's eye.

> —PLUTARCH

He always looked a given horse in the mouth.

—François Rabelais (c. 1494–1553)

Stripped of his rugs, the enormous horse, standing prehistoric in the glare of the naked light-bulb above his manager, showed as near butter-yellow as a steed can be and live. In build, he might have been a model to some equine sculptor of the gigantically symbolic.

—Gilbert Frankau (1884–1952)

The revolution does not choose its paths; it made its first steps toward victory under the belly of a Cossack's horse.

—Leon Trotsky (1879–1940)

His eyes were brilliant; they blazed as though red fire were in them. His nostrils quivered and dilated, his neck was proudly arched. In every line and curve of his body there was a lithe, wild gracefulness, an exultant beauty that was strength and swiftness and freedom.

—HERBERT RAVENEL SASS

It was a horse, yet it looked queer—it had something on its back. So that was a man! Something was wrong with it. It walked on its hind legs. And it wasn't half as big as a horse!

—HENRY HERBERT KNIBBS

No sheriff, royal official, or other person shall take horses or carts for transport from any free man, without his consent.

—MAGNA CARTA, CLAUSE 30

Probably no other living thing has had such an impact on our lives as the horse. Like no other animal has exerted such an influence on the cultural and social development of man.

—ANDY RUSSELL, *HORSES AND HORSEMEN*

Stone, bronze, stone, steel, stone, oak leaves, horses' heels
Over the paving.

—T. S. ELIOT (1888–1965)

I got the horse right here.

—OPENING LINE FROM *GUYS AND DOLLS*

"O my lord, the virtue of this horse is that, if one mount him, it will carry him whither he will and fare with its rider through the air and cover the space of a year in a single day."

—ARABIAN NIGHTS, *THE EBONY HORSE*

My little horse must think it queer
To stop without a farmhouse near.

—ROBERT FROST, *STOPPING BY WOODS ON A SNOWY EVENING*

Every horse is a mystery.

—BILL BARICH, *DREAMING*

Coquette was smuggled out of Abyssinia because Abyssinians do not permit good native mares to leave their country. ... He must have done it with one eye shut and the other on the sweet, tidy lines of her body.

—BERYL MARKHAM, *WAS THERE A HORSE WITH WINGS?*

A lovely horse is always an experience. ... It is an emotional experience of the kind that is spoiled by words.

—BERYL MARKHAM, *WAS THERE A HORSE WITH WINGS?*

We should not even ignore those speculators on Reality who doubted whether a white horse was real because he was white, or because he was solid.

—OKAKURA KAKUZO (1863–1913), *THE BOOK OF TEA*

Things are in the saddle,
And ride mankind.

    —RALPH WALDO EMERSON (1803–1882), *ODE*

<hr>

He will hold thee, when his passion shall have spent its novel force,
Something better than his dog, a little dearer than his horse.

    —LORD ALFRED TENNYSON (1809–1892), *LOCKSLEY HALL*

<hr>

Nothing is more common than birth; a million creatures are born in the time it takes to turn this page, and another million die … There is only time for patience and care, and hope that what is born is worthy and good.

    —BERYL MARKHAM, *WAS THERE A HORSE WITH WINGS?*

<hr>

"I have lost no horse," said Bellerophon … "But I happen to be seeking a very famous one, which, as wise people have informed me about, must be found hereabouts, if anywhere. Do you know whether the winged horse Pegasus still haunts the Fountain of Pirene … ?"

—NATHANIEL HAWTHORNE

⟩⟨

[W]e had a superb view as they came up the straight. The six horses were so close that a carpet could have covered them.

—ARTHUR CONAN DOYLE, *SILVER BLAZE*

⟩⟨

Order your fine horses now.

—*THE PHANTOM OF THE OPERA*

⟩⟨

The Dover mail was in its usual genial position that the guard suspected the passengers, the passengers suspected one another and the guard, they all suspected everybody else, and the coachman was sure of nothing but the horses.

—CHARLES DICKENS, *A TALE OF TWO CITIES*

"What need I go for a horse I would need a bear trap to catch?" Eck said. "Didn't you just see me catch him?"
"I seen you," Eck said. "And I don't want nothing as big as a horse if I go to wrastle with it every time it finds me on the same side of the fence it's on."

—WILLIAM FAULKNER (1897–1962), *SPOTTED HORSES*

Everything is being blown away;
A little horse trots with a letter in its mouth, which is read with eagerness
As we gallop into the flame.

—JOHN ASHBERY, *A LAST WORLD*

I have seen the general dare the combers some closer
And make to ride his bronze horse out into the hoofs and guns of the
storm.

—CARL SANDBURG

[W]hether the tall horse … was desirous of having a little innocent
recreation with Mr. Winkle, or … perform the journey as much to his
own satisfaction without a rider as with one, are points upon which,
of course, we can arrive at no distinct conclusion.

—CHARLES DICKENS

Such horses are
The jewels of the horseman's hands and thighs,
They go by the word and hardly need the rein.

—STEPHEN VINCENT BENÉT, *JOHN BROWN'S BODY*

The civilizing mission of Woman is to reduce the amount of masculinity in the world. Not add to it by wearing trousers. The wearing of trousers—by women—leads inexorably to riding astride a horse. Instead of the modest sidesaddle.

—ERIC OVERMEYER, *ON THE VERGE, OR THE GEOGRAPHY OF YEARNING*

There is a touch of divinity even in brutes, and a special halo about a horse, that should forever exempt him from indignities.

—HERMAN MELVILLE

Because the pleasure-bird whistles after the hot wires,
Shall the blind horse sing sweeter?

—DYLAN THOMAS

I am sick as a horse.

—LAURENCE STERNE

As the traveller who has lost his way, throws his reins on his horse's neck, and trusts to the instinct of the animal to find his road, so must we do with the divine animal who carries us through this world.

—RALPH WALDO EMERSON

Ignorance, madam, pure ignorance.

—SAMUEL JOHNSON (1709–1784), ON BEING ASKED WHY HE HAD
DEFINED PASTERN AS THE KNEE OF A HORSE

Hark! The shrill trumpet sounds to horse! Away!

—COLLEY CIBBER (1671–1757)

The natives had never seen such horses up to this time and thought
the horse and rider were all one animal.

—BERNARD DIAZ DEL CASTILLO, *TRUE HISTORY OF THE CONQUEST
OF NEW SPAIN*

In the neat box stalls round the stable-yard the dozing horses struck
a random hoof against a wooden wall, rattled a tethering chain, sneezed
the hay dust out of a moist black nostril.

—DICK FRANCIS, *A CARROT FOR A CHESTNUT*

He has an invincible hatred of the fighting, hunting, swash-buckling side
of life, symbolized in all his early books by a violent propaganda against
horses.

—GEORGE ORWELL (1903–1950), IN HIS ESSAY *WELLS, HITLER, AND THE WORLD STATE*

A man may well bring a horse to the water but he cannot make him
drink.

—JOHN HEYWOOD (C. 1497–1580)

O the horseman's and horsewoman's joys!
The saddle, the gallop, the pressure upon the seat, the cool gurgling by
     the ears and hair.

    —WALT WHITMAN (1819–1892), *LEAVES OF GRASS*

This poor little one-horse town.

    —MARK TWAIN

The stallion flashed by the stands, going faster with every magnificent
stride. With a sudden spurt he bore down on Sun Raider. For a moment
he hesitated as he came alongside … Into the lead the Black swept, past
the cheering thousands—a step, a length, two lengths ahead—then the
mighty giant plunged under the wire.

    —WALTER FARLEY, *THE BLACK STALLION*

What time she lifteth up herself on high, she scorneth the horse and his rider. Hast thou given the horse strength? Hast thou clothed his neck with thunder?

—JOB 39:18

Death ... on his pale horse.

—JOHN MILTON (1608–1674), *PARADISE LOST*

Show me a man who has no pity on his horse, and I will show you one who is a cruel husband, if he is married, and a tyrannical parent, if he has children; a man that would be Nero if he had the power. He is a coward by nature and a fiend by practice.

—GEORGE ELIOT (1819–1880), *MIDDLEMARCH*

Since childhood we have all had encounters with the Classic Horse.
It is the horse of our dreams, fanciful and airborne, with a long flowing
mane and tail. Its nostrils flare, displaying an inner spirit as magnificent
as the mighty wind.

—ADELE MCCORMICK AND MARLENA MCCORMICK, *HORSE SENSE AND
THE HUMAN HEART*

The sound of hoofs roused him. Here came his horse, throwing up her
head as if enquiring why she was being disturbed … In the movement
of that small head and satin neck was something free and beyond present
company.

—JOHN GALSWORTHY

Agesilaus was very fond of his children, and it is reported that once toying with them he got astride upon a reed as upon a horse, and rode about the room; and being seen by one of his friends, he desired him not to speak of it till he had children of his own.

—PLUTARCH

And here I say to parents, and especially to wealthy parents, don't give your son money. As far as you can afford it, give him horses.

—SIR WINSTON CHURCHILL

The revolution does not choose its paths: it made its first steps toward victory under the belly of a Cossack's horse.

—LEON TROTSKY, *HISTORY OF THE RUSSIAN REVOLUTION*

The sun is coming back after the short days of winter. Now is the time when the horses start losing hair. As they stand in the pasture, long tufts float on the brittle breeze and come down to rest on sharp, gray-frosted grass.

—TERESA TSIMMU MARTINO, *DANCER ON THE GRASS*

A good intention clothes itself with sudden power. When a god wishes to ride, any chip or pebble will bud and shoot out winged feet and serve him for a horse.

—RALPH WALDO EMERSON

Knight, keep well thy head, for thou shalt have a buffet for the slaying of my horse.

—SIR THOMAS MALORY (C. 1405–1471), *LE MORTE D'ARTHUR*

The young horses were splendidly bathed in light. They grouped themselves nobly against the hillside before they swung away from us, with streaming manes and tails, to crest the hill like a wave, and thunder away into the evening.

—MOLLY KEANE

———◆———

A groom used to spend whole days in currycombing and rubbing down his horse, but at the same time stole his oats and sold them for his own profit. Alas! said the horse, if you really wish me to be in good condition, you should groom me less, and feed me more.

—AESOP

———◆———

Pegasus indeed! A winged horse, truly! Why, friend, are you in your senses? … Of what use would wings be to a horse? … To be sure, there might be a little saving in the expense of shoes, but then, how would a man like to see his horse flying out of the stable window?

—NATHANIEL HAWTHORNE, *THE CHIMAERA*

———◆———

I wondered if, after all, the breeding of speed horses was not too cruelly disappointing to those whose heart and soul were in it. The moments of triumph were wonderful, of course. The thrill of any other game was feeble in comparison; but oh, the many and bitter disappointments!

—JOHN TAINTOR FOOTE

By reason of his elegance, he resembles an image painted in a palace, though he is as majestic as the palace itself.

—ABD AL-QADIR

The ego's relation to the id might be compared to that of the rider to his horse. The horse supplies the locomotive energy, while the rider has the privilege of deciding on the goal and of guiding the powerful animal's movement.

—SIGMUND FREUD (1856–1939)

I am emperor. It is I who know what is best for Rome. Not you traitors. Now, let go of my horses!

—ELAGABALUS (C. 203–222), ROMAN EMPEROR

There may have been disillusionments in the lives of the medieval saints, but they would scarcely have been better pleased if they could have foreseen that their names would be associated nowadays chiefly with racehorses and the cheaper clarets.

—SAKI (H. H. MUNRO)

O Lord to You we give thanks
that in time Polish horses ... defeat Nazi tanks.

—SAIOM SHRIVER

What do we, as a nation, care about books? How much do you think we spend altogether on our libraries, public or private, as compared with what we spend on our horses?

—JOHN RUSKIN (1819–1900)

[M]any are the men and horses that stand along the road, each horse and man at the interval of a day's journey; and these are stayed neither by snow nor rain nor heat nor darkness from accomplishing their appointed course with all speed.

—HERODOTUS (c. 484–425 BC)

[V]irtue shall be bound into the hair of thy forelock … I have given thee the power of flight without wings.

—THE KORAN

Nester mounted the gelding by the short stirrup … seated himself in the manner peculiar to coachmen, huntsman, and horsemen, and jerked the reins. The gelding lifted his head to show his readiness to go where ordered, but did not move. He knew that before starting there would be much shouting.

—LEO TOLSTOY, *STRIDER—THE STORY OF A HORSE*

———❖———

The truth is that horses exhibit, in an exaggerated form, many of the worst characteristics of people. They are greedy, envious, spiteful, malicious, slothful, superstitious, and stupid. They are congenital hysterics and each one is, ominously, a prospective homicide. If horses could talk, they would lie.

—OWEN ULPH, *THE FIDDLEBACK: LORE OF THE LINE CAMP*

———❖———

The 'oss that had been standing like a bleeding statue ever since I'd called 'im in the morning, suddenly began to move. Very slowly he came towards us, poked his nose over the door and sniffed. Then suddenly, quick as a monkey, 'e makes a grab and scuttles back into the far corner of his box.

—COLIN DAVY, *THE GOOD THINGS*

I worked like a horse and I ate like a hog and I slept like a dead man.

—RUDYARD KIPLING

Gentle handling, no loud shouts, no jerks on his tender mouth, good food and a cleaned skin—these spelled health and contentment. Kindness had conquered.

—MANUEL BAUKEN, *THE HORSE OF THE SWORD*

Words are as beautiful as wind horses, and sometimes as difficult to corral.

—TED BERKMAN, *THE CHRISTIAN SCIENCE MONITOR*

—◆—

Those terrible grey horses, how they strive!

—NAPOLÉON BONAPARTE (1769–1821)

—◆—

His back, a throne of feathers, will bear you smoothly at the trot and gallop. He'll go where others dare not. He'll stand firm where others flee in terror … And at last you'll understand why he was e'er the chosen one of kings.

—JUAN LLAMAS

—◆—

England is the paradise of women, the purgatory of men, and the hell of horses.

—JOHN FLORIO (1553–1625)

And when he spoke, he felt an affection for the little horse, an exultant pride in his courage, so different in quality from anything he had known before that it could not be described.

—JOYCE CARY (1888–1957)

There are three things that are never boring to see: a swift swimmer swimming, a young girl dancing, and a young horse running. And there are three things that are never tiring to speak of: God, and love, and the racing of horses.

—DONN BYRNE, *THE TALE OF THE GYPSY HORSE*

I who used to swing upside down on a living horse, who always danced when mere walking would have done, so glad was I of life, so full of health.

—JOSEPHINE DEMOTT ROBINSON, *THE CIRCUS LADY*

There are only two classes in good society in England: the equestrian classes and the neurotic classes.

—GEORGE BERNARD SHAW (1856–1950)

Horses have as much individuality and character as people.

—C. W. ANDERSON

I wheeled about, proud and exulting like an untired horse that cares not for his home.

—WILLIAM WORDSWORTH

He flung himself on his horses and rode off madly in all directions.

—STEPHEN LEACOCK

[H]is hoofbeats fall like rain, over and over again.

—RACHEL FIELD

They had built up a tradition that if they had to die it was a fine thing to die on horseback, perhaps in battle, perhaps with the music of hounds or the rattle of guard-rails in their ears. Horsemen and warriors! He thought with a fierce sudden joy.

—RICHARD FINDLAY, *THE DREAM*

All the sounds dear to a horseman were around me-the snort of the horses as they cleared their throats, the gentle swish of their tails, the tinkle of irons as we flung the saddles over their backs-little sounds of no importance, but they stay in the unconscious library of memory.

—WYNFORD VAUGHAN-THOMAS

She doted upon the Assyrians her neighbors, captains, and rulers clothed most gorgeously, horsemen riding upon horses, all of them desirable young men.

—EZEKIEL 23:21

And I looked, and behold a pale horse: and his name that sat on him was Death, and Hell followed with him.

—REVELATIONS 6:8

Mares, she said, had not been altered, in them the blood flowed freely, their life cycles had not been tampered with, their natures were completely their own. The mare usually had more energy than the gelding, could be as temperamental as the stallion, and was, in fact, its superior.

—JOHN HAWKES

With the passion reverberating among the consonants like distant thunder, he laid his hand upon the mane of his horse as though it had been the gray locks of his adversary, swung himself into the saddle and galloped away.

—BRET HARTE (1836–1902)

Now the wild horses play,
Champ and chafe and toss in the spray.

—MATTHEW ARNOLD

There is a touch of divinity even in brutes, and a special halo about a horse, that should forever exempt it from indignities. As for those majestic, magisterial truck-horses of the docks, I would as soon think of striking a judge on the bench, as to lay violent hands upon their holy hides.

—HERMAN MELVILLE

With flowing tail and flying mane,
Wide nostrils, never stretched by pain,
Mouth bloodless to bit or rein,
And feet that iron never shod,
And flanks unscar'd by spur or rod
A thousand horses, the wild, the free,
Like waves that follow o'er the sea,
Came thickly thundering on.

—LORD BYRON

But why discourse
Upon the Virtues of the Horse?
They are too numerous to tell
Save when you have a Horse to Sell.

—JOSH BILLINGS (1818–1885)

[T]ireless, swift as the flowing wind. Shadowfax they called him. By day his coat glistens like silver; and by night it is like a shade, and he passes unseen. Light is his footfall!

—J. R. R. TOLKIEN (1892–1973)

That hoss wasn't built to tread the earth,
He took natural to the air,
And every time he went aloft,
He tried to leave me there.

—TRIBUTE TO AN UNMANAGEABLE HORSE

Once there was an old man who lived in a tiny village. Although poor, he was envied by all, for he owned a beautiful white horse. Even the king coveted his treasure. A horse like this had never been seen before—such was its splendor, its majesty, its strength.

—MAX LUCADO, *THE OLD MAN AND THE WHITE HORSE*

Thou shall be for Man a source of happiness and wealth; thy back shall be a seat of honour, and thy belly of riches; every grain of barley given thee shall purchase indulgence for the sinner.

—THE KORAN

It must be confessed that horses at present work too exclusively for men, rarely men for horses; and the brute degenerates in man's society.

—HENRY DAVID THOREAU

He was the chief of all the horses; and when he snorted, it was a flash of lightning and his eyes were like the sunset star.

—BLACK ELK

Champing his foam, and bounding o'er the plain,
Arch high his neck, and graceful spread his mane.

—SIR RICHARD BLACKMORE (1654–1729)

A large and liquid eye … the swirl of dust around pounding hooves … these, then, are the images that move us.

—ANONYMOUS

Everything is good ... as long as it is unpossessed. Satiety and possession are Death's horses; they run in span.

—JACK LONDON

To many, the words love, hope, and dreams are synonymous with horses.

—OLIVER WENDELL HOLMES, SR.

A kingdom without horses was not a kingdom, and a king without horses was not a king.

—STAN STEINER

Thou must learn the thoughts of the noble horse whom thou wouldst ride.

—JOHANN WOLFGANG VON GOETHE (1749–1832)

What is the price of a thousand horses against a son when there is one son only?

—JOHN MILLINGTON SYNGE (1871–1909), *RIDERS TO THE SEA*

Virtue shall be bound into the hair of thy forelock. I have given thee the power of flight without wings.

—THE KORAN

While everyone else takes his pleasure, and never
Seems happy unless he is riding a horse.

—EDWARD LEAR, *LAUGHABLE LYRICS*

[T]he last sheaf [of wheat] or "Maiden" is carried home in merry procession by the harvesters. It is then presented to the mistress of the house, who dresses it up to be preserved until the first mare foals. The Maiden is then taken down and presented to the mare as its first food.

—SIR JAMES GEORGE FRAZER (1854–1941)

The eyes, circled by his sad and beautiful darkness, were so sorrowful, lonely, gentle, and nobly tragic, that they killed all other emotions except love.

—T. H. WHITE (1906–1964)

[A]nd he whispered to the horse, trust no man in whose eyes you do not see yourself reflected as an equal.

—ANONYMOUS

Let me leap into the saddle once more.

—HERMAN MELVILLE, *WHITE JACKET*

[S]uddenly a chariot of fire and horses of fire appeared.

—2 KINGS 2:11

The horse, mares, and frisking fillies,
Clad, all, in linen white as lilies.

—ROBERT HERRICK (1591–1674)

She was iron-sinew'd and satin-skinn'd.
Ribb'd like a drum and limb'd like a deer,
Fierce as the fire and fleet as the wind—
There was nothing she couldn't climb or clear.

—ADAM LINDSAY GORDON (1833–1870)

I saw Willow and Dick ride out of the stable arch and walk their horses away from sight into the slowly silvering morning. The breathless picture they made is with me still—both sitting a little carefully, perhaps, with saddles still cold on their horses' backs.

—MOLLY KEANE

Little black horse,
Where are you taking your dead rider?

—FEDERICO GARCÍA LORCA (1898–1936)

Steeds, steeds, what steeds! Has the whirlwind a home in your manes?

—NIKOLAI GOGOL

Horses and dogs have been man's most intimate and faithful companions since the dawn of history, but the horse has certainly been the most useful. In sport, agriculture, transport and warfare, the horse has contributed more to human pleasure, ambition and progress than any other animal.

—PRINCE PHILIP, DUKE OF EDINBURGH

And their [horses'] mouths are very clever, so clever with the matter of locks on gates that it is the rare horseman who has had no occasion to be grateful that we have ten fingers and they only one mouth.

—VICKI HEARNE, *ADAM'S TASK*

Since the dawn of civilization, the horse and the Muses have been boon companions in all the heroics of mythology and history.

—ROBERT FROTHINGHAM

The steeds soon perceived that the load they drew was lighter than usual; and as a ship without ballast is tossed hither and thither on the sea, so the chariot, without its accustomed weight, was dashed as if empty.

—*BULFINCH'S MYTHOLOGY*

Horse: A neighing quadruped, used in war, and draught and carriage.

—SAMUEL JOHNSON, *DICTIONARY OF THE ENGLISH LANGUAGE*

I am your equal. I am a wild creature that can never be like you. I have heart, courage, and the game spirit that is my heritage, and I will be respected. I will be taught, and I will please, and maybe in time I will be your intimate. But I will never be your possession.

—ANONYMOUS

England's past has been borne on his back.
All our history is his industry:
We are his heirs, he is our inheritance.
Ladies and gentleman:
The Horse!

—ROBERT DUNCAN, *TRIBUTE TO THE HORSE*, WHICH IS READ AT THE CONCLUSION OF EVERY HORSE OF THE YEAR SHOW IN LONDON

The sunshine's golden gleam is thrown,
On sorrel, chestnut, bay and roan.

—OLIVER WENDELL HOLMES, SR.

When God created the horse he said to the magnificent creature: I have made thee as no other. All the treasures of the earth lie between thy eyes. Thou shalt carry my friends upon thy back. Thy saddle shall be the seat of prayers to me. And thou fly without wings, and conquer without any sword.

—THE KORAN

Their horses were of great stature, strong and clean-limbed; their grey coats glistened, their long tails flowed in the wind, their manes were braided on their proud necks.

—J. R. R. TOLKIEN

Spur not an unbroken horse.

—SIR WALTER SCOTT

Behold, he cometh up as clouds, and his chariots are as the whirlwind; his horses are swifter than eagles—woe unto us. We are undone.

—JEREMIAH 4:13

But he, mighty man, lay mightily in the whirl of dust, forgetful of his horsemanship.

—HOMER, *THE ILIAD*

A horse in the wind, a perfect symphony.

—ANONYMOUS

Over the river and through the wood,
To grandfather's house we go;
The horse knows the way
To carry the sleigh,
Through the white and drifted snow.

—LYDIA M. CHILD (1802–1880)

By reason of his elegance, he resembles an image painted in a palace,
though he is as majestic as the palace itself.

—EMIR ABD-EL-KADER

The Colonel's son has taken a horse, and a raw rough dun was he,
With the mouth of a bell and the heart of Hell and the head
    of the gallows-tree.

—RUDYARD KIPLING

As the wind swept over the saddle, it turned to a mixture of bright colors and painted the world.

—RONAN WARRIORS

Jess stopped laughing but said nothing. He figured Eliza had gone about as far in one day as a woman could in enlarging her appreciation of horseflesh; still he couldn't help smiling when he thought of the sermon that might have been preached in the Bethel Church upon eternal verities.

—JESSAMYN WEST, *FRIENDLY PERSUASION*

Such was the burial they gave to Hector, tamer of horses.

—HOMER, *THE ILIAD*

The horses show him nobler powers;
O patient eyes, courageous hearts!

—JULIAN GRENFELL (1888–1915)

———◈———

Once more upon the waters! yet once more!
And the waves bound beneath me as a steed
That knows his rider.

—LORD BYRON

———◈———

When I looked at life from the saddle and was as near to heaven as it was possible to be.

—DAISY GREVILLE, COUNTESS OF WARWICK

———◈———

I cannot, alas, tell you when I am thirsty, so give me pure, cold water frequently. Do all you can to protect me from the sun; and throw a cover over me—not when I am working, but when I am, standing in the cold.

—CAPTAIN DE CONDENBOVE, FRENCH ARMY, WORLD WAR I.
THIS APPEARED IN *FIELD ARTILLERY MANUAL, VOL. 1*, BY ARTHUR
R. WILSON, CAPT., FIELD ARTILLERY, U.S. ARMY, 1926

The youth walks up to the white horse, to put its halter in and the horse looks up as him in silence. They are so silent, they are in another world.

—D. H. LAWRENCE

Horses: the feeling of absolute ancientness of the English landscape. A landscape that should always, by rights, have horses in it. So, too, should the landscape of the English mind.

—SIMON BARNES

"I see nothing unusual," replied the king.
"You have only to climb on his back and wish yourself anywhere in the world. And no matter how far the distance, in a flash of time too short to count you will find yourself there. It is this, Your Highness, that makes my horse so wonderful."

—*Arabian Nights*

"Remember," he replied, "O perjur'd one,
The horse remember, that did teem with death,
And all the world be witness to thy guilt."

—Dante Alighieri (1265–1321)

Lente, lente currite, noctis equi.
[Translation: Run slowly, slowly, horses of the night.]

—Ovid (43 BC–17 AD)

He [Rumbold] never would believe that Providence had sent a few men into the world ready booted and spurred to ride, and millions ready saddled and bridled to be ridden.

—THOMAS BABINGTON MACAULAY (1800–1859)

———✦———

I have seen soldiers panic at the first sight of battle, and a squire pulling arrows from his body to fight and save his dying horse. Nobility is not a birthright, but is defined by one's actions.

—KEVIN COSTNER IN *ROBIN HOOD, PRINCE OF THIEVES*

———✦———

"Tomorrow, sell your camel and buy a horse. Camels are traitorous: they walk thousands of paces and never seem to tire. Then suddenly, they kneel and die. But horses tire bit by bit. You always know how much you can ask of them, and when it is that they are about to die."

—PAULO COELHO, *THE ALCHEMIST*

———✦———

The horses prance and paw and neigh,
Fillies and colts like kittens play. ...

—OLIVER WENDELL HOLMES, SR.

When the sloops of war are rigged as snows, they are furnished with a horse, which answers the purpose of the try-sail-mast, the fore-part of the sail being attached by rings to the said horse, in different parts of its heighth.

—WILLIAM FALCONER (1732–1769)

One's hepar, or, in vulgar language, liver, ... goes up and down like the dasher of a churn in the midst of the other vital arrangements, at every step of a trotting horse. The brains also are shaken up like coppers in a money-box.

—OLIVER WENDELL HOLMES, SR.

[T]he mare stood kicking slightly with a white hind foot and whisking her tail. Her bright coat shone in the sunlight, and the little shivers and wrinklings passed up and down its satin because of the flies. Then, for a moment, she stood still, ears pricked, eyes on the distance.

—JOHN GALSWORTHY

Yes, there he sat, on the back of the winged horse!

—NATHANIEL HAWTHORNE

The horse knew the route to each house because he had done it so long. What [the mailman] would do, while he was driving, is the horse would just go, and, at every stop, he would read the mail. He would read everybody's mail while he was delivering it.

—ROBERT PATTERSON

Who drives the horses of the sun,
Shall lord it but a day.

—JOHN VANCE CHENEY, *THE HAPPIEST HEART*

Come off to the stable,
all you who are able,
and give your horses some oats and some corn;
for if you don't do it,
your colonel will know it,
and then you will rue it,
as sure as you're born.

—CAVALRY BUGLE CALL

My purpose is, indeed, a horse of that color.

—WILLIAM SHAKESPEARE

[T]hrough his mane and tail the high wind sings,
Fanning the hairs, who wave like feathered wings.

—WILLIAM SHAKESPEARE

The king is come. Deal mildly with his youth;
For young hot colts, being raged, do rage the more.

—WILLIAM SHAKESPEARE

Think, when we talk of horses, that you see them
Printing their proud hooves in the receiving earth;
For tis' your thoughts that now must deck our kings.

—WILLIAM SHAKESPEARE

He's mad, that trusts in the tameness of a wolf, a horse's health,
a boy's love, or a whore's oath.

—WILLIAM SHAKESPEARE

———⟫◆⟪———

Saint George, that swinged the dragon, and e'er since
Sits on his horse back at mine hostess' door.

—WILLIAM SHAKESPEARE

———⟫◆⟪———

Beggars mounted run their horses to death.

—WILLIAM SHAKESPEARE

———⟫◆⟪———

That which is now a horse, even with a thought.
The rack dislimns, and makes it indistinct,
As water is in water.

—WILLIAM SHAKESPEARE

Time travels in divers paces with divers persons. I'll tell you who Time
ambles withal, who Time trots withal, who Time gallops withal and who
he stands still withal.

—WILLIAM SHAKESPEARE

I would my horse had the speed of your tongue.

—WILLIAM SHAKESPEARE

I wish your horses swift and sure of foot;
And so I do command you to their backs.

—WILLIAM SHAKESPEARE

Give me another horse: bind up my wounds.

—WILLIAM SHAKESPEARE

A full-hot horse, who being allow'd his way,
Self-mettle tires him.

—WILLIAM SHAKESPEARE

He is pure air and fire; and the dull elements of earth and water never appear in him, but only in patient stillness while his rider mounts him: he is indeed a horse: and all other jades you may call beasts.

—WILLIAM SHAKESPEARE

When I bestride him, I soar, I am a hawk.
He trots the air, the earth sings when he touches it …

—WILLIAM SHAKESPEARE

A horse, a horse, my kingdom for a horse!

—WILLIAM SHAKESPEARE

O, for a horse with wings!

—WILLIAM SHAKESPEARE

An two men ride of a horse, one must ride behind.

—WILLIAM SHAKESPEARE

He uses his folly like a stalking-horse, and under the presentation of that he shoots his wit.

—WILLIAM SHAKESPEARE

His neigh is like the bidding of a monarch, and his countenance enforces homage. He is indeed a horse.

—WILLIAM SHAKESPEARE

I will not jump with common spirits.

—WILLIAM SHAKESPEARE

Well could he ride, and often men would say,
"That horse his mettle from his rider takes:
Proud of subjection, noble by the sway,
What rounds, what bounds, what course, what stop he makes!"
And controversy hence a question takes,
Whether the horse by him became his deed,
Or he his manage by the well-doing steed.

   —WILLIAM SHAKESPEARE

Vaulted with such ease into his seat,
As if an angel dropp'd down from the clouds,
To turn and wind a fiery Pegasus,
And witch the world with noble horsemanship.

   —WILLIAM SHAKESPEARE

Like unback'd colts, they prick'd their ears,
Advanced their eyelids, lifted up their noses
As they smelt music.

—WILLIAM SHAKESPEARE

Let the galled jade wince, our withers are unwrung.

—WILLIAM SHAKESPEARE

Gallop apace, you fiery-footed steeds,
Toward Phoebus' lodging.

—WILLIAM SHAKESPEARE

Sometime he trots, as if he told the steps,
With gentle magesty and pride;
Anon, he rears upright, curvets and leaps,
As who should say 'Lo, thus my strength is tried.'

— WILLIAM SHAKESPEARE

Think, when we talk of horses, that you see them
Printing their proud hoofs i' the receiving earth.

—WILLIAM SHAKESPEARE

So did this horse excel a common one
In shape, in courage, color, pace and bone.
What a horse should have he did not lack,
Save a proud rider on so proud a back.

—WILLIAM SHAKESPEARE

What a piece of work is a horse! How noble in reason! How infinite in faculty! In form and moving how express and admirable! In action how like an angel! In apprehension how like a man! The beauty of the world! The paragon of animals!

—JAMES AGATE (1877–1947)

CHAPTER SEVEN

"The Horse Is Never Wrong": Philosophies of Horsemanship

I hope someday to learn about dressage and all the other equine disciplines. But to date my learning has been confined to the school of natural horsemanship, and so for the keynote of this chapter I have borrowed one of that school's cornerstone principles—namely, that "the horse is never wrong."

It's an outlook that takes some getting used to. I mean, what is the single most repeated comment we humans make to any of our domesticated animals? Probably has to be "bad dog," right? Well, it's my experience that it's very difficult not to bring the exact same outlook with us when we start to work with this very different animal. Luckily, however, it doesn't take long for even the densest beginning horseman to realize that hollering "bad horse" won't get him anywhere.

Think about it: the horse ... is *never* ... wrong.

Take that precept to heart and everything starts to change. It *has* to. Or at least it did for me. For example: early on, whenever Koda and I would be working in the round pen, there would typically come a point when I'd be cross and frustrated because I didn't have a lot of time to spare, but I wanted to feel like we were accomplishing something and yet it seemed to be taking Koda a whole lot longer than it should to learn whatever it was I was trying to teach him. "Bad horse!" would indeed be right on the tip of my tongue.

But then I started thinking in the-horse-is-never-wrong terms and gradually began to be able to share the kind of wise perspective found in these remarks by Mark Rashid and Craig Cameron, respectively: first, "it doesn't matter to [our horses] if we have to be somewhere at three o'clock. They don't. They cannot be forced into understanding or doing something faster just because we're running out of time"; and second: "The horse is a rhythmical, balanced, patient, trusting and consistent animal. It's you who needs to develop feel, timing, rhythm, balance, patience, consistency and understanding."

I've made sure that on the following pages you'll discover at least a handful of quotations that memorably state tenets of natural horsemanship. But a wide variety of other perspectives are also represented, different ways of thinking about horses, and our relationship with them. What I hope unites the chapter, its common thread, is the belief that any horse-human partnership will improve when the latter takes the trouble to try to figure out why the former does what he or she does. I think Buck Brannaman says it best when he summarizes his long experience with horses in the following words: "I've tried every physical means to contain my horse in an effort to keep from getting myself killed. I started to realize that things would come much easier for me once I learned why a horse does what he does."

Realize that horsemanship is all about working on yourself, not so much working on the horse. The horse is a rhythmical balanced, patient, trusting, and consistent animal. It's you who needs to develop feel, timing, rhythm, balance, patience, consistency, and understanding.

—CRAIG CAMERON, *RIDE SMART*

The one great precept and practice in using a horse is this—never deal with him when you are in a fit of passion.

—XENOPHON

So many people nowadays don't know how to "read" a horse. I guess they are so used to a mechanized world that they don't think about a horse having ideas of his own.

—MARY TWELVEPONIES

The horse is never wrong.

—TOM DORRANCE

One of the cardinal rules of natural horsemanship is to ask the horse "as gently as possible, but as firmly as necessary." Notice that failure to get the response is not an option.

—DR. ROBERT M. MILLER AND RICK LAMB, *THE REVOLUTION IN HORSEMANSHIP*

The bottom line on what true horsemanship is: Communication. … How well can you get your horse to understand what it is you want him to do? How well can you get your horse to understand what it is you don't want him to do? That's horsemanship.

—CRAIG CAMERON, *RIDE SMART*

Because we are predators, ironically there is nothing "Natural" about "Natural Horsemanship." The term is used for want of a better phrase. Maybe creative or progressive horsemanship would be a better phraseology. Our unnatural relationship can be creatively developed between prey and predator by understanding their world.

—PETER FULLER

[A] horse never lies. The horse will be exactly as good as his human. When he has a choice, the horse will always make his own decision. And that decision will always be a reflection of you, the human.

—DENNIS REIS

I've started horses since I was twelve. … I've tried every physical means to contain my horse in an effort to keep from getting myself killed. I started to realize that things would come much easier for me once I learned why a horse does what he does.

—BUCK BRANNAMAN

The paradox of horses is that they do not *have* to carry us, but they agree to do so.

—TERESA TSIMMU MARTINO, *DANCER ON THE GRASS*

A definite purpose, like blinders on a horse, inevitably narrows its possessor's point of view.

—ROBERT FROST

Everything that's fun in life is dangerous. Horse races, for instance, are very dangerous. But attempt to design a safe horse and the result is a cow (an appalling animal to watch at the trotters). And everything that isn't fun is dangerous too. It is impossible to be alive and safe.

—P. J. O'ROURKE, *REPUBLICAN PARTY REPTILE*

A good horse is hard to find.

—BOOTS REYNOLDS

Grab life by the reins.

—ANONYMOUS

One must get off one's horse over its head; to step off is merely weak.

—MAO TSE-TUNG

Horses have as much individuality and character as people.

—C. W. ANDERSON

But America is a great, unwieldly Body. Its Progress must be slow. … The fleetest Sailors must wait for the dullest and slowest. Like a Coach and six—the swiftest Horses must be slackened and the slowest quickened, that all may keep an even Pace.

—JOHN ADAMS (1735–1826)

———

Once a word leaves your mouth, you cannot chase it back even with the swiftest horse.

—PROVERB

———

It doesn't matter to [our horses] if we have to be somewhere at three o'clock. They don't. They cannot be forced into understanding or doing something faster just because we're running out of time. This in itself is probably the biggest reason why people have problems with their horses.

—MARK RASHID, *CONSIDERING THE HORSE: TALES OF PROBLEMS SOLVED AND LESSONS LEARNED*

———

The tygers of wrath are wiser than the horses of instruction.

—WILLIAM BLAKE (1757–1827)

It left you a lot of time to hang around and listen to horse talk … you'd find out about horses and men and pick up a lot of stuff you could use all the rest of your life, if you had some sense and salted down what you heard and felt and saw.

—SHERWOOD ANDERSON

Sickness comes on horseback, but goes away on foot.

—PROVERB

To me, horses and freedom are synonymous .

—VERYL GOODNIGHT

The horse, with beauty unsurpassed, strength immeasurable and grace unlike any other, still remains humble enough to carry a man upon his back.

—AMBER SENTI

A cursed horse has a shining coat.

—CORSICAN PROVERB

The great advantage of a dialogue on horseback: it can be merged at any distant into a trot or canter, and one might escape from Socrates himself in the saddle.

—GEORGE ELIOT

Horses change lives. They give our young people confidence and self esteem. They provide peace and tranquility to troubled souls—they give us hope!

—TONI ROBINSON

On the back of a horse you will find Paradise.

—STELLA A. WALKER

My horses are my friends, not my slaves.

—REINER KLIMKE

The only time some people work like a horse is when the boss rides them.

—GABRIEL HEATTER

It is the horse's gift to connect us with Heaven and our own footsteps.

—RONNI SWEET

Only when you see through the eyes of the horse, can you lead the dance of the mind.

—PETE SPATES

Industry is a better horse to ride than genius.

—WALTER LIPPMANN

A horse can lend its rider the speed and strength he or she lacks—but the rider who is wise remembers it is no more then a loan.

—PAM BROWN

My most trustworthy saddle horse … clamped on my upper leg …
I threw him down on the ground … and put the tarp over him. I let him
up two hours later; he thought I was the greatest man in the world, one
he wouldn't think of biting. Horses only remember the end of the story.

—TOM MCGUANE

The only science that has ever existed in the world, relative to the
breaking of horses, that has been of any value, is that true method which
takes them in their native state, and improves their intelligence.

—JOHN RAREY (1827–1866), AMERICAN HORSE TRAINER

I can remember looking up at the sky and, however simplistic it may
seem now, wondering if there was a God up there. … I find myself
asking "big" questions when I'm … riding alone on horseback, and I'm
here to tell you there is a God.

—BUCK BRANNAMAN

The cow, a large animal with horns on its head; its flesh and milk are excellent food. The horse, a large animal. Men sit upon his back and ride; he has no horns on his head.

—DAVID MALO (C. 1793–1853), *HAWAIIAN ANTIQUITIES*

———◆———

The horse. Here is nobility without conceit, friendship without envy, beauty without vanity. A willing servant, yet never a slave.

—RONALD DUNCAN

———◆———

Hay is for horses.

—AMERICAN PROVERB, A GENTLE REBUKE THAT ONE SHOULDN'T GREET ANOTHER WITH THE EXPRESSION "HEY, YOU!"

———◆———

A beggar upon horseback lashes a beggar on foot.

—WILLIAM BUTLER YEATS

A man sentenced to death obtained a reprieve by assuring the king he would teach his majesty's horse to fly within the year. ... "Within a year ... the king may die, or I may die, or the horse may die ... who knows? Maybe the horse will learn to fly." My philosophy is like that man's.

—BERNARD BARUCH

It's no use closing the stable door after the horse has bolted.

—JAPANESE SAYING

When your ship comes in, it just might be a horse.

—JAN JASION CROSS

If a horse won't eat it, I don't want to play on it.

—DICK ALLEN, ON ARTIFICIAL TURF.

If you call a tail a leg, how many legs does a horse have? Four. Calling a tail a leg does not make it a leg.

—ABRAHAM LINCOLN (1809–1865)

[H]aving heard the neigh of the horse, they were so enchanted with the sound, that they tried to imitate it; and, in trying to neigh, they forgot how to sing. Moral: The desire for imaginary benefits often involves the loss or present blessings.

—AESOP

No hour of life is wasted that is spent in the saddle.

—WINSTON CHURCHILL

———◆———

The ears never lie.

—DON BURT

———◆———

There is no need of spurs when a horse is running away.

—PUBLILIUS SYRUS (C. FIRST CENTURY BC)

———◆———

Horses lend us the wings we lack.

—PAM BROWN

———◆———

Men without horses are nothing.

—JEREMY JAMES, *THE BYERLEY TURK: THE INCREDIBLE STORY OF THE WORLD'S FIRST THOROUGHBRED*

I say it is better to see a horse as a monster than to see it only as a slow substitute for a motor-car. If we have got into that state of mind about a horse as something stale, it is far better to be frightened of a horse because it is a good deal too fresh.

—G. K. CHESTERTON (1874–1936)

Nothing is more sacred as the bond between horse and rider ... no other creature can ever become so emotionally close to a human as a horse. When a horse dies, the memory lives on because an enormous part of his owner's heart, soul, very existence dies also ... but that can never be laid to rest, it is not meant to be.

—STEPHANIE M. THORN

I am not saying that you should not "love on" your horse. Go to it! But do it on your terms, not hers. You set the rules, and the most important rule is that she never invades your space. So many other good things in your relationship will flow from that simple rule.

—CHARLES WILHELM, *STARTING BABY JAZ*

No philosophers so thoroughly comprehend us as dogs and horses.

—HERMAN MELVILLE

We kept him until he died ... and sat with him during the long last minutes when a horse comes closest to seeming human.

—C. J. MULLEN

For one to fly, one needs only to take the reins.

—MELISSA JAMES

There is no secret so close as that between a rider and his horse.

—ROBERT SMITH SURTEES (1803–1864)

Reckless automobile driving arouses the suspicion that much of the horse sense of the good old days was possessed by the horse.

—ANONYMOUS

In their eyes shine stars of wisdom and courage to guide men to the heavens.

—JODIE MITCHELL

There's nothing so good for the inside of a man as the outside of a horse.

—RONALD REAGAN

After God we owe it to the horses.

—ADOLF SCHREYER (1828–1899)

A dog looks up to a man, a cat looks down on a man, but a patient horse looks a man in the eye and sees him as an equal.

—ANONYMOUS

A ragged colt may prove a good horse. And so may an untoward slovenly boy prove a decent and useful man.

—JAMES KELLY

I have not permitted myself, gentlemen, to conclude that I am the best man in the country; but I am reminded, in this connection, of a story of an old Dutch farmer who remarked to a companion once that "it was not best to swap horses while crossing streams."

—ABRAHAM LINCOLN

The sun it was, ye glittering gods, ye took to make a horse.

—DIRGHATAMAS

Reason lies between the spur and the bridle.

—GEORGE HERBERT (1593–1633)

A fly, sir, may sting a stately horse, and make him wince; but one is but an insect, and the other a horse still.

—SAMUEL JOHNSON

I find the Englishman to be him of all men who stands firmest in his shoes. They had in themselves what they value in their horses, mettle and bottom. Mettle: spirited; bottom: capacity to endure strain.

—RALPH WALDO EMERSON

[The horse possesses] a singular body and a noble spirit, the principle thereof is a loving and dutiful inclination to the service of Man, wherein he never faileth in Peace nor War … and therefore … we must needs account it the most noble and necessary of all four-footed beasts.

—EDWARD TOPSELL

Men without horses are worse than nothing: they are the rayah, the cattle, the common herd. ... They know nothing of the purity of the hoof and the breath of our sacred horses.

—JEREMY JAMES, *THE BYERLEY TURK: THE INCREDIBLE STORY OF THE WORLD'S FIRST THOROUGHBRED*

Bread may feed my body, but my horse feeds my soul.

—ANONYMOUS

Horse sense is actually the animal's instinct for self-preservation.

—GORDON WRIGHT

Wild horses couldn't drag a secret out of a woman. However, women seldom have lunch with wild horses.

—IVERN BOYETT

Horses are the dolphins of the plains, the spirits of the wind; yet we sit astride them for the sake of being well-groomed, whereas they could have all the desire in the world to bolt, but instead, they adjust their speed and grace, only to please us, never to displease.

—LAUREN SALERNO

When a harvester grows weary of his work, it is said "He has the fatigue of the Horse." The first sheaf, called the "Cross of the Horse," is placed on a cross of boxwood in the barn, and the youngest horse on the farm must tread on it.

—SIR JAMES GEORGE FRAZER, *THE GOLDEN BOUGH*

Don't ride the high horse. The fall, when it comes, is hard.

—AMERICAN PROVERB

If God had intended man to walk, he would have given him four legs. Instead, he gave him two—one to put on either side of a horse.

—MONTANA RANCHER

The wagon rests in winter, the sleigh in summer, the horse never.

—YIDDISH PROVERB

What the colt learns in youth he continues in old age.

—FRENCH PROVERB

A horse with two heads wins no races.

—AMERICAN PROVERB

Many people have sighed for the "good old days" and regretted the "passing of the horse," but today, when only those who like horses own them, it is a far better time for horses.

—C. W. ANDERSON

Intimate acquaintance with the horse's knowledge … mark the faces of some older riders with the look that I have also seen on the faces of a few poets and thinkers, the incandescent gaze of unmediated awareness that some might be tempted to call innocence.

—VICKI HEARNE, *ADAM'S TASK*

Belief? What do I believe in? I believe in sun. In rock ... and broom-tailed horses.

—EDWARD ABBEY

Keep five yards from a carriage, ten yards from a horse, and a hundred yards from an elephant; but the distance one should keep from a wicked man cannot be measured.

—INDIAN PROVERB

People on horses look better than they are. People in cars look worse than they are.

—MARYA MANNES

The primeval instincts of the horse are nowhere more pronounced than in the bond between the mare and the foal, for the maternal instinct is the strongest in nature. It is the instinct that ensures the survival of the species and determines the character of them are and her attitude towards other horses and toward man.

—H. H. Isenbart

Horses and children, I often think, have a lot of the good sense there is in the world.

—Josephine Demott Robinson

Heaven is high and earth wide. If you ride three feet higher above the ground than other men, you will know what that means.

—Rudolf C. Binding

A horse is the projection of peoples' dreams about themselves—strong, powerful, beautiful—and it has the capability of giving us escape from our mundane existence.

—PAM BROWN

Let us look beyond the ears of our own horses so that we may see the good in one another's.

—OLD EQUINE EXPRESSION

Men are not hanged for stealing horses but that horses may not be stolen.

—SIR GEORGE SAVILE (1726–1784)

In ceremonies of the horsemen, even the pawn must hold a grudge.

—BOB DYLAN

God first made Man. He thought better of it and made Woman. When he got time he made the Horse, which has the courage and spirit of Man and the beauty and grace of Woman.

—BRAZILIAN SAYING

A tree might be a show in Scotland as a horse in Venice.

—SAMUEL JOHNSON

The cat lets Man support her. But unlike the dog, she is no hand-licker. Furthermore, unlike Man's other good friend, the horse, the cat is no sweating serf of Man. The only labor she condescends to perform is to catch mice and rats, and that's fun.

—VANCE PACKARD

If a mule gets a leg caught in a barbed-wire fence, she will either figure out how to free herself without injury or will wait stoically and patiently for help. … A horse veterinarian once told me that if everyone rode mules she would soon be out of business.

—JOHN HAUER, *THE NATURAL SUPERIORITY OF MULES*

Do not confuse motion and progress. A rocking horse keeps moving, but does not make any progress.

—ALFRED MONTAPERT

We ought to do good to others as simply as a horse runs.

—Marcus Aurelius (121–180)

The only constant thing in life is change, and things can change rapidly when you're dealing with horses.

—Pat Parelli

Quality is like buying oats. If you want nice, clean, fresh oats, you must pay a fair price. However, if you can be satisfied with oats that have already been through the horse … that comes a little cheaper.

—Anonymous

Soft grass for an old horse.

—Bulgarian proverb

A Hibernian sage once wrote that there are three things a man never forgets: The girl of his early youth, a devoted teacher, and a great horse.

—C. J. J. MULLEN

A horse is worth more than riches.

—SPANISH PROVERB

Good people get cheated, just as good horses get ridden.

—CHINESE PROVERB

Spending that many hours in the saddle gave a man plenty of time to think. That's why so many cowboys fancied themselves Philosophers.

—CHARLES M. RUSSELL (1864–1926)

A horse is simply a horse.

—AVICENNA (C. 980–1037)

A horse is a vain thing for safety.

—PSALMS 33:17

The horse is God's gift to mankind.

—ARABIAN PROVERB

The daughter who won't lift a finger in the house is the same child who cycles madly off in the pouring rain to spend all morning mucking out a stable.

—SAMANTHA ARMSTRONG

A Horseman should know neither fear, nor anger.

—JAMES RAREY

A nod is as good as a wink to a blind horse.

—IRISH PROVERB

Horsemanship through the history of all nations has been considered one of the highest accomplishments. You can't pass a park without seeing a statue of some old codger on a horse. It must be to his bravery, you can tell it's not to his horsemanship.

—WILL ROGERS

[Fate is] a little like a horse with a loose rein. It can meander calmly, or break into a gallop without warning, leaving you to hang on for dear life.

—*STAR TREK: THE NEXT GENERATION*

There is one respect in which beasts show real wisdom ... their quiet, placid enjoyment of the present moment.

—ARTHUR SCHOPENHAUER (1788–1860)

From a workaday drudge, [the Shetland pony] became a fun-loving playmate. No door was closed to him, for he had taught himself how to slide bolts, open gates, rattle latches. His long lips became expert at plucking caps from children's heads or handkerchiefs from pockets.

—MARGUERITE HENRY

No matter what you weigh, the little fellow is your equal on a horse.

—WILL ROGERS

Never were abilities so much below mediocrity so well rewarded; no, not when Caligula's horse was made Consul.

—JOHN RANDOLPH, REGARDING RICHARD RUSH'S APPOINTMENT AS SECRETARY OF THE TREASURY

Lend a horse, and you may have back his skin.

—ENGLISH PROVERB

What we are seeking so frantically elsewhere may turn out to be the horse we have been riding all along.

—HARVEY COX, *TURNING EAST*

The labor of women in the house, certainly, enables men to produce more wealth than they otherwise could; and in this way women are economic factors in society. But so are horses.

—CHARLOTTE P. GILMAN

———◆———

When you hear hoof beats in Texas, think horses not zebras.

—ANONYMOUS

———◆———

A man trying to sell a blind horse always praises its feet.

—GERMAN PROVERB

———◆———

The hardest thing to do on a horse is nothing at all.

—ANONYMOUS

———◆———

Don't spur a willing horse.

—PROVERB

Brooks too wide for our leaping, hedges far too high. Loads too heavy for our moving, burdens too cumbersome for us to bear. Distances far beyond our journeying. The horse gave us mastery.

—PAM BROWN

If an ass goes traveling it will not come home a horse.

—PROVERB

I can make a General in five minutes but a good horse is hard to replace.

—ABRAHAM LINCOLN

Animals do not admire each other. A horse does not admire its companion.

—ATTRIBUTED TO VARIOUS

The ox longs for the gaudy trappings of the horse; the lazy pack-horse would fain plough.

—PROVERB

Never gallop Pegasus to death.

—ALEXANDER POPE (1688–1744)

Don't approach a goat from the front, a horse from the back, or a fool from any side.

—JEWISH PROVERB

Hurry! At a gallop! To Paradise.

—PRINCESS LOUISE-MARIE OF FRANCE (1812–185), HER LAST WORDS
BEFORE DYING

———⬦———

The speed of a runaway horse counts for nothing.

—JEAN COCTEAU (1889–1963)

———⬦———

A good horse will never return to graze on grass it has already passed by.

—CHINESE PROVERB

———⬦———

A mule is just like a horse, but even more so.

—PAT PARELLI

———⬦———

It was yer hosses done likked us!

—CONFEDERATE SOLDIER

The horse is an archetypal symbol which will always find ways to stir up deep and moving ancestral memories in every human being.

—PAUL MELLON

Being born in a stable does not make a man a horse.

—ARTHUR WELLESLEY, FIRST DUKE OF WELLINGTON, ON LEARNING
HE HAD BEEN DESCRIBED AS IRISH BECAUSE HE HAS BEEN BORN
IN DUBLIN

A good horse makes short miles.

—GEORGE ELIOT

All I say is, if you cannot ride two horses you have no right in the circus.

—JAMES MAXTON (1885–1946), AFTER BEING TOLD HE COULDN'T BE IN
TWO POLITICAL PARTIES

There are instances when we are like horses, we psychologists, and grow restless: we see our own shadow wavering up and down before us.

—FRIEDRICH NIETZSCHE

A man, a horse and a dog never get weary of each other's company.

—ANONYMOUS

Horsepower was a wonderful thing when only horses had it.

—ANONYMOUS

No man ought to looke a given horse in the mouth.

—JOHN HEYWOOD

———◆———

I am, always suspicious of a horse … without guile.

—ERNEST THOMPSON SETON (1860–1946)

———◆———

Set the cart before the horse.

—ANONYMOUS

———◆———

The conqueror and king in each one of us is the knower of truth. Let the knower awaken in us and drive the horses of the mind, emotions, and physical body on the pathway which that king has chosen.

—GEORGE S. ARUNDALE

———◆———

Whenever I was upset by something in the papers, [Jack] always told me to be more tolerant, like a horse flicking away flies in the summer.

—JACKIE KENNEDY ONASSIS

You want your horse to look good but you also want it not to have to eat grass.

—CHINESE PROVERB

While the grasse groweth the horse starveth.

—JOHN HEYWOOD

If one hasn't a horse, one is one's own horse.

—VINCENT VAN GOGH (1853–1890)

The American Saddle Horse, with his refinement of gaits and his animation and beauty, does not belong just to his owner or trainer. He belongs to the show ring, where he can bring joy and thrill to thousands of "ringside riders."

—MARGUERITE HENRY

———◆———

Few girls are as well shaped as a good horse.

—CHRISTOPHER MORLEY

———◆———

A fence should be horse high, hog tight, and bull strong.

—ANONYMOUS

———◆———

Will is to grace as the horse is to the rider.

—SAINT AUGUSTINE (354–430)

———◆———

Ride a cow until you ride a horse.

—JAPANESE PROVERB

Words are as beautiful as wild horses, and sometimes as difficult to corral.

—TED BERKMAN

Some people regard private enterprise as a predatory tiger to be shot. Others look on it as a cow they can milk. Not enough people see it as a healthy horse, pulling a sturdy wagon.

—WINSTON CHURCHILL

Man was created to complete the horse.

—EDWARD ABBEY

England's past has been borne on his back;
All our history is his industry.
We are his heirs; he our inheritance.

—RONALD DUNCAN, *THE HORSE*

Sleep after selling horses and elephants.

—HINDU PROVERB

You cannot judge of the horse by the harness.

—PROVERB

Marriage may often be a stormy lake, but celibacy is almost always a muddy horse pond.

— THOMAS LOVE PEACOCK (1785–1866)

Your tongue is like a horse—if you take care of it, it takes care of you; if you treat it badly, it treats you badly.

— SAUDI ARABIAN PROVERB

Dumb animals we call them, while they bark and neigh and moo. They talk as much as we do—to them we seem dumb too.

— REBECCA MCCANN

Trends, like horses, are easier to ride in the direction they are going.

— JOHN NAISBITT

Some people think horses are dumb. Ability and intelligence are in all horses, regardless of breed. Their so-called stupidity stems from our poor communication.

—JOHN LYONS, *LYONS ON HORSES*

You never know how a horse will pull until you hook him to a heavy load.

—PAUL "BEAR" BRYANT

A horseshoe that clatters needs a nail.

—SPANISH PROVERB

If wishes were horses, beggars would ride.

> —JAMES ORCHARD HALLIWELL-PHILLIPS (1820–1889), *THE NURSERY RHYMES OF ENGLAND*

———◆———

I have thought that to breed a noble horse is to share with God in one of his mysteries, as well as one of his delights.

> —TOM LEA, *THE HANDS OF CANTU*

———◆———

Horse sense means seeing things two ways—how you want them to be and how they have to be.

> —JUNE SMITH

———◆———

The same philosophy is a good horse in the stable, but an errant jade on a journey.

—OLIVER GOLDSMITH (C. 1730–1774)

If you see a piebald horse, make a wish before you see his tail.

—GYPSY SAYING

A good horse runs even at the shadow of the whip.

—*THE GATELESS GATE*, A COLLECTION OF FORTY-EIGHT ZEN KOANS COMPILED IN THE EARLY THIRTEENTH CENTURY

Men still dominate the worlds of polo and racing, and a greater percentage of them show and train professionally. To a woman, however, horses often represent something more profound than sport or hobby.

—LINDA KOHANOV, *THE TAO OF EQUUS*

Horses do think. Not very deeply, perhaps, but enough to get you into a lot of trouble.

—PATRICIA JACOBSON AND MARCIA HAYES

Lots of ground has been plowed by balky horses.

—ANONYMOUS

Raise your horse as a son, ride him as an enemy.

—ARABIAN PROVERB

I'm hostile to men, I'm hostile to women, I'm hostile to cats,
to poor cockroaches, I'm afraid of horses.

—NORMAN MAILER

⟞◆⟝

Take care to sell your horse before he dies. The art of life is passing losses
on.

—ROBERT FROST

⟞◆⟝

Most nations ... should be dealt with like a spirited horse, whom
a judicious rider will keep steady, by maintaining an exact balance in his
seat, showing neither fear nor cruelty, occasionally giving and checking
with the rein, while he prudently and resolutely corrects with the spur,
or kindly blandishes with his hand.

—FRANCIS GENTLEMAN (1728–1784)

⟞◆⟝

Old minds are like old horses; you must exercise them if you wish to keep them in working order.

—John Adams

⟨⟩

HORSE, (n): stable thinking.

—Unknown

⟨⟩

Competitions are for horses, not for artists.

—Béla Bartók (1881–1945)

⟨⟩

A wise man looks upon men as he does on horses; all their comparisons of title, wealth, and place, he consider but as harness.

—Robert Cecil (1563–1612)

⟨⟩

I have also observed that if you refuse a high price for a favorite horse, he will go and lay down somewhere and die.

—MARK TWAIN

Men, my dear, are very queer animals, a mixture of horse-nervousness, ass-stubbornness, and camel-malice—with an angel bobbing about unexpectedly like the apple in the posset, and when they can do exactly as they please, they are very hard to drive.

—THOMAS HUXLEY (1825–1895)

It is not the horse that draws the cart, but the oats.

—RUSSIAN PROVERB

For centuries we have been famed for our skill in horsemanship,
so that the Magyar has no need to have his horses dance with crossed legs,
Spanish fashion.

—KING MATHIAS, CORVINUS OF HUNGARY

The burden is equal to the horse's strength.

—THE TALMUD

In dealing with a girl or a horse, one lets nature take its course.

—FRED ASTAIRE IN *TOP HAT*

Betwixt the stirrup and the ground,
Mercy I asked, mercy I found.

—WILLIAM CAMDEN (1551–1623)

Science is not a sacred cow. Science is a horse. Don't worship it. Feed it.

—AUBREY EBEN

—◆—

As judges of horseflesh they [the Irish tinkers] are hard to beat, and make their living trading horses or "finding" them before the owner has lost them.

—DOROTHEA DONN BYRNE, *THE TURN OF THE WHEEL*

—◆—

If wishes were fishes we'd all be throwing nets. If wishes were horses we'd all ride.

—DOUG HORTON

—◆—

[A] cavalry charge is very much like ordinary life. So long as you are all right, firmly in the saddle, your horse in hand and well armed, lots of enemies will give you a wide berth. But as soon as you ... are wounded, or your horse is wounded ... from all quarters enemies rush upon you.

—SIR WINSTON CHURCHILL, *SENSATIONS OF A CAVALRY CHARGE*

Don't draw another's bow, don't ride another's horse, don't mind another's business.

—PROVERB

Nothing is so abject and pathetic as a politician who has lost his job, save only a retired stud-horse.

—H. L. MENCKEN

One can't shoe a running horse.

—DUTCH PROVERB

It excites me that no matter how much machinery replaces the horse, the work it can do is still measured in horsepower.

—MARGUERITE HENRY

Emotions are wild horses.

—PAULO COELHO

Nature will never disclose all her secrets to us, and the horse will forever have in store for us novelties, surprises, springing from life itself.

—GENERAL ALEXIS L'HOTTE

Horses have hoofs to carry them over frost and snow; hair, to protect them from wind and cold. They eat grass and drink water, and fling up their heels. ... Such is the real nature of horses.

—ZHUANGZI

———◆◆———

You can learn a lot about people by being around them and their horses.

—CLAY WALKER

———◆◆———

We are like horses who hurt themselves as soon as they pull on their bits—and we bow our heads. We even lose consciousness of the situation, we just submit. Any re-awakening of thought is then painful.

—SIMONE WEIL

———◆◆———

The soul is like a pair of winged horses and a charioteer joined in natural union.

—PLATO

Happiness is not a horse, you cannot harness it.

—RUSSIAN PROVERB

Time is the rider that breaks youth.

—GEORGE HERBERT, *JACULA PRUDENTUM*

A man trying to sell a blind horse always praises its feet.

—GERMAN PROVERB

What good is grass when the horse is already dead?

—FILIPINO PROVERB

Life is a horse: either you ride it or it rides you.

—GREGORY MCDONALD

It's what you learn after you know it all that's important.

—JIMMY WILLIAMS

A good resolution is like an old horse, which is often saddled but rarely ridden.

—MEXICAN PROVERB

We can judge the heart of a man by his treatment of animals.

—IMMANUEL KANT (1724–1804)

We judge a horse not only by its pace on a racecourse, but also by its walk, nay, when resting in its stable.

—MICHEL DE MONTAIGNE (1533–1592)

Horses carry the history of mankind on their broad backs.

—LUCINDA PRIOR PALMER

The grey mare is the better horse.

—JOHN HEYWOOD

Our greatest glory is not in never falling, but in rising every time we fall.

    —CONFUCIUS (C. 551–479 BC)

God forgive you for the galloping when trotting's not a sin.

    —SCOTTISH PROVERB

A young trooper should have an old horse.

    —H. G. BOHN

We tolerate shapes in human beings that would horrify us if we saw them in a horse.

    —W. R. INGE (1860–1954)

As old wood is best to burn; old horses to ride; old books to read; old wine to drink; so are old friends most trusty to use.

—LEONARD WRIGHT

Conquering the world on horseback is easy; it is dismounting and governing that is hard.

—GENGHIS KHAN (C. 1162–1227)

Courage is being scared to death and saddling up anyways.

—JOHN WAYNE

The horse is, like man, the most beautiful and the most miserable of creatures.

—ROSA BONHEUR (1822–1899)

One must plow with the horses one has.

—GERMAN PROVERB

———◆◆◆———

He that will venture nothing must not get on horseback.

—SPANISH PROVERB

———◆◆◆———

Not the fastest horse can catch a word spoken in anger.

—CHINESE PROVERB

———◆◆◆———

The horse loves his oats more than his saddle.

—RUSSIAN PROVERB

———◆◆◆———

He that hath love in his heart hath spurs in his sides.

—ENGLISH PROVERB

Trust yourself and your horse.

—CROATIAN PROVERB

For bringing us the horse we could almost forgive you for giving us whiskey. Horses make a landscape more beautiful.

—LAME DEER

The slow horse reaches the mill.

—IRISH PROVERB

It's difficult to water a horse that won't lower its head.

—FINNISH PROVERB

The horse that pulls the most is usually given the least amount of oats.

—GERMAN PROVERB

Every horse is good for something.

—CHRIS COOPER AS TOM SMITH IN *SEABISCUIT*

Horses do change, you know; a lot of the … ponies really give the able-bodied grooms a hard time, but if you put a disabled child or adult on their back they're as gentle as lambs.

—JACKIE CROOME

The empire was won on horseback, but you cannot govern on horseback.

—Yeh-lu T'su T'sai, Chinese general

—◆—

Human reason is like a drunken man on horseback; set it up on one side and it tumbles over on the other.

—Martin Luther (1483–1546)

—◆—

In the choice of a horse and a wife, a man must please himself, ignoring the opinion and advice of friends.

—George John Whyte-Melville (1821–1878)

—◆—

Sell the cow, buy the sheep, but never be without the horse.

—Irish proverb

—◆—

I think that the most important thing for me in life is to learn from whatever I'm doing … I don't really like to participate in things that I'm not learning something from and getting something out of. With horses, you learn constantly and you get so much back.

—CLAY WALKER

The horse is not judged of by the saddle.

—GERMAN PROVERB

One may ride a free horse to death.

—SCOTTISH PROVERB

In buying a horse or taking a wife, shut your eyes tight and commend yourself to God.

—TUSCAN PROVERB

Anyone who is concerned about his dignity would be well advised to keep away from horses.

—PRINCE PHILIP, DUKE OF EDINBURGH

Never give up. For fifty years they said the horse was through. Now look at him—a status symbol.

—FLETCHER KNEBEL

The riders in a race do not stop short when they reach the goal. There is a little finishing canter before they come to a standstill … The canter that brings you to a standstill need not be only coming to rest. It cannot be while you still live.

—OLIVER WENDELL HOLMES, JR., JUSTICE OF THE SUPREME COURT, REFLECTING ON RETIREMENT IN A RADIO ADDRESS ON HIS NINETIETH BIRTHDAY

If a man works like a horse for his money, there are a lot of girls anxious to take him down the bridal path.

—MARTY ALLEN

May your descendants ride in chariots.

—CHINESE FORTUNE

Show me your horse and I will tell you what you are.

—ENGLISH PROVERB

If time were the wicked sheriff in a horse opera, I'd pay for riding lessons and take his gun away.

—W. H. AUDEN (1907–1973)

Evidently, if you fall on the ground and there is a horse charging at you, he won't step on you; he'll jump over you.

—BRUCE BERESFORD

Nature has not placed us in an inferior rank to men, no more than the females of other animals, where we see no distinction of capacity, though I am persuaded if there was a commonwealth of rational horses ... it would be an established maxim amongst them that a mare could not be taught to pace.

—LADY MARY WORTLEY MONTAGU (1689–1762)

In order to go fast, one must go slow.

—DOMINIQUE BARBIER

The horse is prepared against the day of battle: but safety is of the Lord.

—PROVERBS 21:31

Let us put Germany in the saddle, so to speak—it already knows how to ride.

>—OTTO VON BISMARCK (1815–1898), IN A SPEECH TO THE
>GERMAN REICHSTAG

Straight from the horse's mouth.

>—OLD EXPRESSION

Horses have hooves to carry them over frost and snow; hair, to protect them from wind and cold. They eat grass and drink water, and fling up their heels over the campaign. Such is the real nature of horses. Palatial dwellings are of no use to them.

>—ZHUANGZI

Who buys a horse buys care.

—SPANISH PROVERB

Another man's horse and your own spurs outrun the wind.

—GERMAN PROVERB

When the mule is beaten, the horse is scared.

—CHINESE PROVERB

[T]o emphasize the afterlife is to deny life. To concentrate on Heaven is to create hell … religious multitudes are gambling the only life they may ever have on a dark horse in a race that has no finish line.

—TOM ROBBINS, *SKINNY LEGS AND ALL*

Tomorrow your horse may be lame.

—YIDDISH PROVERB

A husband is very much like a house or a horse.

—ANTHONY TROLLOPE

[A] blind horse fears no dangers, because he sees none.

—PHILIP DORMER STANHOPE (1694–1773)

Fix this sentence: He put the horse before the cart.

—STEPHEN PRICE

I have just read your dispatch about sore tongued and fatigued sick horses. Will you pardon me for asking what the horses of your army have done since the battle of Antietem that fatigues anything?

—ABRAHAM LINCOLN, LETTER TO GEN. GEORGE B. MCCLELLAN

There is no greater pleasure than a nice ride on a nice horse on a beautiful day.

—JUDY RICHTER

Heretofore, every peasant knew only too well that when he had a horse he could manage his homestead and that without a horse he could not make a living.

—NIKITA KHRUSHCHEV

The kick of a quiet horse strikes strong.

—ARMENIAN PROVERB

The punters know that the horse named Morality rarely gets past the post, whereas the nag named Self-Interest always runs a good race.

—GOUGH WHITLAM

In partnership with a horse, one is seldom lacking for thought, emotion, and inspiration. One is always attended by a great companion.

—CHARLES DE KUNFFY

A short horse is soon curried.

—JOHN HEYWOOD

If the horse is good, you don't mind paying the rental fee.

—JAPANESE PROVERB

—⊰◆⊱—

Put a beggar on horseback and he'll ride to hell.
Put a beggar on horseback and he'll go on a gallop.

—IRISH PROVERBS

—⊰◆⊱—

The burden is equal to the horse's strength.

—TALMUD

—⊰◆⊱—

It's hard to lead a cavalry charge if you think you look funny on a horse.

—ADLAI E. STEVENSON

—⊰◆⊱—

Equestrian art, however, is something else which involves complete harmony between horse and rider, and that makes the rider feel that there have been moments of beauty and greatness which make a flight possible from all that is ordinary and mediocre.

—Nuno Oliveira

If you can't get in by the front door, try the stable door.

—Prince Edward, Duke of Windsor

Do not mistake a goat's beard for a fine stallion's tail.

—Irish proverb

I would rather ride on an ass that carries me than a horse that throws me.

—GEORGE HERBERT

———◆———

When the good times come around, they gallop in like wild horses.
You just try to stay on them for as long as you can. And when they throw
you off ... you just wait in the shade until they come around again.

—JIMMY BUFFETT

———◆———

A donkey appears to me like a horse translated into Dutch.

—GEORG CHRISTOPH LICHTENBERG (1742–1799)

———◆———

Horses symbolize the personal drive for freedom shared by people
of all nations.

—VERYL GOODNIGHT

———◆———

A bad foaling might still produce a fine horse.

—FRENCH PROVERB

It's better to want the horse you don't have than to have the horse you don't want.

—ANONYMOUS

The human mind is not rich enough to drive many horses abreast and wants one general scheme, under which it strives to bring everything.

—GEORGE SANTAYANA (1863–1952)

An old friend is like a saddled horse.

—AFGHAN PROVERB

Behold, we put bits in the horses' mouths, that they may obey us;
and we turn about their whole body.

—JAMES 3:3

For the student there is, in its season, no better place than the saddle.

—FRANCIS PARKMAN (1823–1893)

Horses and poets should be fed, not overfed.

—CHARLES II OF ENGLAND (1630–1685)

Money is not found under a horse's hoof step.

—FRENCH PROVERB

It is fair to say the country could not have grown the way it did were it not for the service of horses.

—DONNA SNYDER-SMITH, *THE ALL-AROUND HORSE AND RIDER*

So, I can tell when the horse is right because I spent eighteen years on, not horses, but spaceships and spacesuits.

—ALAN BEAN

No horseman or horsewoman has ever finished learning.

—MARY GORDON-WATSON

Good horses make short miles.

—GEORGE HERBERT

Who's born as donkey can't die as horse.

—ITALIAN PROVERB

My father once said, "You want to know what is around you?
Ask the horses."

—TERESA TSIMMU MARTINO

The old horse will not mistake the road.

—PROVERB

Organization is the art of getting men to respond like Thoroughbreds.
When you cluck to a Thoroughbred, he gives you all the speed and
strength of heart and sinew he has in him. When you cluck to a jackass,
he kicks.

—C. R. HOUSE

The will is a beast of burden. If God mounts it, it wishes and goes as God wills; if Satan mounts it, it wishes and goes as Satan wills; Nor can it choose its rider … the riders contend for its possession.

—MARTIN LUTHER

With horses as with warriors, you can't judge from their appearance.

—JAPANESE PROVERB

If there's a lot of try in the human, there's a lot of forgiveness in a horse.

—WALTER JOSEY

The wind flew. God told the wind to condense itself and out of the flurry came the horse. But with the spark of spirit the horse flew by the wind itself.

—MARGUERITE HENRY

———◆———

The horse's death makes the cow fatter.

—ENGLISH PROVERB

———◆———

A nail may save the horseshoe, the horseshoe may save the horse, the horse may save the rider, and the rider may save the kingdom.

—TURKISH PROVERB

———◆———

Talking to a horse's ear.

—Japanese expression (meaning to say something that falls
    on deaf ears)

Fat is the best color.

—Horseman's adage

Horses are karmic, and they come to us in our lives karmically, when
it is time for us to truly learn.

—Dominique Barbier

I ended the war a horse ahead.

—Nathan Bedford Forrest (1821–1877)

A fool and his horse are soon parted.

—ANONYMOUS

———◆———

It is the horse's gift to connect us with Heaven and our own footsteps.

—RONNI SWEET

———◆———

You will find it is always easier to walk if there is a horse between your legs.

—ANONYMOUS

———◆———

You can lead a horse to water … if you got a horse.

—ENGLISH PROVERB

———◆———

There is a natural affinity between women and horses, something so basic it creates as immediate foundation for a relationship and a launching pad for almost everything we want to do with a horse.

—MARY D. MIDKIFF

He that riseth late, must trot all day, and shall scarce overtake his business at night.

—BENJAMIN FRANKLIN

He that can travel well afoot, keeps a good horse.

—BENJAMIN FRANKLIN

Be not elated at any excellence that is not your own. If the horse in his
elation were to say, "I am a beautiful horse," it could be endured;
but when you say in your elation, "I have a beautiful horse," rest assured
that you are elated at something good that belongs to a horse.

—EPICTETUS (C. 55–135)

He had got inside the very soul of the poor beast and taken me with him.
I could not refrain from remarking: "I say, Leo Nikolayevich, beyond
any doubt, you must have been a horse once yourself."

—IVAN TURGENEV (1818–1883), COMMENTING ON WATCHING
LEO TOLSTOY WHISPER TO AN OLD HORSE

A wild horse cares not how fast a man may run.

—ARMENIAN PROVERB

Is it possible, at certain moments we cannot imagine, a horse can add its sufferings together—the non-stop jerks and jabs that are its daily life—and turn them into grief? What use is grief to a horse?

—PETER SHAFFER, *EQUUS*

Of all creatures, the horse is the noblest.

—GERVASE MARKHAM (C. 1568–1637)

"There's life here," the boy said to the alchemist. "I don't know the language of the desert, but my horse knows the language of life."

—PAULO COELHO, *THE ALCHEMIST*

A night reddish sky, prepare the horses for the race.

—MALTESE PROVERB

If economists wished to study the horse, they wouldn't go and look at horses. They'd sit in their studies and say to themselves, "what would I do if I were a horse?"

—ELY DEVONS

A good person has many friends, a good horse has many masters.

—TYWA PROVERB

Horses become acquainted by neighing, people by talking.

—KHAKAS PROVERB

All the treasures of this earth lie between thine eyes. Thou shalt cast mine enemies beneath thy hooves … This shall be the seat from whence prayers rise unto me.

—THE KORAN

Behold, he shall come up as clouds, and his chariots shall be as a whirlwind: his horses are swifter than eagles. Woe unto us! for we are spoiled.

—JEREMIAH 4:13

To err is human, to whinny equine.

—CHERYL FARNER

If we were to go back in time … and ask a farmer what he'd like … he'd probably say he wanted a horse that was twice as strong and ate half as many oats. He would not say he wanted a tractor … technology changes things so fast.

—Philip Quigley

Some things, of course, you can't change. Pretending that you have is like painting stripes on a horse and hollering "Zebra!"

—Eddie Cantor

The first horse to drink doesn't get the dirty water.

—Nigerian proverb

A horse knows how to be a horse; the rider has to learn how to become a rider. A horse without a rider is still a horse; a rider without a horse is no longer a rider.

—ANONYMOUS

You sometimes hear the old saying, "Fat is the best color." This means, of course, that fat covers a multitude of conformation faults and therefore looks good—especially to the less discerning horseman.

—ELEANOR F. PRINCE AND GAYDELL M. COLLIER

Spring and summer are riding on a piebald mare.

—RUSSIAN PROVERB

A mule will labor ten years willingly and patiently for you, for the privilege of kicking you once.

—WILLIAM FAULKNER

———————

A horse has no future. It cannot greet the sun and say today will be better. It can only reflect upon days of past experiences. It is our job to create a positive past.

—KAREN WEST

———————

A mule is an animal that has neither pride nor hope of prosperity.

—ANONYMOUS

———————

The stable wears out the horse more than the road does.

— FRENCH PROVERB

⇒◦⇐

The sound of hoofbeats and the occasional whinny of a horse complement the scene instead of destroying it.

— DAN AADLAND

⇒◦⇐

A horse is both intelligent enough and stupid enough to do what we demand of him.

— GEORGE GAYLORD SIMPSON

⇒◦⇐

Dead horses don't kick.

— BULGARIAN PROVERB

⇒◦⇐

Tell it to the Horse Marines.

—ANONYMOUS

All the king's horses and all the king's men can't put the past together again. So let's remember: Don't try to saw sawdust.

—DALE CARNEGIE

Imagination is a good horse to carry you over the ground—not a flying carpet to set you free from improbability.

—ROBERT DAVIES

Watching a seasoned pony carry its young rider, one senses the pony is doing the teaching. With an uncanny sense of the rider's limitations and often genuine kindness, ponies seem to possess an intelligence you don't always see in horses.

—NINA DURAN

The snorting of his horses was heard from Dan: the whole land trembled at the sound of the neighing of his strong ones; for they are come, and have devoured the land, and all that is in it; the city, and those that dwell therein.

—JEREMIAH 8:16

Mules will test your horsemanship. You must be patient, kind, gentle, consistent, and very persuasive in order to train mules and get along with them. They separate the "men from the boys" when it comes to horse training. This is one of the reasons that I am a mule fan.

—ROBERT M. MILLER, D.V.M.

We all want everything to be wonderful. Every woman wants to sit upon a horse dressed in bells and go riding off through the boundless green and sensual forest.

—CLARISSA ESTES

While there are many things you can fake through in this life, pretending that you know horses when you don't isn't one of them.

—COOKY MCCLUNG

With their mystery and magic, the horses have taught me the speech that transcends verbal language. The horses have shown me spirit and family and leadership.

—TERESA TSIMMU MARTINO

If you see someone riding a horse, and don't have the money to buy one don't get a donkey for yourself.

—PAKISTANI PROVERB

————◆————

War is no place for horses.

—SIR MICHAEL ANSELL

————◆————

Distance tests a horse's strength. Time reveals a person's character.

—CHINESE PROVERB

————◆————

No horse gets anywhere until he is harnessed. No stream or gas drives anything until it is confined.

—HARRY EMERSON FOSDICK (1878–1969)

————◆————

CHAPTER EIGHT

And They're Off!: At the Track and On the Track

There was an article in the paper today about the man who won the 2007 National Harness Handicapping Championship. I was particularly struck by his assertion that "handicapping is a skill. There is a bit of luck involved, but it's not like other forms of gambling, like playing slot machines or blackjack at a casino, which are based predominantly on luck."

I've always suspected as much—even while acting as if I didn't. That is, over the last couple of decades I've turned into the kind of occasional horseplayer who, when he visits the track, makes absolutely no effort to study form but instead places one sort of crazy bet after another. Two bucks on the six horse because his name rings a bell, ten on the two because his *dam*'s name rings a *different* bell, ten more on the eight, an impossible long shot, because—what a coincidence!—he hails from the town where we waited overnight, during that college-era road trip, for the Rambler to have its push-button transmission repaired, and so on.

But you know what? I look back on the dough I've basically thrown away at tracks from Suffolk Downs and Saratoga to Lexington's fabled Red Mile and I consider my losses a small price to have paid for the wonderful times I've enjoyed at those tracks. Because ever since a couple of pre-teen bus trips to Belmont with my grandparents way back in the sixties, I've loved being at the races with family and friends. And I honestly can't think of a single time I didn't have fun at the flats or the trotters—or made any money, to be perfectly honest.

Some of the people you'll find quoted in this chapter devoted to racing and betting and attendant subjects sound as if they share my fondness for being at the track, win or lose. For instance, the great sportswriter Red Smith certainly liked attending the Kentucky Derby, which he called "the one assignment of the sports year which I would most deeply regret missing." And Bill Barich seems to write with similarly genuine affection for the way "a racetrack exists as a world apart, rich in its own mysteries and subject to laws of its own devising."

But just to keep things honest, you'll also hear from folks who are a little more cynical about the whole enterprise. Such as Frank Richardson, who admits that because he knows nothing about racing, "any money I put on a horse is a sort of insurance policy to prevent it winning."

Nice to have the contrasting viewpoints, of course. It's what makes for a horse race, after all.

To me, [the Kentucky Derby] is the one assignment of the sports year which I would most deeply regret missing. It is a noisy, wearing, sleepless week of work and play and a fellow feels like a litter case coming home, and I love it.

—RED SMITH

One way to stop a runaway horse is to bet on him.

—ATTRIBUTED TO VARIOUS

The race is not always to the swift, nor the battle to the strong, but that's the way to bet.

—DAMON RUNYON (1884–1946)

Sadie's right, that track is crooked! Lora May, it isn't the track, it's the horses. They fix things up amongst themselves.

—JOSEPH L. MANKIEWICZ, DIRECTOR OF *A LETTER TO THREE WIVES*

I hope I break even, I need the money.

—JOE E. LEWIS, ON BETTING

A racehorse is an animal that can take several thousand people for a ride at the same time.

—MARJORIE JOHNSON

[T]he only way Breezing Along can lose the race is to have somebody shoot him at the quarter pole, and of course nobody is shooting horses at the quarter pole at Hialeah, though many citizens often feel like shooting horses at the half.

—DAMON RUNYON, *PICK THE WINNER*

Betting is the manure to which the enormous crop of horse-races and racehorse breeding in this and other countries is to a large extent due.

—RICHARD BLACKMORE

Racetrack! Well ... what am I doin' here?

—GROUCHO MARX

No horse can go as fast as the money you put on it.

—EARL WILSON

———⊳◆⊲———

A horse that relieves himself on the track will relieve you of your money.

—C. N. RICHARDSON, *SMALL TRACK BETTING*

———⊳◆⊲———

A man in passion rides a horse that runs away with him.

—THOMAS FULLER (1608–1661)

———⊳◆⊲———

Beauty, delicacy and position—these were the foundations of courtly equestrianism.

—HENNING EICHBERG

———⊳◆⊲———

There is moreover something magnificent, a kind of majesty in his whole frame, which exalts his rider with pride as he outstrips the wind in his course.

—PAULUS JOVIUS

———◆———

The rhythm of the ride carried them on and on, and she knew that the horse was as eager as she, as much in love with the speed and air and freedom.

—GEORGESS MCHARGUE

———◆———

In the saddle is heaven on earth.

—ANONYMOUS

———◆———

We were gamblers … whether we admit it or not. What other sort of person would stake a dollar bill on an animal that runs on one toe at a time.

—SALLY JENKINS

A tout is a guy who goes around the race track giving out tips on the races, if he can find anybody who will listen to his tips, especially suckers, and a tout is nearly always broke. If he is not broke, he is by no means a tout, but a handicapper, and is respected by one and all.

—DAMON RUNYON

A mostly British expression urging someone to stick to the thing he knows best, "horses for courses" comes from the horse racing world, where it is widely assumed that some horses race better on certain courses than on others.

—ROBERT HENDRICKSON, *ENCYCLOPEDIA OF WORD AND PHRASE ORIGINS*

I lived so close to Aqueduct that I would slip under the fence and do my running right on the track.

—EDWARD L. BOWEN, *NASHUA*

———◆———

The American male, at the peak of his physical powers and appetites, driving 160 big white horses across the scenery of an increasingly hopeless society, with weekend money in his pocket and with little prior exposure to trouble and tragedy, personifies "an accident going to happen."

—JOHN SLOAN DICKEY

———◆———

If you bet on a horse, that's gambling. If you bet you can make three spades, that's entertainment. If you bet cotton will go up three points, that's business. See the difference?

—BLACKIE SHERROD

———◆———

Making a choice is like backing a horse—in a hundred years, they may decide you picked wrongly.

—EDWARD CARPENTER

The horse I bet on was so slow, the jockey kept a diary of the trip.

—HENNY YOUNGMAN

If you have any questions, I'll try to answer them. If it's not inconvenient, I might even tell you the truth … Ocala's my assistant, but don't bother him, he's a son of a bitch. And try to stay out of the way. I'm a working horse trainer, not a … tourist destination.

—P. G. JOHNSON

The Oracle looks at the book … no one … ventures to speak … "Well … of course there's only one in it—if he's wanted" … No one likes to expose … ignorance by asking which horse he refers to as the "only one in it"; and the Oracle goes on to deal out some more wisdom in a loud voice.

—A. B. "Banjo" Paterson, *The Oracle*

Everyone knows that horse racing is carried out mainly for the delight and profit of fools, ruffians, and thieves.

—George Gissing (1857–1903)

[T]here are times when you catch glimpses of the racetrack … elegant and formal, a universe of bright surfaces where honor, decorum, and order prevail.

—Eric Rachlis, Blossom Lefcourt, and Bert Morgan, *Horse Racing: The Golden Age of the Track*

Lord Hippo suffered fearful loss,
By putting money on a horse;
Which he believed, if it were pressed,
Would run faster than the rest.

—HILAIRE BELLOC (1870–1953)

And so there I was, sitting up in the grandstand … looking down on the swipes coming out with their horses … I liked … sitting up there and feeling grand.

—SHERWOOD ANDERSON

No, I'm not a horse bettor. Every once in a while somebody will give me a sure thing and of course it's not.

—M. EMMET WALSH

I would come to look upon such mornings at the racetrack as my strongest ties to earth and place, my strongest link to the kind of heritage I would read about in the library.

—CAREY WINFREY, *TIP ON A LOST RACE*

Lady Godiva put everything she had on a horse.

—W. C. FIELDS

The only decent people I ever saw at the racecourse were horses.

—JAMES JOYCE (1882–1941)

When I started playing the horses and trying to comprehend the mysteries of the game, I thought I was searching for great, immutable truths. I thought there must be a set of principles that governed the outcome of races and were waiting to be discovered.

—ANDREW BEYER, *THE WINNING HORSEPLAYER*

The best horse is not necessarily the best bet. In order to evaluate a bet, we must know … the probability of winning the bet, and the payoff if we win. …[I]t is the relationship between these two factors which determines the expected return of the bet.

—STEVEN L. BRECHER, *BEATING THE RACES WITH A COMPUTER*

A beginning horseplayer picking a cold trifecta is like a guy who's never held a dart shooting three straight bull's-eyes.

—TED MCCLELLAND, *HORSEPLAYERS*

Horses have never hurt anyone yet, except when they bet on them.

—STUART CLOETE (1897–1976)

———⊰◆⊱———

Thursday afternoon Tricksy Wilcox scratched his armpit absentmindedly and decided Claypits wasn't worth backing in the 2:30. [Later that day] Tricksy watched Claypits win the 2:30 with insulting ease and drank down his dented self-esteem with the last of the beer.

—DICK FRANCIS, *A ROYAL RIP-OFF AT KINGDOM HILL*

———⊰◆⊱———

There he lives from noon to five P.M. on every day when there is racing, ceaselessly receiving scraps of paper stating that someone (for initials only are used) is eager to wager 2s 6d on Blue Moon in the two-thirty P.M. race at Wye.

—C. C. L. BROWNE, *THE INSIDE VIEW*

———⊰◆⊱———

You can eat your betting money, but never bet your eating money.

—SIGN IN MANY RACETRACK CAFETERIAS

From New York City, you drive north for about 175 miles, turn left on Union Avenue and go back one hundred years.

—RED SMITH, WHEN ASKED FOR DIRECTIONS TO SARATOGA RACE COURSE

The racing people were busy discussing prospects for the final day. The first day's racing had been interesting; some long shots had come home, and a few among the crowd in the lounge were conscious as they talked of fatter, heavier wallets hanging in their inside pockets.

—MAURICE GEE, *THE LOSERS*

Who makes the most money? Horse bettors first, followed by sports bettors. Then poker, golf hustlers, and blackjack and backgammon players.

—RICHARD W. MUNCHKIN IN *GAMBLING WIZARDS*

This is the only place where the windows clean the people.

—JOE E. LEWIS, ON RACETRACKS

Saratoga is forever known as the "Graveyard of Champions."

—BILL HELLER, *SARATOGA TALES: GREAT HORSES, FEARLESS JOCKEYS, SHOCKING UPSETS AND INCREDIBLE BLUNDERS AT AMERICA'S LEGENDARY RACE TRACK*

There are not immutable truths, no absolute rights and wrongs, because the only meaningful measure of any handicapping method is its profitability. Certain systems may produce profits for a while, but as the betting public catches on to them the odds drop and the systems eventually cease to work.

—ANDREW BEYER, *THE WINNING HORSEPLAYER*

[T]he racetrack is strikingly romantic. It has a kind of grandeur, even an epic quality. The horses, too, are blessed with a heroic dimension.

—ERIC RACHLIS, BLOSSOM LEFCOURT, AND BERT MORGAN, *HORSE RACING: THE GOLDEN AGE OF THE TRACK*

On arrival at the course, the Oracle is in great form. Attended by his string of satellites, he plods from stall to stall staring at the horses. Their names are printed in big letters on the stalls, but the Oracle doesn't let that stop his display of knowledge.

—A. B. "BANJO" PATERSON, *THE ORACLE*

Keeping horses in order to have a bet is not job for a poor man.

—COLIN DAVY, *THE MAJOR*

——◆——

Friday afternoon, having pinched a tenner from his wife's holiday fund in the best teapot, Tricksy Wilcox went to the races.

—DICK FRANCIS, *A ROYAL RIP-OFF AT KINGDOM HILL*

——◆——

Well, I am not going to bother you the details of the race, but this horse Breezing Along is nowhere. In fact, he is so far back that I do not recollect seeing him finish, because by the time the third horse in the field crosses the line, Hot Horse Herbie and me are on our way back to town.

—DAMON RUNYON

——◆——

The horse racing handicapping system does not reward brilliance, it punishes it. If tennis were run along these lines, Roger Federer would start his matches two sets down. But tennis is not a betting sport in the way that racing is. Nothing is.

—CLARE BALDING

Chuck and I felt our very presence among the drunken, happy hordes of the Churchill Downs infield was a victory, no matter what happened for us at the betting windows.

—ELIZABETH MITCHELL, *THREE STRIDES BEFORE THE WIRE*

Horse sense is what keeps horses from betting on what people will do.

—RAYMOND NASH, *PEARLS OF WISDOM*

A longshot wins a race. A disappointed bettor consults his Form and discovers that the longshot had been timed at 36 seconds in a breezing three-furlong workout a couple of days ago. No other horse in the race had worked so rapidly so recently. Powie! A new system is born!

—TOM AINSLIE, *AINSLIE'S COMPLETE GUIDE TO THOROUGHBRED RACING*

———

"I never bet," I ses, "an' I take no interest in horse-racing an', moreover," I ses, "she can't give Bountiful Boy seven pounds over a mile an' a quarter."

—EDGAR WALLACE

———

Never bet on a sure thing unless you can afford to lose.

—ANONYMOUS

———

Anything can happen in a handicap … All good horses might fall—you never know.

—DICK FRANCIS

———◆———

[T]he grandstand had the empty, aimless feeling of a shopping mall. I spread out my program on a table and ran my eyes across lines of statistics … I had learned to handicap—to dope out the winners of a horse race—when I was just a small child.

—TED MCCLELLAND, *HORSEPLAYERS*

———◆———

In 1999 *Sports Illustrated* named Saratoga Race Course "as one of the Top Ten sporting venues in the world." Two years later, *ESPN Magazine* called Saratoga "the loveliest racetrack in the country."

—BILL HELLER, *SARATOGA TALES: GREAT HORSES, FEARLESS JOCKEYS, SHOCKING UPSETS AND INCREDIBLE BLUNDERS AT AMERICA'S LEGENDARY RACE TRACK*

———◆———

At the track, the odds are not set by the house, as they are in a casino. They're set by the amount of money bet on each horse. The more money bet, the lower the odds. This is known as pari-mutuel wagering.

—TED MCCLELLAND, *HORSEPLAYERS*

It is during the last race meeting at Saratoga, and one evening I am standing out under the elms in front of the Grand Union Hotel thinking what a beautiful world it is, to be sure, for what do I do in the afternoon at the track but grab myself a piece of a ten-to-one shot.

—DAMON RUNYON

I once asked my dad to tell me about his life. "Pretty simple," he answered. "Went to the races, got married, got divorced; went to the races, got married, got divorced; went to the races, got married, got divorced. Went to the races."

—VICTORIA VANDERBILT

Every gambler relies on such gimmicks. My own trick is never to hold on to a losing ticket, for fear it will contaminate my aura and keep me from ever cashing a bet.

—BILL BARICH, *DREAMING*

Playing the races appears to be the one business in which men believe they can succeed without special study, special talent, or special exertion.

—*RACING MAXIMS AND METHODS OF "PITTSBURGH PHIL"*

Poor devil, poor devil, he's best gone out of a life where he rides his rocking-horse to find a winner.

—D. H. LAWRENCE

Perhaps he should delay his return home and we should go to the Derby, because surely that was the lesson of life: that, within reason, you never regret what you do, but only what you fail to do.

—ELIZABETH MITCHELL, *THREE STRIDES BEFORE THE WIRE*

Horse racing is animated roulette.

—ROGER KAHN

It has been my custom … to rise at dawn and to proceed to the track to see the horses train … one can learn … if one has ears and eyes. It is … a beautiful sight … to see the horses jogging around the track, past the deserted grandstand, more beautiful than a picture.

—J. P. MARQUAND

[A] bet is the placing of a wager on a "contender" to finish first in the race. This is the "win bet." Other bets are "quinella," "exacta," "trifecta" or "triple," "daily double," "pick three."

—M. PAUL ANDERSON, *WAGERING TO WIN*

I'd been a fan of racing all my life … since my grandfather took me to see the flamingos in the infield at beautiful old Hialeah in Florida. I'd never thought about being a sportswriter, but it seemed natural enough to write about a horse race.

—MAX WATMAN, *RACE DAY*

The earliest owner of Saratoga Race Course was a boxer-turned-gambler named James Morrissey. Morrissey developed the track for a specific crowd, making it attractive to the high rollers—he even camouflaged the gambling that was present by naming the casino the "Club House."

—NANCY STOUT, *HOMESTRETCH*

The weeks passed, Pennyfeather … humorously thanked his stars that he was old enough not to risk his bank balance on anything with four legs.

—J. C. SQUIRE, *THE DEAD CERT*

Many of the early tracks were tracks in the same way raisins can be considered fruits—technically, and only in a manner of speaking.

—BERT SUGAR AND CORNELL RICHARDSON, *HORSE SENSE: AN INSIDE LOOK AT THE SPORT OF KINGS*

Nobody has ever bet enough on a winning horse.

—AMERICAN PROVERB

One of the worst things that can happen to you in life is to win a bet on a horse at an early age.

—Danny McGoorty

Ascot is so exclusive that it is the only racecourse in the world where the horses own the people.

—Art Buchwald

Saratoga … was always embraced for its summer racing—so much so that summer racing at Saratoga became an institution.

—Nancy Stout, *Homestrecth*

A racetrack is a place where the human race is secondary.

—Anonymous

[H]e had seen almost nothing of a horse; his racecourse hours were spent ferreting among a bawling, perspiring crowd. … [H]e never went near a race-meeting … yet his conversation seldom deviated for more than a minute at a time from that physically unknown animal the horse.

—JOHN GALSWORTHY, *HAD A HORSE*

When Protagonist rallied to beat Stonewalk by two lengths, I could not explain the outcome of the race in any way that was consistent with my own philosophy.

—ANDREW BEYER

A profit at the race track isn't a profit until you spend it somewhere else.

—CHARLES CARROLL, *HANDICAPPING SPEED*

He is called Hot Horse Herbie because he can always tell you about a horse that is so hot it is … all readied up to win a race, although sometimes Herbie's hot horses turn out to be so cold they freeze everybody within fifty miles of him.

—DAMON RUNYON, *PICK THE WINNER*

Betting the ponies is done in various methodical ways by professionals, haphazardly by some enthusiasts, and often in a rather bizarre fashion by others just out for a day's lark.

—COOKY MCCLUNG, *HORSEFOLK ARE DIFFERENT*

After all, if you remove the gambling, where is the fun in watching a bunch of horses being whipped by midgets?

—IAN O'DOHERTY

The quaint custom of moving an entire household from the city to a cooler place in the country during the hottest month of summer brought racing fans to Saratoga. ... People flocked to Saratoga for the cool pine forests of the Adirondack Muntains and the therapeutic mineral springs.

—NANCY STOUT, *HOMESTRECTH*

If it can happen, it happens at Saratoga.

—GEORGE CASSIDY

There are a million miles of difference between the words "win" and "beat." We don't ever allow the word "beat" on this farm. Because when you start talking about beating someone, you've lost your concentration. You're thinking about the opposition.

—HELEN CRABTREE

He disliked looking back in a race because this action was apt to make one's horse unbalanced, but in this case the knowledge thus gained would make a difference to the way in which he would jump the fence.

—RICHARD FINDLAY, *THE DREAM*

Competitive riding should be classical riding at its best.

—CHARLES DE KUNFFY

When you're riding, only the race in which you're riding is important.

—BILL SHOEMAKER

479

I hope you'll always love Thoroughbred racing and the Kentucky Derby. And never feel embarrassed about shedding a tear or two when "My Old Kentucky Home" is played at Churchill Downs on the first Saturday in May. I wouldn't have it any other way.

—BILLY REED, *MY FAVORITE DERBY STORIES*

The hot thing kicked … as we went down to the start. It jumped the first fence so fast that I did not have time to fall off. At the second it … turned itself into a … corkscrew. I went sailing away. The ground came up to meet me with an almighty bang.

—JOHN WELCOME, *MY FIRST WINNER*

The Whitbread Gold Cup, scheduled for six weeks ahead was the last race of the season. To have a horse fit to run it, and to have Derek Roberts ride it, seemed to be the pinnacle in her racing life that she had never envisaged. Her horizons, her joy, expanded like flowers.

—DICK FRANCIS, *SPRING FEVER*

Losers walking around with money in their pockets are always dangerous, not to be trusted. Some horse always reaches out and grabs them.

—BILL BARICH, *LAUGHING IN THE HILLS*

They were off like rockets as the barrier shot, and the bay filly flashed into the lead. Her slender legs seemed to bear her as though on the breast of the wind. She did not run—she floated—yet the gap between herself and her struggling schoolmates grew even wider.

—JOHN TAINTOR FOOTE, *BLISTER*

When I started riding, winning wasn't thought to be all that important. It was simply something that happened if you worked hard ... *Having fun* was the important thing.

—WILLIAM STEINKRAUS

Sometimes I make the wrong move and it turns out to be the right move. The point is you have to have someone between the shafts. Horses are all about the same. It's just some are faster than others. I'm out there to win money. Not for the love of this or that. The money.

—HERVE FILION

The sun has not yet risen over Saratoga Race Course, but the glory of impending dawn paints the sky lavender. Fog wanders the infield in wisps, slipping over the inside rail and onto the track. While the town lies silent, most occupants asleep, the track awakens.

—BARBARA D. LIVINGSTON, *BARBARA D. LIVINGSTON'S SARATOGA*

Not all jockeys loved horses; for many, they were merely animals, tools for making a living and maybe getting rich. But Jimmy Winkfield not only loved them, he needed them.

—ED HOTALING, *WINK: THE INCREDIBLE JOURNEY LIFE AND EPIC JOURNEY OF JIMMY WINKFIELD*

I love watching a good horse do what he's bred to do—I guess that's what I like the most about it. And I love to see good athletes do what they're bred to do.

—WILFORD BRIMLEY

———✦———

There appears to be no immunity to this dangerous germ. If as a parent you observe your little precious pick up a toy horse, make galloping noises, and plop it over a block, screaming "Win!" you've had it. The jumping rider's disease is loose in your house.

—RAYMOND WOOLFE, JR.

———✦———

The best horse doesn't always win the race.

—IRISH PROVERB

———✦———

"The fastest two minutes in sports."

—ON THE KENTUCKY DERBY

——•——

You win, you're happy; you lose, you're disappointed—but don't let either one carry you away.

—BUSTER WELCH

——•——

[L]ike any race, once the Derby starts, any horse can win.

—FUNNY CIDE TEAM AND BARRY MOSER, *A HORSE NAMED FUNNY CIDE*

——•——

[A] winning formula. A very simple one, much favored by trainers at the race track, is to have the best horse.

—WILLIAM STEINKRAUS

——•——

Those sweet young things performed ... every lawless act known to the equine brain. They reared. They plunged. They bucked. They spun. They surged together. They scattered like startled quail. I heard squeals, and saw vicious shiny hoofs lash out in every direction.

—JOHN TAINTOR FOOTE

Well out by herself she was, an' there she kept right along the straight to the distance. There was no chance of the others catchin' her, an' they were easin' up when suddenly from the rails came a report like the snap of a whip, an' the Belle staggered, swerved, an' went down all of a heap.

—EDGAR WALLACE

[O]ne of the few names that I remember was Jimmy Winkfield. My grandfather called him "Wink." He would often say, "Boy, before there was a Jackie Robinson or a Jessie Owens, we ... had a sport where we made the difference. Horse racing!"

—C. N. RICHARDSON

Because we have the best hay and the best oats and the best horses.

—Col. Sir Harry Llewellyn, on why the British show jumping
team was so successful in the 1952 Olympics

—⟫•⟪—

A key winning component that can even compensate partially for some
other deficiencies is simply to have the best competitive attitude.

—William Steinkraus

—⟫•⟪—

Some athletes don't care what kind of shoes they wear, or how many fans
they have. They don't even care that they're on television from coast to
coast. They just want to run.

—Anonymous, on horses

—⟫•⟪—

The only trouble with that horse is that it doesn't like jockeys. Once it's thrown its jockey it goes like the wind.

—HENRY CECIL

The only sport I'm not interested in is horse racing. That's because I don't know the horses personally.

—NAT KING COLE

[S]eemed to be some kind of prehistoric throwback, a living legend of the days when horses were hunted, when fear and hunger ruled their lives. In a classy stable of calm, earnest animals, Sunday Silence was Al Capone singing in the Vienna Boys Choir.

—JAY HOVDEY

[T]rainer Michael Matz ignored Kentucky Derby tradition by sending a good horse to Churchill Downs after not having raced him in the previous five weeks … no horse in half a century had won the Derby after a five-week layoff. The wailing persisted until Barbaro rolled to victory by six and a half lengths.

—TIM LAYDEN

There is no feeling that equals the one that overcomes you on your way to the winner's circle … All of the joy and heartache that accompany raising a racehorse can never be expressed in words, but it all comes together in that tiny piece of dirt.

—CAROL WADE KELLY

Thoroughbred: This is the racehorse *par excellence.*

—COLIN VOGEL, *COMPLETE HORSE CARE MANUAL*

Everyone talks about the last quarter-mile of the Derby, but the race is really won in the first quarter-mile, between the gate and the first turn.

—KENT DESORMEAUX

The child who is fortunate enough to be associated with horses during his formative years can look back on fond memories, and those who continue to ride, hunt, or show during their lifetime seldom experience anything more gratifying than the thrill of winning their first ribbon.

—STEPHEN O. HAWKINS

[H]elping horses to achieve their full potential and working to achieve your own are satisfying and fulfilling, and if you can come close to accomplishing this, winning as such will take care of itself.

—WILLIAM STEINKRAUS

Wink guided his colt along the north side of the grandstand, trotted onto the track, and got a thrill l known to only a few hundred humans before him. It was May 3, 1900, and he was riding at Churchill Downs on Derby Day.

>   —ED HOTALING, *WINK: THE INCREDIBLE JOURNEY LIFE AND EPIC JOURNEY OF JIMMY WINKFIELD*

We are led into the starting gate. ... Then my horse is still. The bell rings, the doors fly open, and with an incredible lurch that all but throws me from the saddle, we are off.

>   —CAREY WINFREY

Most good horses know when they'd won: filled their lungs and raised their heads with pride. Some were definitely depressed when they lost. Guilt they never felt, nor shame not regret nor compassion.

>   —DICK FRANCIS

A horse gallops with his lungs,
Perseveres with his heart,
And wins with his character.

—FEDERICO TESIO (1869–1954)

It is not best that we should all think alike; it is a difference of opinion that makes horse races.

—MARK TWAIN

Remember that the horse that finishes a neck ahead wins the race.

—ANONYMOUS

To finish is to win.

—ENDURANCE RIDING MOTTO

The harrowing uncertainty of the turf.

—RED SMITH

———◆———

A horse never runs so fast as when he has other horses to catch up and outpace.

—OVID

———◆———

An exhibitor went up to a horse show judge to complain about being placed below someone who made some sort of mistake … The judge's explanation: "The other guy did it better wrong than you did it right."

—ANONYMOUS

———◆———

I let the horse do the work. I guide him. If the horse gets beat, it's not my fault. If he wins, it's not my fault.

—HERVE FILION

Don't fuss too much about your start. It's no odds getting off in a tear-away. What you got to do is to jump round and jump clean and go as fast as you can when you know what you're doing. But wait till you know what you're doing before you hurry.

—ENID BAGNOLD

It's simply my creed that an executive of a race track might bring certain censure upon the sport by owning horses that campaign at his track, or by betting on the outcome of races at a track where he is supervisor.

—MATT WINN (1861–1949)

I had acquired some small … proficiency in the business of sitting a horse at racing pace over fences and making a pretence of staying on him if things went wrong. This had not been achieved without a considerable amount of bruising and breaking, hard work, dedication, disappointment, toil, and sweat.

—JOHN WELCOME

I was more nervous than when I played before 55,000 at Old Trafford.

—MICK QUINN, EX-SOCCER PLAYER ON SENDING OUT HIS FIRST RUNNER AS A HORSE TRAINER AT SOUTHWELL IN 1997

[H]e trots down the straight to win the race. Lord, Cap, you should have heard the people cheer! I never heard anything like it, not even on Derby Day.

—COLIN DAVY

A few years ago, I gave an interview in which I referred to sport as a crucible. My point was that if things are done correctly, the heat and pressure generated within the crucible of competition should burn away all that is base and false, leaving only the pure and true.

—JAMES C. WOFFORD

———◆———

Julie Krone rides Thoroughbreds as well as anyone. … She rides the way Bill Shoemaker rode. Waiting, watching, waiting for the time to move. Racetrackers call it sitting chilly.

—DAVE KINDRED

———◆———

He had watched her … when she raced, but only from the … stands. … Up close … he'd begun to realize … [s]he had the uncanny ability to seem calm and excited at the same time. Perfectly at ease, and … eager, intense, wired. He had never seen that in a horse … or … in a person either.

—JANE SCHWARTZ, *RUFFIAN: BURNING FROM THE START*

———◆———

Anybody can win unless there happens to be a second entry.

—George Ade

⎯⎯◆⎯⎯

He should have lived with the wild horses of the prairie where he could have been boss. There the issue would have been settled quickly; he would have ruled or died. … Finally he did what they asked but not because he had changed his mind.

—J. A. Estes, on Throughbred racehorse Display

⎯⎯◆⎯⎯

When you peel back the layers of racing, you are left with the horse and the groom.

—Charlsie Canty

⎯⎯◆⎯⎯

One of the wonderful things about our equestrian sport is the great diversity of breeds and disciplines.

—HALLIE MCEVOY, *HORSE SHOW JUDGING FOR BEGINNERS*

I don't think of Julie as a girl. I think of her as a rider. A great rider. She has courage that cannot be measured.

—NICK ZITO, ON JULIE KRONE

Actors are the jockeys of literature. Others supply the horses, the plays, and we simply make them run.

—RALPH RICHARDSON

The spirited horse, which will try to win the race of its own accord, will run even faster if encouraged.

—OVID

A cutting competition is nothing more than a contest of "oh shits" and "attaboys." And the person with more attaboys is the winner.

—BUSTER WELCH

I had never grown up around horses, never owned a horse, never knew anyone who owned horses. To conceive of the dream, as I did, of … owning champion racehorses was truly ludicrous. Yet I was driven to make it happen.

—GEORGE ROWAND

Every horseman and horsewoman alive … wants to believe that among the babies in the barn that are just beginning racing careers there is *the* one. … The magical equine athlete who in the springtime of his third year on this earth can … win one—or, better, all three—of the races that make up the Triple Crown.

—JOE DRAPE, *THE RACE FOR THE TRIPLE CROWN: HORSES, HIGH STAKES, AND ETERNAL HOPE*

The wild horse race was usually no race at all but a kind of maniacal musical chairs played with mustangs.

—MONTY ROBERTS, *THE MAN WHO LISTENS TO HORSES*

The bell rang, an' there was a yell. "They're off!"

—EDGAR WALLACE

———✦———

The best horse usually wins, but not always.

—TOM AINSLIE, *AINSLIE'S COMPLETE GUIDE TO THOROUGHBRED RACING*

———✦———

I've had one hundred people tell me, "You shouldn't do this. You don't have the money, you don't have the talent, you're not going to make it." There are always doubters, but I don't worry about what other people think.

—NONA GARSON

———✦———

Politics is like a racehorse. A good jockey must know how to fall with the least possible danger.

—Édouard Herriott (1872–1957)

Not only did Barbaro win the Derby, he demolished what was supposed to be one of the toughest fields in years. The six-and-a-half-length winning margin was the largest since 1946, when Assault won by eight lengths and went on to sweep the Triple Crown.

—SI.com

Barbaro left no doubt he was the class of an already classy group.

—Maryjean Wall

Horses and jockeys mature earlier than people—which is why horses are admitted to racetracks at the age of two, and jockeys before they are old enough to shave.

—DICK BEDDOES

＊

When I turned him loose, he took off like a rocket.

—EDGAR PRADO, BARBARO'S JOCKEY

＊

In practice do things as perfectly as you can; in competition, do what you have to do.

—WILLIAM STEINKRAUS

＊

There are few things I enjoy more in this world than watching
Thoroughbreds compete … we all try to catch a flash of brilliance here
or there, a hint of promise that tomorrow big dreams will come true, that
the horses we're watching today will be champions.

—MICHAEL COMPTON

If you're lucky enough to draw a good horse, you still have to ride him,
then the next ones. So it's probably 80 percent luck and 20 percent skill.

—CHRIS LEDOUX

[T]ook the next fence like a rocket. I shook the reins at him. Away we
went down the straight with myself giving the best imitation I could of
riding a finish. No challenge came. The judge's box flashed. It all seemed
too easy. It was.

—JOHN WELCOME

The Oxford English Dictionary defines "classic," from the French *classique*, and Latin *classicus*, as meaning "of the first rank or authority," which gets its racing sense exactly; but the word is not used to describe races until 1885 … in the phrase "classic races."

—GERALD HAMMOND

Buck thought of the crowds that cheered her every time she ran. If only they could see her now. She was a towering filly, and had always looked magnificent on those bright afternoons when she raced. … But at night … she was even more striking.

—JANE SCHWARTZ, *RUFFIAN: BURNING FROM THE START*

I imagined galloping down the stretch. I could hear the thundering hooves and the roaring crowd. I imagined them laying the roses across my lap. It was a great feeling of romance.

—JULIE KRONE

We were all shocked. The heart of the average horse weighs about nine pounds. This was almost twice the average size, and a third larger than any equine heart I'd ever seen. All the chambers and valves were normal. It was just larger. I think it told us why he was able to do what he did.

—Dr. Thomas Sweczek, after performing an autopsy on Secretariat

How the horse dominated the mind of the early races, especially of the Mediterranean! You were a lord if you had a horse.

—D. H. Lawrence

[A] dark horse which had never been thought of, and which the careless St. James had never even observed in the list, rushed past the grand stand in sweeping triumph.

—Benjamin Disraeli (1805–1881)

[L]et's talk about the death of Seabiscuit the other night. It isn't mawkish to say, there was a racehorse, a horse that gave race fans as much pleasure as any that has ever lived and one that will be remembered as long and as warmly.

—RED SMITH

After one of them has won the Derby, any breeding expert can sit down and show you just why he won, from his pedigree. The only trouble is, the expert can't do it before the race.

—PHIL CHINN

Monastic Calm beat the other quad by twenty lengths, and was never going more than half-speed neither.

—COLIN DAVY, *THE GOOD THINGS*

You have to bear in mind that Mr. Autry's favorite horse was named Champion. He ain't ever had one called Runner Up.

—GENE MAUCH

———✦———

Since the earliest of years, humans have studied what they call "common sense." We in horsedom call it "horse sense." What it means is that things are not always as they appear. Try reading the *Daily Racing Form* and picking the winners, and you'll know what I mean.

—ROBERT L. MERZ

———✦———

The archives of statistics … demonstrate that the most certain way of breeding stakes performers is to send stakes-winning and/or producing mares to proven, top-echelon sires. Done repetitively, this will improve the odds of getting a good horse.

—TIMOTHY T. CAPPS, *SPECTACULAR BID*

———✦———

He's diseased with speed.

—JOHN TAINTOR FOOTE

⊷•⊷

[O]n the morning of the Belmont Stakes he had burst from the barn like a stud horse going to the breeding shed.

—WILLIAM NACK

⊷•⊷

If the horse is used for the purpose of the rider's ego in winning competition points, dressage is no longer an art but an abuse of a generous long-suffering animal.

—SALLY O'CONNOR

⊷•⊷

It is damnably hard to know for certain which horse will win … but a trainer, jockey, or groom can often be very sure indeed that a horse will lose.

—MATTHEW ENGEL

She was perfect. … Always first. Always on the lead. Perfect.

—JANE SCHWARTZ, *RUFFIAN: BURNING FROM THE START*

The first time he saw Seabiscuit, the colt was walking through the fog at five in the morning. Smith would say later that the horse looked right through him, as if to say, "What the hell are you looking at? Who do you think you are?"

—DAVID MCCULLOUGH, NARRATOR IN *SEABISCUIT*

When I play football, it's more controlled; at horse racing I'm an outsider. You just have to hope they go well, really.

—STEVE MCMANAMAN

—◆—

Don't fall off.

—HOLLIE HUGHES, TO RON TURCOTTE, SECRETARIAT'S JOCKEY, BEFORE THE 1973 BELMONT STAKES

—◆—

The skies were all blue as the bottom of a freshly painted pool. The white clapboard steeples of Churchill Downs, which had loomed over Thoroughbred races since the turn of the century, were brilliant in the sunshine.

—ELIZABETH MITCHELL

—◆—

If Carrie Ford wins the National I'll bare my backside to the wind and let everyone kick it.

—GINGER MCCAIN

A racetrack exists as a world apart, rich in its own mysteries and subject to laws of its own devising.

—BILL BARICH

[T]he most famous race in the world is the Kentucky Derby, held on the first Saturday of May at Churchill Downs in Louisville at the distance of one-and-a-quarter miles.

—JOE DRAPE, *THE RACE FOR THE TRIPLE CROWN: HORSES, HIGH STAKES, AND ETERNAL HOPE*

I'm so shaken. It's just a gift from God.

—JOHN SERVIS'S WIFE SHERRY, AFTER SMARTY JONES WON THE
SOUTHWEST STAKES

Of the more than six million horses in the United States, almost two
million are used for showing. More than seven million people are
involved in the horse industry and more than three and a half million are
involved in showing.

—VICKY MOON

Racing in France is largely a silent ritual, played out for the benefit of a
rich elite who have no particular interest in attracting the public to the
track.

—ANDREW LONGMORE

I knew nothing about Standardbreds beyond the fact that they were long-bodied, harness-racing horses, sometimes called trotters because they raced at a trot.

—SUSAN RICHARDS, *CHOSEN BY A HORSE: A MEMOIR*

Horse races are short—two and a half minutes tops. They begin in mystery and probability. ... A hundred and twenty seconds later, possibility will have metamorphosed into truth, fiction into fact, suspicion into realization.

—MAX WATMAN

I watched the race ... but I only remember the last 200 yards, when the horses were charging past my seat. Flash Light took the lead and hurtled down the stretch like a running back headed for the end zone ... this was the biggest thrill I'd had in months.

—TED MCCLELLAND, *HORSEPLAYERS*

If certainty about the past is so limited, must not certainty about the future be terribly slight? How can anybody wrench a profit from such confusion?

—TOM AINSLIE

No other sport is as profoundly affected by the start of a new year as Thoroughbred racing.

—T. D. THORNTON, *NOT BY A LONG SHOT*

If the horse is not familiar with its rider, or does not like that person, or if the rider is not attuned to the animal, the race can be lost during the post parade.

—TOM AINSLIE

In the sport of kings, Jerry Bailey is the king of kings.

—CHARLIE ROSE

I bought five more horses. Two are with the Canadian mounted police. One's directing traffic out on Union Avenue. One is up at Cornell; they can't figure out if it's a male or female. And a last one a friend bought for $5,000 to spare me further embarrassment.

—SAM RUBIN

Galloped because he was asked to gallop, because he knew it was the right place for it. A great horse, with a great racing heart.

—DICK FRANCIS

There's always a moment in a race where a horse has to decide to press on. A Thoroughbred is likelier than not to press on. That's what we ask of them. But … at what cost? We rely on them … to press on anyway. That's heart. … They have great hearts.

—JANE SMILEY, *HORSE HEAVEN*

To the rest of the country, the advance signs of spring are the warble of birdies that sing. … But in the bluegrass country of Kentucky, there is only one true harbinger of spring: the Kentucky Derby.

—BERT SUGAR AND CORNELL RICHARDSON, *HORSE SENSE: AN INSIDE LOOK AT THE SPORT OF KINGS*

Take one of those every half-mile and call me if there is any change.

—FROM *A DAY AT THE RACES*, MEDICAL ADVICE GIVEN TO A SICK RACE HORSE

With a gallantry that deserted him at the critical moment ... his rider turned a somersault over his head and landed ... sitting on the fence facing his horse's nose ... he remained on the bank, towed the horse over, scrambled on to his back again and started afresh.

—SOMERVILLE AND ROSS

Ritual and routine are everything at the races. So to me, there is but one way to enter Suffolk Downs first thing in the morning—by a prescribed yet meandering route.

—T. D. THORNTON, *NOT BY A LONG SHOT*

Barclay Tagg, was not exactly the sort that typically stands in the winner's circle smiling after the million-dollar race. Tagg is the kind of smart, hardworking reserved trainer that horsemen love.

—MAX WATMAN

If a horse has four legs, and I'm riding it, I think I can win.

—ANGEL CORDERO, JR.

All that he remembers of the race at the turn was a jumble of colours, a kaleidoscope of horses and riders hanging on to the horses' necks.

—A. B. "BANJO" PATERSON

I was a racing fanatic … As a boy, I would drag the piano bench into my bedroom, fasten a Western riding saddle to it and envision myself in the greatest races of the day aboard any number of the greatest racehorses of the day.

—KY MORTENSEN

Man o' War, the Kentucky-bred who became a Kentucky legend, never raced in Kentucky—not in the Derby and not in any other race.

—THE BLOOD-HORSE STAFF, *THOROUGHBRED CHAMPIONS*

I may be romantic, but I do like to have ideals. I like to think that the average race is straight, and I believe it is. Maybe a race is straight because a horse is straight if he has a proper family tree. He's there to run because his kind have run. He's there to run because he's honest.

—J. P. MARQUAND

I'll be around as long as horses think I'm smarter than they are.

—JAMES E. "SUNNY JIM" FITZSIMMONS

A good jockey is one who settles his mount into a rhythm that even the most casual observer can notice. If a jockey is bouncing around on a horse like a pinball machine, then the horse has something else to think about other than running.

—C. N. RICHARDSON, *SMALL TRACK BETTING*

I never knew how to kiss rich people's asses, and I got too old to learn. If no owner was going to give me a big horse, I figured I'd have to find one myself.

—P. G. JOHNSON

A small red box with gold snap-lock and hinges sits atop a tall green safe. … It contains a triangular, three-sided, sterling silver vase approximately eight inches tall, which symbolizes the epitome of achievement for a three-year old Thoroughbred. It is the Triple Crown of American turfdom.

—MARVIN DRAGER, *THE MOST GLORIOUS CROWN*

You have to remember that about seventy percent of the horses running don't want to win. Horses are like people. Everybody doesn't have the aggressiveness or ambition to knock himself out to become a success.

—EDDIE ARCARO

Ask racing fans to name the greatest two horses of the twentieth century, and more times than now, you'll hear the names of Secretariat and Man o' War in either order. Though they raced more than fifty years apart, they are forever linked.

—BILL HELLER

The Kentucky Derby is a monument to him. It's his baby, and his alone. He will always be part of it, even more a part of it than the spired towers at Churchill Downs.

—ARTHUR DALEY, ON MATT WINN

That's a dam nice horse … you might depind your life on him …

—SOMERVILLE AND ROSS

———◆———

I never met a Kentucky Derby I didn't like.

—JOE HIRSCH

———◆———

Well, when I thought it over, I realized what that added up to. *We'd got the fastest horse in the world.* With the seven stone in the Cambridgeshire, 'e'd be like a racing car against push-bicycles.

—COLIN DAVEY

———◆———

There just can't be anything smarter than a smart cutting horse. He can do everything but talk Meskin—and he understands that.

—Joe Evans, *A Corral Full of Stories*

Racing is a thrilling sport. It is a colorful spectacle. Follow the crowds to the race course on the day of any classic fixed event or big special and you will see why it has grown so largely in popularity and public favor. It calls its devotees from every walk of life.

—Tom R. Underwood

I promised mother I'd quit the racehorses for good. There's a lot of things you've got to promise a mother because she don't know any better.

—Sherwood Anderson

It's called Derby Fever. Catch it.

—STEVE HASKIN

——◆——

It was a magical time in Saratoga's history, a time when Secretariat, Ruffian, Forego, and Affirmed and Alydar wrote the headlines.

—BARBARA D. LIVINGSTON, *BARBARA D. LIVINGSTON'S SARATOGA*

——◆——

The criminal trial today is … a kind of show-jumping contest in which the rider for the prosecution must clear every obstacle to succeed.

—ROBERT MARK, COMMISSIONER, LONDON METROPOLITAN POLICE

——◆——

The rain was lashing down with a cold, relentless fury that discouraged hope. ... On a day like this only the stouthearted won races. They had to conquer their own feelings as well as their horses' before they could begin to think about besting the others.

—C. C. L. BROWNE

Regarding racing ... the United States' first president, George Washington, dispassionately wrote in his diary that he was a consistent and persistent loser.

—NANCY STOUT, *HOMESTRETCH*

I'm pleased to proclaim April 11 as Rainbow Blue Day in Delaware to honor one of the greatest horses ever and to honor the Teague family for their hard work and dedication to horse racing in Delaware.

—RUTH ANN MINNER

The first Saturday in May is almost here, which means a bunch of three-year-old horses with Onewordnamesaslongastheirtails will be running for the roses. Ah, the Kentucky Derby. The most exciting two minutes in sports and the only day of the year anyone drinks mint juleps.

—Woody Woodburn, *Unbelievable Kentucky Derby Tale*

—◆—

Apart from the big days, American racing is a wonderful cure for insomnia, and the prospect of four furlong races reminds me of those crash, bang performers in the bedroom—over in a flash, turn off the light, and goodnight!

—Geoff Lester, on the introduction of U.S.-style four-furlong races to the British scene

—◆—

Sheehy's colt was facing the wrong way at the moment when I dropped the flag, but a friend turned him with a stick, and, with a cordial and timely whack, speeded him on his way onto sufficiently level terms.

—Somerville and Ross

—◆—

How is that grand colt of yours? I declare he is the best-looking three-year-old I've seen out in ten years and he moves just as sweet as he looks. He is the kind of a horse I like to have a look at once in a while just to keep my eye in.

—GORDON GRAND, *A NIGHT AT THE OLD BERGEN COUNTY RACE-TRACK*

Kentucky Derby mud. Real Derby mud. Put it in your pocket and keep it. You'll want it because I'm going to win this race someday.

—JULIE KRONE

Saratoga is the wildest, most unpredictable constant in my life.

—SEAN CLANCY, *SARATOGA DAYS*

You have to make split-second decisions. If you have to think about them, it's too late. A mistake on the run to the turn, and your chances of winning end right there.

—KENT DESORMEAUX

<hr>

I … remember my father and I listening to Clem McCarthy's call of the 1948 Kentucky Derby, won by Citation, Eddie Arcaro aboard, with Calumet stablemate Coaltown finishing second.

—JOE MCGINNISS, *THE BIG HORSE*

<hr>

Two words not commonly related to winning or losing at the horseshow ring correlate to the color of the ribbons received. The two words are "act" and "react." Winners act. Nonwinners react.

—DON BURT, *WINNING WITH THE AMERICAN QUARTER HORSE*

<hr>

A pheasant jumped out of a tree and he [the chestnut] whipped round that quick that even the horse fell over.

—FRANKIE DETTORI, ON A BIZARRE RACE EVENT

He [Seabiscuit] was a small horse, barely fifteen hands. He was hurting too. There was a limp in his walk, a wheezing when he breathed. Smith didn't pay attention to that. He was looking the horse in the eye.

—DAVID MCCULLOUGH, NARRATOR IN *SEABISCUIT*

He had never come close to losing a race, often intimidating opponents with his mere appearance, hoofs pounding and nostrils flaring.

—JOHN EISENBERG, *THE GREAT MATCH RACE*

I think a lot of people picked wrong in the Derby and it created a reaction that, instead of saying they were wrong, they knocked the horse.

—JERRY MOSS

The race went off. The announcer rattled off the names of the horses from the front of the pack to the trailers.

—ELIZABETH MITCHELL, *THREE STRIDES BEFORE THE WIRE*

I know nothing about racing, and any money I put on a horse is a sort of insurance policy to prevent it winning.

—FRANK RICHARDSON

The best pedigree in the world won't sell a lame racehorse.

—ANONYMOUS

How grand racing at Saratoga is!

—BARBARA D. LIVINGSTON, *BARBARA D. LIVINGSTON'S SARATOGA*

[Steeplechasing] is one of the real sports that's left, isn't it? A bit of danger, a bit of excitement and the horses—the best thing in the world.

—QUEEN ELIZABETH, THE QUEEN MOTHER (1900–2002)

I was nuts about the horses … There's something about it, when they come out and go up the track to the post.

—ERNEST HEMINGWAY

A racing horse is not like a machine. It has to be tuned up like a racing car.

—CHRIS POOL

A million things have to go right to win a race. Only one thing has to go wrong to lose it.

—BARCLAY TAGG

Pedigrees that are to kill for on paper and in the auction ring so often turn out to be road kill on the race track.

—TIMOTHY T. CAPPS, *SPECTACULAR BID*

A horse's ability to stay a distance cannot be accepted until proven by the test of a race. Most horses have one distance at which they produce their best form.

—PETER BRADDOCK, *BRADDOCK'S COMPLETE GUIDE TO HORSE RACE SELECTION AND BETTING*

It's the most exciting thing in racing, to come down the stretch with two powerful horses and two good jockeys. There's no feeling like that.

—CHRIS MCCARRON

[He] was blessed to have forgotten his binoculars.

—TOM CALLAHAN, ON CHARLIE WHITTINGHAM WHEN HIS HORSE FERDINAND WON THE KENTUCKY DERBY

In some village in La Mancha, whose name I do not care to recall, there dwelt not so long ago a gentleman of the type wont to keep an unused lance, an old shield, a skinny old horse, and a greyhound for racing.

—MIGUEL DE CERVANTES, *DON QUIXOTE*

People say that it was degrading for an Olympic champion to run against a horse, but what was I supposed to do? I had four gold medals, but you can't eat four gold medals. There was no television, no big advertising, no endorsements then. Not for a black man, anyway.

—JESSE OWENS (1913–1980)

Assault, the colt, turned to see his friend gallop away, her full, dark tail flying behind her. He raced after her, feeling the warm wind, enjoying the sound of their hooves thundering across the pasture.

—MARJORIE HODGSON PARKER, *ASSAULT: THE CRIPPLED CHAMPION, THE KING RANCH RACEHORSE*

They feed their horses hay and grain, and change their stable rugs for the rugs they wear outside. After the horses eat, they cheerfully follow their grooms out to their individual paddocks in front of the barn.

—SUSAN NUSSER, *IN SERVICE TO THE HORSE*

"My dear boy," Lady Honour was indeed in earnest, "provided you don't actually fall off the mare the race is a gift to us. The mare's fit, she won't fall down and she has the legs of the lot of them; what more do you want?"

—MOLLY KEANE (1904–1996)

Sir Charles came to a halt a half-mile from the finish. The southern horse stood forlornly on the grassy track, his sinewy right foreleg dangling awkwardly as his grooms raced to help him. His thousands of supporters abruptly fell silent, shocked by his abject failure.

—JOHN EISENBERG, *THE GREAT MATCH RACE*

You are the only ambassador in the world to race a horse named after your country's foreign policy.

—DAVID LANGE, PRIME MINISTER OF NEW ZEALAND, TO U.S. AMBASSADOR H. MONROE BROWNE, WHO OWNED A RACEHORSE CALLED LACKA REASON

I've been in one Derby, and this is my third Belmont. But I've never thought of the fact that I haven't won a Triple Crown race. I'm not like that. I always look at the sunshine of things.

—JULIE KRONE

A difference of opinion is what makes horse racing and missionaries.

—WILL ROGERS

"Slow, huh?"
"He ain't Count Fleet"
"But you say he's sound?"
"Sure. Doesn't run fast enough to hurt himself."

—DAVE FELDMAN, *WOULDA, COULDA, SHOULDA*

The performance of a quality jockey can be the difference between winning and losing a race at all types and levels of racing.

—PETER BRADDOCK, *BRADDOCK'S COMPLETE GUIDE TO HORSE RACE SELECTION AND BETTING*

The world should be postponed for a whore and a horse race.

—HORACE WALPOLE, FOURTH EARL OF ORFORD (1717–1797)

Epic Steam [a race horse] is easily offended. He has high standards of behavior with regard to his own person, and every human he has met so far has offended them … Epic Steam would like to see a person, just one, who can pay attention and meet his standard.

—JANE SMILEY, *HORSE HEAVEN*

No matter how good a trainer may be, he isn't going to win the big race unless he has a horse with the talent and other traits to be there in first place. And the trainer who doesn't understand horses won't win the big race even if he has the best horse in the world.

—CARL A. NAFZGER, *TRAITS OF A WINNER*

If the horse is good enough, he'll win with the rider facing his tail.

—DONN BYRNE, *THE TALE OF THE GYPSY HORSE*

The pace was beginning to improve, and the other horses drew away … they charged the bank at full gallop, the black mare and the chestnut flying it perilously, with a windmill flourish of legs and arms from their riders.

—SOMERVILLE AND ROSS

"When you win one Derby, people can say it was a fluke … They don't say it when you win two."

—BARCLAY TAGG

I didn't care about going off favorite—the horse has no idea what price he is!

—RUBY WALSH, ON HEDGEHUNTER, WINNER OF 2005 GRAND
    NATIONAL

If he has the heart to go, he goes; and no ninety-pound boy on him is going to stop him much and no electric shocks and dope will make him go much faster. If he has the heart, he goes; if he hasn't he fades out. No, sir, it's the horse who wins the race.

—J. P. MARQUAND

I can't stand the pressure of watching, but I can't stand not to follow Joey to the track. He knows he's going to work. He knows I'm out there watching him.

—MERRI MELDE, *FOR THE LOVE OF RACEHORSES*

Sportsmanship is the ideal of racing.

—TOM R. UNDERWOOD, *THOROUGHBRED RACING AND BREEDING: THE STORY OF THE SPORT AND BACKGROUND OF THE HORSE INDUSTRY*

"Races are won with that seat, sir."
"Be damned to that," said my uncle Valentine. "If the horse is good enough, he'll win with the rider facing his tail."

—DONN BYRNE, *DESTINY BOY*

The horses are at the post; a distant cluster of crowded animals with little dots of color on their backs. Green, blue, yellow, purple, French grey, and old gold … They're off! The long line of colors across the track becomes a shapeless clump and then draws out into a long string.

—A. B. "BANJO" PATERSON, *THE ORACLE*

I had made my way from the paddock with my sister and our trainer, and all of us were focused intently in a five-year-old mare named Miss Josh. … Parading before the stands, she was nibbling on the mane of her lead pony—a good sign. She was eager.

—GEORGE ROWAND

All Thoroughbred race horses are given an official birthday of 1st January, irrespective of what date in the year they were actually born. A horse foaled in February and a horse foaled in June will both be officially considered a year old on 1st January of the following year.

—PETER BRADDOCK, *BRADDOCK'S COMPLETE GUIDE TO HORSE RACE SELECTION AND BETTING*

The money.

—TOMMY HITCHCOCK'S ANSWER TO A NEWSPAPERMAN'S QUESTION ABOUT WHAT WENT FIRST IN POLO: THE HORSE OR THE PLAYER'S KNEES, BACK, LEGS, REFLEXES, ETC.

[J]ocks riding hell out of the horses.

—ERNEST HEMINGWAY

Any man who wins a race, whether point-to-point, steeplechase, or on the flat is, for that brief moment, a hero and a good jockey. Let him be beaten by a better horse and a short head when riding the race of his life, and his stock is down at once.

—MOLLY KEANE

If it can't be expressed in figures, it is not science; it is opinion. It has long been known that one horse can run faster than another—but which one? Differences are crucial.

—ROBERT A. HEINLEIN, *TIME ENOUGH FOR LOVE*

The horse will run because that is his nature.

—CARL A. NAFZGER

There's no sense in whipping a tired horse, because he'll quit on you. More horses are whipped out of the money than into it.

—EDDIE ACARO

They must get to the end and go, "We were just here." What's the point of that?

—JERRY SEINFELD, ON WHAT A HORSE MUST THINK AFTER A RACE IS OVER

What it comes down to is that anybody can win with the best horse. What makes you good is if you can take the second- or third-best horse and win.

—VICKY ARAGON

———◆———

[S]omething happened that made me so mad, Sir, that I could hardly look at the race, for the boy on our colt drew his whip and went to it, and he did go to it. It was terrible, for I was just thinking how fine and game the colt had been, and to see anyone hit him seemed more than I could stand.

—GORDON GRAND, *A NIGHT AT THE OLD BERGEN COUNTY RACE-TRACK*

———◆———

Untold numbers of horse,
have broken legs on the racecourse,
whipped into dangerous speed by drugs and jockeys' force.

—O ANNA NIEMUS

———◆———

The nostrils of a racer are like petals of a rose. … The ears, inward pointing, are lilies in trembling water, and the whole body of the mystical … horse sways with the supple strength of wind, sun, and sand.

—GERALD HAUSMAN AND LORETTA HAUSMAN, *THE MYTHOLOGY OF HORSES: HORSE LEGEND AND LORE THROUGHOUT THE AGES*

⇒◆⇐

The utter joy of riding Template lay in the immense power which he generated. … He had enough reserve strength for his jockey to be able to carve up the race as he wishes, and there was nothing in racing, I thought, more ecstatic than that.

—DICK FRANCIS

⇒◆⇐

On November 1, 1938, two legendary racehorses geared up for the most exciting horse race in history. Over 40,000 fans packed into Baltimore, Maryland's Pimlico Race Course to witness Seabiscuit vs. War Admiral.

—KAT SHEHATA, *SEABISCUIT VS. WAR ADMIRAL*

⇒◆⇐

Rarely in sport has a game's most brilliant competitor ... seized the day by delivering a performance so original, so stunning in its clarity, that it raised to a new level the standard by which all who followed would be measured. And Secretariat, plunging toward the far turn, was raising it right then.

—WILLIAM NACK

I love two-year-old racing. I'm fascinated by its freshness and its promise, and I've gained valuable insights about speed, class, distance potential, and trainers through watching these young horses progress from race to race.

—STEVE DAVIDOWITZ, *BETTING THOROUGHBREDS*

Owning a Standardbred racehorse is undoubtedly that most unique experience in professional sports.

—PAUL D. SIEGEL, *HOW TO OWN WINNING STANDARDBRED RACEHORSES*

One man's wrong lead is another man's counter-canter.

—STEVEN D. PRICE

But when someone is on a winning horse, and everything looks wonderful, it's very hard as an outsider to persuade them something is wrong.

—JAMES WOLFENSOHN

It was the majesty of the Thoroughbred and the beauty of the historical track. ... Saratoga's racing past was filled with titans of the sport. Man o' War ran here; so did Exterminator and the "gray ghost" Native Dancer.

—BARBARA D. LIVINGSTON, *BARBARA D. LIVINGSTON'S SARATOGA*

The racecourse is as level as a billiard ball.

—JOHN FRANCOMBE

⟨⟩

Each leg in its gallop seems to stream with a rush of speed as though from a bucket of water poured o'er the field.

—ANONYMOUS

⟨⟩

My mouth was completely dry in anticipation. I hovered somewhere between wanting the race to be over and the outcome known and wanting it never to start.

—GEORGE ROWAND

⟨⟩

Until you go to Kentucky and with your own eyes behold the Derby, you ain't never been nowheres and you ain't never seen nothing.

—IRVIN COBB (1876–1944)

The racetrack empty, viewed from the grandstand, up the track, suggests every dream worth imagining, whether discredited, or still unknown.

—BRENDAN BOYD, *RACING DAYS*

Watching the horses … was the only thing Mrs. Betham enjoyed at the races. They were so clean and so polished looking, so sleek and yet so powerful. They seemed to dominate the men, and she wondered how the jockeys ever found courage to climb on their backs.

—MAURICE GEE, *THE LOSERS*

I think that boxing and horse racing are the sports that probably produce the greatest characters. Part of the reason is that in both sports, no matter where you turn, the scent of larceny is in the air. That's a very sweet odor that lends itself to characters and funny situations.

—DICK SCHAAP

He was a sprinkle of light on a dark canvas, the only grey horse in a dizzy tumble of bays, blacks, and chestnuts coming down the stretch.

—JOHN EISENBERG, *NATIVE DANCER*

[L]ong before I owned my first horse, much less started writing about harness racing, I was a fan, faithfully attending the races virtually every Saturday.

—PAUL D. SIEGEL, *HOW TO OWN WINNING STANDARDBRED RACEHORSES*

Early records are spotty but most historians believe that organized racing in the United States of America was first staged during the early to mid-seventeenth century in the southern colonies, with the fastest horses in one community competing against those of another.

—GEORGE ENNOR, *WORLD ENCYCLOPEDIA OF HORSE RACING*

You can take an old mule and run him and feed him and train him and get him in the best shape of his life, but you ain't going to win the Kentucky Derby!

—PEPPER MARTIN

The Thoroughbred horse is that idol of racing enthusiasts. He is the matchless embodiment of speed and gameness. He is the symbol of fair play. The Thoroughbred typifies stamina. He strives to his utmost in heart, nerve and muscle.

—TOM R. UNDERWOOD, *THOROUGHBRED RACING AND BREEDING: THE STORY OF THE SPORT AND BACKGROUND OF THE HORSE INDUSTRY*

If you could call the thing a horse. If it hadn't shown a flash of speed in the straight, it would have gotten mixed up with the next race.

—P. G. WODEHOUSE (1881–1975), *VERY GOOD, JEEVES*

In this game there are millions of ways to get beaten but only one way to win; by finishing first.

—BILL MOTT

Playing polo is like trying to play golf during an earthquake.

—SYLVESTER STALLONE

If you start getting nervous about getting hurt you will be. … If you are worrying about the danger it's time to give up.

—JASON WEAVER

It is Australian innocence to love the naturally excessive and be proud of a thoroughbred bay gelding who ran fast.

—PETER PORTER

———⤜◆⤛———

There is something about breeding good horses that makes it the Sport of Kings.

—STANLEY HARRISON

———⤜◆⤛———

Muscular and riveting, with a gargantuan stride and an unyielding will, he had ambled along in the middle of the pack in every race … until he was told it was time to sprint to the finish line; then … he lowered his head … accelerated past his rivals, and left them behind.

—JOHN EISENBERG, *NATIVE DANCER*

———⤜◆⤛———

The blood runs hot in the Thoroughbred and the courage runs deep. In the best of them, pride is limitless. This is their heritage and they carry it like a banner.

—C. W. ANDERSON

If I'm not on a racetrack, I'm not alive.

—JULIE KRONE

There are a hundred ways to lose a race, but only one way to win one.

—RACING MAXIM

We look for a "been there, done that" kind of horse. Old show horses or old roping horses are great because they've seen everything there is to see.

—ANN LARSON

Racing is all I know.

—J. P. MARQUAND

A hoss is a gen'leman, kid. It hurts him to lose a race, it breaks him—permanent—to see a race.

—LINCOLN STEFFENS

Life is like a horse race, there are winners and losers.

—PROVERB

Comin' across the flat … it were like flying.

—COLIN DAVY, *THE GOOD THINGS*

In racing, to insult a man's horse is worse than insulting a wife.

—JOHN OAKSEY

Polo is a disease for which the only cure is money.

—ANONYMOUS

"This is the great thing about racing," trainer D. Wayne Lucas once said. "There's always another race."

—BILLY REED, *THOROUGHBRED: A CELEBRATION OF THE BREED*

"Here comes the number 4."

—Vic Stauffer, track announcer at Hialeah in 1993, calling a race with a horse named Altmagraenguida, after two vain attempts at pronouncing the horse's name, he surrendered during the stretch run

It was a typical racing crowd, composed mostly of men dressed in coats and hats, with a smattering of women and no children. Belmont's grandstand, opened in 1905, seated just 17,500, so every inch of the aisles … was filled. … Racing was at a spectacular zenith of popularity.

—John Eisenberg, *Native Dancer*

The boy hadn't more than touched the colt when he shot past the chestnut horse as though he had been tied.

—Gordon Grand, *A Night at the Old Bergen County Race-Track*

Kentucky. Saturday. May. An iridescent sky. A stampede of horses. The chance of a lifetime in a lifetime of chance. Everyone in pastels and hats and flowers, 144,110 people gathered in glad circumstances.

—DAVE KINDRED, *LIVING TO RIDE*

I feel as a horse must feel when the beautiful cup is given to the jockey.

—EDGAR DEGAS (1834–1917), ON SEEING ONE OF HIS PAINTINGS SOLD AT AUCTION

His horse suddenly faltered with that horrible little dip and lurch that tells of a tendon gone; and that was that. Ted pulled him up to a walk and they made their sad, limping progress back to the stables … the horse to pass out of the racing scene, for a season if it was lucky and forever if it was not.

—C. C. L. BROWNE, *THE INSIDE VIEW*

It isn't important who is ahead at one time or another, in either an election or a horse race. It's the horse that comes in first at the finish that counts.

—ATTRIBUTED TO VARIOUS

Run for the Roses.

—BILL CORUM, FIRST TO USE THIS EPITHET FOR THE KENTUCKY DERBY

I would rather sit at home and play in the manure than go into the show ring and deal with the bullshit!

—KRIS PATSOLIC

It doesn't get any better than this.

> —ALAN KING ON A RARE BIG-RACE TREBLE WITH MY WAY DE SOLZEN, VOY POR USTEDES, AND KATCHIT

The more you know, the more you win. That is the allure of horse race handicapping.

> —CHARLES CARROL, *HANDICAPPING SPEED*

I had the best buffalo horse that ever made a track.

> —BUFFALO BILL

Melody is the essence of music. I compare a good melodist to a fine racer, and counterpoints to hack post-horses.

> —WOLFGANG AMADEUS MOZART (1756–1791)

People make a lot of fuss about the so-called heroic courage of jump jockeys, which is nonsense. We all know the risk and we accept them. Nothing can match the thrill of riding good horses at speed over fences—nothing! I don't see that courage has anything to do with it. It's simply a job we all enjoy doing.

—BOB CHAMPION, WINNER OF THE GRAND NATIONAL

Winfrey offered Guerin a leg up with the advice he always gave: "Just ride him with confidence."

—JOHN EISENBERG, *NATIVE DANCER*

But if we offer prizes for races with ridden horses—young and half-grown colts as well as full-grown beasts—we shall be cultivating a sport well in keeping with the nature of our enemy.

—PLATO

There is a law in the benighted state of New York which bars children from racetracks in the afternoon, the archaic theory being that frequenting a gambling hall is an occasion of sin for minors. Wherefore a small boy, if he is to be reared properly, must be taken to the track for morning works.

—RED SMITH

Out on the Texas plains a fellow had to be a smart horseman to win a race and a smarter one to win a bet—and collect it!

—SAMUEL CLAY HILDRETH (1866–1929)

Every jockey makes mistakes … and no one holds them against him as long as he gets his share of winners. … When a jockey is going down, people remember his mistakes.

—WILLIAM FAIN

There is no better buzz than racing—it gives me a bigger kick than football when I have a winner.

—KEVIN KEEGAN

⟫◆⟪

Eventing has been called the ultimate equestrian challenge ... The event horse is the embodiment of courage, speed, dexterity, power, scope, precision, durability, and a resolute will to prevail. The event rider ... must be able to elicit from a horse ... the willingness to deliver its talents on request, no matter how challenging the obstacle.

—GARY J. BENSON

⟫◆⟪

For better it is to dare mighty things, to win glorious triumphs, even though checkered by failure, than to rank with those poor spirits who neither enjoy much nor suffer much because they live in the gray twilight that knows neither victory or defeat.

—THEODORE ROOSEVELT

⟫◆⟪

Frank Hayes was aboard a horse named *Sweet Kiss* at Belmont Park …
he rode *Sweet Kiss,* a twenty-to-one shot, to victory. The applause turned
to silence, however, when his lifeless body still atop the steed made him
the first and, thus far, the only jockey to win a race while dead.

—C. N. RICHARDSON, *SMALL TRACK BETTING*

Often referred to as the three "jewels" in the Triple Crown, they are the
Kentucky Derby, the Preakness Stakes, and the Belmont Stakes, three of
the oldest classics of America's king of sports.

—MARVIN DRAGER, *THE MOST GLORIOUS CROWN*

They are unpredictable—horses are like women.

—JIMMY PIKE, OWNER OF KAWAGINO, FIFTH AT 100-1 IN THE
CHAMPION HURDLE AND FOURTH (33-1) IN THE COUNTY HURDLE
THREE DAYS LATER.

CHAPTER NINE

"They Don't Call It Sitting":
On Riding

Mary Twelveponies laid it on the line: "there are no problem horses," she said, "only problem riders."

This problem rider can only agree. When I ride my horse it is usually at a walk. He must find it awfully boring. Try as I might, I can't really relax in the saddle, and my apprehensiveness must further add to Koda's distaste for the experience. The way he feels under me—well, I sense that we're both thinking how different it is when I am *not* on his back. Out in the field with his stable mates he will canter with effortless grace. Catching a downhill slope he'll take advantage of the headlong momentum and kick up his heels. With his ears pinned back he'll prance at and around Tadik, playing dominance games. Or all at once he, Tadik, and Sasha will decide it's time to race to the gate, and then Koda's prodigious quarter-horse haunches come into action as he works up into an earth-pounding, flat-out gallop.

Ruefully I call to mind those images of my young and athletic horse while I'm slowly circling the round pen with him. Here again, I recognize that my late start as a rider is going to limit my potential for development. I'm sure never going to be, oh, Stacy Westfall, let's say, who wins reining championships riding bareback and bridleless. All I can realistically hope for, I suppose, is that one day I'll be riding Koda and discover that we are actually moving as if I wasn't there—*that* naturally. Indeed, if just once the two of us could gallop up from the bottom field to the paddock gate, well, I won't ever have to wonder again if my life had been worth the living.

But you know what *is* good about being a late-starting rider? I am *never* going to take it for granted that I, a predator, am sitting atop an incredible prey animal. *That* is "an amazing fact," as Craig Cameron rightly declares. "You sit up there for one reason only—through his good grace." (Speaking of which, do you know that song by Mary Ann Kennedy, "When You Carry Me"? My wife thinks I'm a sap because it always gets me misty-eyed, but check it out and see if it doesn't make your heart ache a little at the beauty and wonder of the very idea that horses let themselves be ridden.)

Reading about riding can be helpful—to a point. There's obviously nothing that can substitute for time spent on board. So have a look at the words that follow, and when you find some inspiration and practical guidance take it with you. Maybe it'll be the key to your horse thinking "problem solved" next time you ride.

Never take it for granted that this prey animal allows a predator to ride on his back. That's an amazing fact. You sit up there for one reason only—through his good grace.

—CRAIG CAMERON, *RIDE SMART*

It takes a bit of basic courage to ride beyond the status quo, but with each stride the view along that road becomes more and more exquisite.

—LESLIE DESMOND, *HORSE HANDLING AND RIDING THROUGH FEEL*

In order to have a saddle that is comfortable for the horse it has to be a little too big for the horse, especially at the front. This is because when a horse moves, his shoulder and back muscles have to bulge upwards. If a saddle fits snugly at rest it's actually too small when the horse starts to move.

—LINDA PARELLI

Unlike some of today's trendy methods (which rely on gimmicks, gadgets, or fatigue), dressage is rooted solidly in centuries of history: it was developed out of wartime maneuvers that required horses to respond calmly and instantly to a warrior's command—or face fatal consequences.

—LYNN PALM

It's the aspirin of horseback riding; it cures everything.

—NUNO OLIVERA, ON THE "SHOULDER-IN" DRESSAGE MOVEMENT

The first ten minutes of your ride [are] the "golden moments" where you show your horse your ability as a leader. And during that time, the only conversation you should have with the horse goes like this: "Hello. This is your Captain speaking!"

—JULIE GOODNIGHT

A saddle is something special just between you and your horse.

—STÜBBEN, SADDLE DEALERS

Holding our breath is something we all do when we're scared. But your breathing is noticeably copied by the horse, so good breathing is good first aid for releasing tensions in both of you in scary situations.

—GINNY SELF BUCKLIN, *MORE HOW YOUR HORSE WANTS YOU TO RIDE*

To err is human, but to blame the horse is even more human.

—PAT PARELLI

People who say they have no fear of horses are unsafe to be around.

—JOHN LYONS

A horse doesn't care how much you know until he knows how much you care.

—PAT PARELLI

———

There is a secret pleasing and cherishing of the horse with the bridle, which the rider must accomplish with so unperceiving a motion that none but the beast may know it.

—GERVAISE MARKHAM

———

I never encountered a horse in whose soul there was no harmony to call on.

—VICKI HEARNE

———

Anyone who has sat astride a horse will tell you that after their first time in the saddle, they found themselves incredibly sore and stiff. But any discomfort soon fades away, to be replaced by the joy of making new discoveries and experiencing revelations that are far more lasting.

—MOIRA C. HARRIS AND LIS CLEGG, *RIDING*

They don't call it sitting, they call it riding.

—CRAIG CAMERON, *RIDE SMART*

Personally, the only horse who I ever set on their back throwed me off on my bosom before I had road him twenty feet and did the horse wait to see if I was hurt, no.

—RING LARDNER, *TIPS ON HORSES*

In riding these wild, vicious horses ... especially at night, accidents are always occurring. A man who is merely an ordinary rider is certain to have a pretty hard time.

—THEODORE ROOSEVELT

Horses see in black and white, and riders ride in grey.

—CINDY ISHOY

Developing a dependable source of remounts has plagued man ever since he began to ride horseback thousands of years ago. As a hunter and warrior, he was only as good as the horse under him.

—PHIL LIVINGSTON AND ED ROBERTS, *WAR HORSE: MOUNTING THE CAVALRY WITH AMERICA'S FINEST HORSES*

No one ever promised that the fastest horse in the race was the easiest one to ride.

—ERIC J. JOINER JR.

———◆———

[A]ll that I could do in a race was to sit still and try to stay on, and that this was exactly the sort of rider the old horse needed to get the best out of him.

—JOHN WELCOME, *A GLASS OF PORT WITH THE PROCTOR*

———◆———

Always smile when you are riding because it changes your intent.

—JAMES SHAW

———◆———

Riders ... know in their head what they did wrong. ... If you allow yourself to make excuses, you're not going to get better.

—STEVE ASMUSSEN

When one is on horseback he knows all things.

—GEORGE HERBERT

Riding teaches him self-esteem and control of himself and of something else—this animal.

—GENE SMITH, *THE CHAMPION*

When riding a horse we leave our fear, troubles, and sadness behind on the ground.

—JUDI CARLSON

Did you come to hide or did you come to ride?

—PAUL ZARZYSKI, *GOOD HORSE KEEPING*

A horse which stops dead just before a jump and thus propels its rider into a graceful arc provides a splendid excuse for general merriment.

—PRINCE PHILIP, DUKE OF EDINBURGH

When life hands me lemons, I don't make lemonade, I go for a ride; horses are my family.

—JUDY RICHTER

It lies in the hands of every single rider whether horse and rider feel relaxed. It must be every rider's supreme aim to create relaxation of mind and body.

—KLAUS BALKENHOL

Horses had never scared him because he had been born to the saddle and had grown up mastering everything on four legs with contemptuous ease. He believed in his heart that no one could really ride better than he could.

—DICK FRANCIS, *A CARROT FOR A CHESTNUT*

And the horse was never saddled that the Geebungs couldn't ride.

—A. B. "BANJO" PATERSON, *THE GEEBUNG POLO CLUB*

Never a pony couldn't be rode, never a cowboy couldn't be throwed.

—PAUL ZARZYSKI, *GOOD HORSE KEEPING*

I ride because I rode as a child when life was simpler and somehow more complete.

—M. ADELIA RAMEY, *ALWAYS THERE ARE HORSES*

Had I but known about breathing in my youth, how much simpler my competitive riding life would have been.

—VICTOR HUGO-VIDAL

Before you swing a leg over a horse, you should know why you're swinging it.

—Marlene McRae, *Barrel Racing 101: A Complete Program for Horse and Rider*

———

Riding is a partnership. The horse lends you his strength, speed and grace, which are greater than yours. For your part, you give him your guidance, intelligence, and understanding, which are greater than his. Together, you can achieve a richness that alone neither can.

—Lucy Rees, *The Horse's Mind*

———

He rode a splendid horse that was born for a racer and fed and lodged like a gentleman; kept him at his utmost speed for ten miles, and then ... the transfer of rider and mail-bag was made in the twinkling of an eye.

—Mark Twain

———

Get pitched off, climb right back on.

—PAUL ZARZYSKI, *GOOD HORSE KEEPING*

———◆———

There is nothing in which a horse's power is better revealed than in a neat, clean stop.

—MICHEL DE MONTAIGNE

———◆———

The horse and rider are elemental. They ride at the heart of the wind of God.

—J. PHILIP NEWELL

———◆———

There is something about riding down the street on a prancing horse that makes you feel like something, even when you ain't a thing.

—WILL ROGERS

———◆———

A horse's eye disquiets me: it has an expression of alarm that may at any moment be translated into action.

—E. V. Lucas

We have almost forgotten how strange a thing it is that so huge and powerful and intelligent an animal as a horse should allow another, and far more feeble animal, to ride upon its back.

—Peter Gray

Speak your mind, but ride a fast horse.

—Anonymous

She had ridden with Grey Horse before she could walk, held firmly in his arms as he cantered back and forth from the herd. By the age of ten, she was constantly riding at his side from camp to camp.

—TYLER TAFFORD, *THE STORY OF BLUE EYE*

You'll never know how much you love to be on a horse … until you fall off!

—ANONYMOUS

Many riding accidents would never have happened if people could control the false pride that makes them almost ashamed to ask for a quiet horse.

—GORDON WRIGHT, *LEARNING TO RIDE, HUNT, AND SHOW*

This is the time I ride Colonel every day. I told you how he waits for me. He knows the time.

—ANN RINALDI, *A RIDE INTO MORNING: THE STORY OF TEMPE WICK*

When you are on a great horse, you have the best seat you will ever have.

—SIR WINSTON CHURCHILL

In riding a horse we borrow freedom.

—HELEN THOMSON

To ride a horse well, you have to know it as well as you know your best friend.

—KATIE MONAHAN PRUDENT

Do in *your* body what you want your horse to do in *his*. That's the whole simple secret to riding with fluidity.

—LINDA PARELLI

———◦◦———

I've spent most of my life riding horses. The rest I've just wasted.

—ANONYMOUS

———◦◦———

Her gaits were so smooth that I felt like we were flying. She seemed able to do whatever I asked, responding with enthusiasm and a little extra spunk.

—CHRISTA IACONO, *THE PERFECT HORSE*

———◦◦———

A horse's behavior will be in direct proportion to the number of people watching you ride him.

—Cooky McClung

It felt as though she unfurled an invisible sail between strides, so that when her feet were off the ground she rode the wind at her back.

—Yates Kennedy, on Ruffian

[O]nce a rider has found trust in his horse's abilities, he can develop the confidence needed to achieve special accomplishments.

—Elizabeth Furst

The rider of a responsive Western horse must anticipate and lead the horse with a weight-shift cue. If in turning to the right, the rider turns her body and looks to the right, she leads the horse, and the responsive horse moves under the rider's weight, bringing them back into balance.

—DON BLAZER, *NATURAL WESTERN RIDING*

A good rider can hear his horse speak to him. A great rider can hear his horse whisper.

—ANONYMOUS

I want my horse to look and feel his best.

—MARLENE MCRAE, *BARREL RACING 101: A COMPLETE PROGRAM FOR HORSE AND RIDER*

To expect to ride without encountering difficulties and worries, as well as risks and dangers, is only to look for something that cannot possibly be attained.

—*RIDING FOR LADIES*, 1887

Spoiled horses, difficult horses, and even rogues, can teach us much that is important; the rider who is too well mounted may never really learn to ride.

—WILLIAM C. STEINKRAUS, *RIDING AND JUMPING*

Feeling down? Saddle up. It is the only cure.

—ANONYMOUS

Don't be the rider who gallops all night and never sees the horse that is beneath him.

—RUMI (1207–1273)

If the horse does not enjoy his work, his rider will have no joy.

—H. H. ISENBART

We shall take great care not to annoy the horse and spoil his friendly charm, for it is like the scent of a blossom—once lost it will never return.

—ANTOINE DE PLUVINEL (1552–1620)

[The mare] set off for home with the speed of a swallow, and going as smoothly and silently. I never had dreamed of such a motion, fluent and graceful, and ambient, soft as the breeze flitting over the flowers, but swift as the summer lightning.

—RICHARD DODDRIDGE BLACKMORE (1825–1900)

Riding: The art of keeping a horse between you and the ground.

—ANONYMOUS

Ride the horse in the direction that it's going.

—WERNER ERHARD

It is not enough for a man to know how to ride; he must know how to fall.

—MEXICAN PROVERB

Horses are uncomfortable in the middle and dangerous at both ends.

—ATTRIBUTED TO VARIOUS

Most persons do not ride; they are conveyed.

—M. F. MCTAGGART

[T]here is a secret pleasing and cherishing of the horse with the bridle, which the rider must accomplish with so unperceiving a motion that none but the beast may know it.

—GERVASE MARKHAM

I never mount a horse without experiencing a sort of dread that I may be setting out on that last mysterious journey which all of us must take sooner or later, and I never come back in safety from a horseback trip without thinking of my latter end for two or three days afterward.

—MARK TWAIN

When pride rideth in the saddle, destruction rideth on the crupper.

—ANONYMOUS

It is a disease for which there is no cure. You will go on riding even after they have to haul you on a comfortable wise old cob, with feet like inverted buckets and a back like a fireside chair.

—MONICA DICKENS (1915–1992)

Well, suh, about the head of a truly great hawse there is an air of freedom unconquerable. The eyes seem to look on heights beyond our gaze. It is the look of the spirit that can soar.

—John Taintor Foote, *The Look of Eagles*

The chestnut horse galloped through sun and wind, stars and snow, looking for a place where there was no Death.

—Sally Pomme Clayton, *Tales Told in Tents: Stories from Central Asia*

When I rode for myself, that's when I got better. It's a matter of confidence and getting used to showing.

—Linda Zang

The worst part is over
Now, get back on that horse and ride.

—JAMES MERCER

A canter is a cure for every evil.

—BENJAMIN DISRAELI

At its finest, rider and horse are joined not by tack, but by trust. Each is totally reliant upon the other. Each is the selfless guardian of the other's well-being.

—ANONYMOUS

Men are better when riding, more just and more understanding, and more alert and more at ease and more under-taking, and better knowing of all countries and all passages; in short and long all good customs and manners cometh thereof, and the health of man and of his soul.

—ATTRIBUTED TO VARIOUS

Ridin' for the brand is an often misunderstood concept in that it requires an obligation from both parties.

—WADDIE MITCHELL

Being with my horses gives me a sense of inner calm and satisfaction that I can carry with me. It improves my ability to handle the stresses of my job and gives me a wonderful perspective on life.

—SPRING SWINEHART

To ride a horse well, you have to know it as well as you know your best friend.

—KATIE MONAHAN PRUDENT

⸺◆⸺

[T]he stopping of a horse dramatically so that it would not move. That was called ... *jading* a horse; and ... the horsemen sometimes earned the name of *horse-witches* because they were able to make the horse stand as though it were paralyzed or bewitched.

—ANTHONY DENT, *THE HORSE THROUGH FIFTY CENTURIES OF CIVILIZATION*

⸺◆⸺

There is something about jumping a horse over a fence, something that makes you feel good. Perhaps it's the risk, the gamble. In any event it's a thing I need.

—WILLIAM FAULKNER

⸺◆⸺

There is nothing like a rattling ride for curing melancholy!

—WINTHROP MACKWORTH PRAED (1802–1839)

Listen to the horses clipping, clopping, hoofbeats everywhere never stopping. ...

—RAFFI

When riding a high-strung horse, pretend you are riding an old one.

—DOMINIQUE BARBIER

He bows his nose to his chest and prances, his tail lifted proudly and he cocks his head toward me as he passes. I'm smitten and he knows it.

—MERRI MELDE, *FOR THE LOVE OF RACEHORSES*

Riding becomes a break from reality, a time when I know why I am.

—GaWaNi Pony Boy, *Of Women and Horses*

⟨◆⟩

The rhythm of the ride carried them on and on, and she knew that the horse was as eager as she, as much in love with the speed and air and freedom.

—Georgess McHargue

⟨◆⟩

"I'd rather ride for the devil himself," said he, "than ride a horse for Cousin Honour."

—Molly Keane

⟨◆⟩

There's a variety of horse minds as big as there is among human minds. Some need more persuading than others, and a few of 'em, no matter how firm they're handled, will have to be showed again and again that they can't get away with this or that.

—WILL JAMES, *SMOKY THE COWHORSE*

The sport of show jumping turns a glamorous face to the world.

—NANCY JAFFER

In a second or two it becomes a horse and rider, rising and falling, rising and falling—sweeping towards us nearer and nearer—growing more and more distinct, more and more sharply defined—nearer and still nearer, and the flutter of the hoofs comes faintly to the ear ...

—MARK TWAIN, *ROUGHING IT*

I think jumping is the biggest thrill of all. It's the closest thing to flying. Nothing feels better than galloping down a big jump and having a horse take flight. It's like being superhuman.

—NONA GARSON

The horse you get off is not the same as the horse you got on. It is your job as a rider to ensure that as often as possible, the change is for the better.

—CORMAC MCCARTHY, *CITIES OF THE PLAIN*

No ride is ever the last one. No horse is ever the last one you will have. Somehow there will always be other horses, other places to ride them.

—MONICA DICKENS

On the worst day, I think I have the best job in the world.

—NONA GARSON, ON SHOW JUMPING

Riders who force their horses by the use of the whip only increase their fear for they then associate the pain with the thing that frightens them.

—XENOPHON

May your horse never stumble.

—SALLY POMME CLAYTON, *TALES TOLD IN TENTS: STORIES FROM CENTRAL ASIA*

Women who ride, as a rule, ride better than men. They, the women, have always been instructed; whereas men usually come to ride without any instruction.

—ANTHONY TROLLOPE, *THE LADY WHO RIDES TO HOUNDS*

Sing, riding's a joy! For me I ride.

—ROBERT BROWNING, *THE LAST RIDE TOGETHER*

I ride because of all the horses I shall never ride.

—M. ADELIA RAMEY

Fear almost always arises—in horses as well as in people—from concern about what might happen, and much more rarely from what IS happening.

—Mary Wanless

The way a person sits on a horse is exactly the way a mountain lion would … it's easy to understand why a horse wouldn't be that interested in a person crawling up on top of him like some would-be mountain lion clamping down his feet!

—Buck Brannaman

He who would ride a horse must learn to fall.

—Spanish proverb

Equestrian art, however, is something else which involves complete harmony between horse and rider, and that makes the rider feel that there have been moments of beauty and greatness which make a flight possible from all that is ordinary and mediocre.

—NUNO OLIVEIRA

I add riding to my list of things that look easier than they are!

—MELISSA SOVEY-NELSON, *IF I HAD A HORSE*

There are times when you can trust a horse, times when you can't, and times when you have to.

—ANONYMOUS

He soared over every fence as if he had wings.

—STEPHEN BUDIANSKY, *TALLYHO AND TRIBULATION*

He wheeled the cart up to him, got him harnessed to it, and in two minutes that pony was walking, trotting, anything I wanted—can't explain why—one of the mysteries of horseflesh.

—SOMERVILLE AND ROSS

I, who travel most often for my pleasure, do not direct myself so badly. If it looks ugly on the right, I take the left; if I find myself unfit to ride my horse, I stop. ... Have I left something unseen behind me? I go back; it is still on my road. I trace no fixed line, either straight or crooked.

—MICHEL DE MONTAIGNE

I sit astride life like a bad rider on a horse. I only owe it to the horse's good nature that I am not thrown off at this very moment.

—LUDWIG WITTGENSTEIN (1889–1951)

Half the failures of this world arise from pulling in one's horse as he is leaping.

—JULIUS HARE (1795–1855), *GUESSES AT TRUTH*

Equitation is not the search for public acclaim and self satisfaction after applause. Nor is it the pleasure of every prize or a judge or jury's admiration at a show. It is the head-to-head dialogue with the horse and the search for communication and perfection.

—NUNO OLIVEIRA

Henry Miller once said that a hero is a man who has conquered his fears. … I began to be a heroine when I sat on the back of a horse for the first time …

—INGRID SOREN, *ZEN AND HORSES*

Lord Ronald said nothing; he flung himself from the room, flung himself upon his horse and rode madly off in all directions.

—STEPHEN LEACOCK, *GERTRUDE THE GOVERNESS*

[T]he lad with the ankle-length boots and spurs two inches long and his breeches worn over his stockings, riding a savage of a brown horse that had killed one man and frightened several so badly that they never wanted to ride again.

—MOLLY KEANE, *PRIME ROGUES*

•

Green on green makes black and blue.

>—AMERICAN PROVERB, ABOUT WHAT HAPPENS WHEN A GREEN, OR
> NOVICE, RIDER RIDES A GREEN HORSE.

Love, not force, rides the horse.

>—SAIOM SHRIVER

Those who love horses are impelled by an ever-receding vision, some enchanted transformation through which the horse and the rider become a third, much greater thing.

>—THOMAS MCGUANE

If the horses knew their strength we should not ride anymore.

—MARK TWAIN

Each handicap is like a hurdle in a steeplechase, and when you ride up to it, if you throw your heart over, the horse will go along too.

—LAWRENCE BIXBY

It seems no coincidence … that the history of our country is bound up with that of the horse; the very act of riding continuing the chronicle of horsemen and horsewomen who have left their marks on history from the saddle in years past.

—DONNA SNYDER-SMITH, *THE ALL-AROUND HORSE AND RIDER*

[R]iding preserves during the physical development a precise balance between strength and suppleness. This special quality, which naturally involves moral values too, leads to more balanced and disciplined training. Thus riding—the complete sport *par excellence*—tempers the body as it does the spirit.

—COMMANDANT JEAN LICART

The horse never knows I'm there until he needs me.

—WILLIE SHOEMAKER

So sudden is it all, and so like the flash of unreal fancy ... we might have doubted whether we had seen any actual horse and man at all, maybe.

—MARK TWAIN

A man in passion rides a horse that runs away with him.

—THOMAS FULLER

Think of riding as a science, but love it as an art.

—GEORGE MORRIS

It was on horseback that man would first experience the exhilaration of the whipping wind and the flashing landscape.

—FULVIO CINQUINI, *MAN AND HORSE: AN ENDURING BOND*

Find your horse. Discover the direction the horse is going. Ride the horse in that direction.

—PETER MCWILLIAMS

I had lived with horses all my life. I seemed to be constitutionally incapable of sitting on one over a fence. This happens to a few unlucky people and I was one of them.

—JOHN WELCOME

Good riders constantly improve their riding skills.

—CHARMAYNE JAMES, *CHARMAYNE JAMES ON BARREL RACING*

My early riding days were spent on the wooden, or rocking variety of mount. Armchairs, bedsteads, all served in my apprenticeship—in fact, my parents' furniture still bears the mark of my whip and improvised spurs!

—ALAN OLIVER

Never ride your horse more than five-and-thirty miles a day, always taking more care of him than of yourself; which is right and reasonable, seeing as how the horse is the best animal of the two.

—GEORGE BORROW (1803–1881)

No horse gets anywhere until he is harnessed.

—HARRY EMERSON FOSDICK

I have seven horses. I'm known to go off on my horse for about six hours in the wilderness.

—ARMAND ASSANTE

The rhythm of the ride carried them on and on, and she knew that the horse was as eager as she, as much in love with the speed and air and freedom.

—GEORGESS MCHARGUE

The horse provides the locomotor energy, and the rider has the prerogative of determining the goal and of guiding the movements of his powerful mount towards it. But all too often … the rider is obliged to guide his horse in the direction in which it itself wants to go.

—SIGMUD FREUD

Listen to its hooves hitting the ground, a living drum. Each hoof-beat resounds in a four-beat quatrain, the rhythm many great poets use to turn words into music.

—ADELE MCCORMICK AND MARLENA MCCORMICK, *HORSE SENSE AND THE HUMAN HEART*

Awareness takes you beyond the mechanics of your riding.

—JILL KEISER HASSLER, *BEYOND THE MIRRORS*

A catcher and his body are like the outlaw and his horse. He's got to ride that nag till it drops.

—JOHNNY BENCH

And he will ride this year! He is fixed to that purpose. He will ride straight—and, if possible, he will like it.

—ANTHONY TROLLOPE

If you're riding a horse and it dies, get off …

—JIM GRANT AND CHAR FORSTEN

Every time you ride, you're either teaching or un-teaching your horse.

—GORDON WRIGHT

—◆—

They rode with great speed; and both men and horses were covered with dust and blood.

—JAMES BALDWIN (1924–1987)

—◆—

A man who rode good horses was usually a good man.

—WESTERN EXPRESSION

—◆—

Horses can be scary animals to work with, due to their size and apparent skittishness, but often fear of an animal is just covering up other personal issues that the person is trying to deal with.

—BUCK BRANNAMAN

—◆—

There are few things more exciting than releasing a band of young horses from a corral where they have been confined for some time into open space and watching the explosion of movement as these meteors take an open country.

—THOMAS MCGUANE

It is also well known that good horses bring happiness to the heart of the riders, if they are at least reasonably skilled.

—EDWARD OF PORTUGAL (1391–1438)

When riding a horse we leave our fear, troubles, and sadness behind on the ground.

—JULIE CARLSON

If anybody expects to calm a horse down by tiring him out with riding swiftly and far, his supposition is the reverse of the truth.

—XENOPHON

Women who have had the same opportunities as men of learning to ride, ride quite well. ... But as a rule they do not *get* the chance of excelling, not are they "set right" by unpalatable home truths being told them without favor or affection.

—ALICE HAYES, *THE HORSEWOMAN*

Riding is simple ... it's just not easy.

—ANONYMOUS

Just sit back. If you lie back you'll only be upright to the ground. Don't jerk his head whatever you do. It's a long way down but he'll land steady. Just keep him as still as if you were a dummy, and put confidence into him.

—ENID BAGNOLD

To judge a horse by its rider, is to judge a book by its cover.

—ANONYMOUS

No gymnastics could be better or harder exercise, and this and the art of riding, are of all the arts the most befitting a free man.

—PLATO

Most persons do not ride; they are conveyed.

—M. F. McTaggart

⸺⸱⸱⸺

The quality of the jump is determined by the quality of the approach to the fence, which is itself determined by the quality of the getaway from the previous fence and the turns between the two jumps.

—Mary Wanless, *The Natural Rider*

⸺⸱⸱⸺

Whenever difficulties appear, the rider must ask himself: does the horse not want to execute my demands, does he not understand what I want, or is he physically unable to carry them out? The rider's conscience must find the answer.

—Alois Podhajsky (1898–1973)

⸺⸱⸱⸺

As a good horse is not very apt to jump over a bank, if left to guide himself, I let mine pick his own way.

—BUFFALO BILL

There are two important rules in horse-riding. The first is to mount the horse. The second is to stay mounted.

—ANONYMOUS

The horse thinks one thing and he who saddles him another.

—ATTRIBUTED TO VARIOUS

Tricks have no place in the art of riding, since in moments of crisis, when effective action is most needed, the superficial "trick" never succeeds.

—LT. COL. A.L. D'ENDRODY, *GIVE YOUR HORSE A CHANCE*

No one ever came to grief—except honorable grief—through riding horses.

—Sir Winston Churchill

＊＊＊

There comes a point in every rider's life when he has to sit back and wonder, Am I Nuts?

—Kelly Stewart

＊＊＊

I can tell you what judges like. They like a well-turned-out rider, smart as a whip, riding every ounce of his horse and looking as though he was glad to be in the ring.

—Helen Crabtree, *Saddle Seat Equitation*

＊＊＊

But if I must choose, I ride because I have dreams yet to live. I ride because I have dreams yet to have and what exactly they will be tomorrow I cannot say … but always there will be the horses.

—M. ADELIA RAMEY

A bad ride is much better than a good walk.

—PETER GRACE

The caveson my way held in the rider's hand gives the true ply to the horse; and there is nothing like it, for it bends him from nose to tail.

—WILLIAM CAVENDISH

To ride or not to ride, this is a stupid question.

—BRANDY MICHELLE

Let the best horse leap the hedge first.

—Thomas Fuller, M.D.

⟫⟪

[H]ow to stay aboard is the most important piece of knowledge the rider will ever acquire in the course of her entire riding career.

—Heather Moffett, *Enlightened Equitation*

⟫⟪

The noblest task of the riding teacher is to form the mind of the student as well, so that the latter comes to depend on the teacher less and less.

—Waldemar Seunig, *Horsemanship*

⟫⟪

It's hard enough to strike off at a canter from a walk with one horse. But to have eight horses doing this at the same time without the slightest raggedness is a work of art.

—Visitor to the Spanish Riding School, Vienna

I was sort of afraid she'd fall off the goddam horse, but I didn't say anything or do anything. The thing with kids is, if they want to … you have to let them do it, and not say anything. If they fall off they fall off, but it's bad if you say anything to them.

—J. D. Salinger, *The Catcher in the Rye*

Young men have often been ruined through owning horses, or through backing horses, but never through riding them; unless of course they break their necks, which, taken at a gallop, is a very good death to die.

—Sir Winston Churchill

I had a horse, always, and I'd ride the horse in the summertime, sometimes bare back—gentle horse, you understand.

—SAM DONALDSON

And I think that if everybody maintains a strong determination and will, only very few would not be able to become reasonable horsemen through lack of the minimal physical condition.

—EDWARD OF PORTUGAL

There's nothing like the first horseback ride to make a person feel better off.

—HERBERT V. PROCHNOW

It is important to learn to control our emotions and to present a picture of complete confidence to the horse.

—KELLY MARKS, *RIDE WITH CONFIDENCE!*

———✦———

Max possessed several serious quirks which we would need to iron out. … As soon as Max knew I was aiming for the saddle, he would be off. … It was not uncommon to see me leaping onto the saddle from the hood of a car … or even a rooftop.

—NEAL SHAPIRO

———✦———

Just grab tight with your knees and keep your hands away from the saddle, and if you get throwed, don't let that stop you.

—JOHN STEINBECK, *THE RED PONY*

———✦———

Riding is a unique sport in that it requires not only the participation of a human athlete, but also the active involvement and cooperation of a horse.

—THE BRITISH HORSE SOCIETY

A feeling of quiet ecstasy surrounds many female riders ... as is they've resurrected a lost part of themselves while galloping ...

—LINDA KOHANOV, *THE TAO OF EQUUS*

Keep one leg on one side, the other leg on the other side, and your mind in the middle.

—HENRY TAYLOR

But if a rider teach his horse to go with the bridle loose … he would thus lead him to do everything in … pleasure and pride.

—SIR JOHN ASTLEY (1687–1772)

The trot is the foundation of the gallop.

—RICHARD BERENGER

On horseback you could ride through the cattle and they would pay no attention. But the minute you dismount, you become a threat.

—DAVID J. MYERS

Dressage riding comprises many skills, several of which are acquired by jumping and riding cross-country, or on trails.

—CHARLES DE KUNFFY

Long before we rode horses, we hunted them, killed them, and ate them. … Given all this, it's rather remarkable that horses can ever learn to trust and willingly obey humans.

—SARAH BLANCHARD, *THE POWER OF POSITIVE HORSE TRAINING*

A horseman is one who not only rides (although some fine horseman do not ride at all) but also seeks to know the horse—its nature, needs and management—and feels a deep responsibility for his horses, the care they get, and the life they lead.

—SUSAN HARRIS

As a horse runs, think of it as a game of tag with the wind.

—TRE TUBERVILLE

A good rider on a good horse is as much above himself and others as the world can make him.

—EDWARD HERBERT (1583–1648)

I wouldn't mind starting to ride some more if I had a really good horse to just work a little bit with every day.

—ROBERT DUVALL

But it would be enough that, when riding beasts, they behave like men and not like beasts.

—EDWARD OF PORTUGAL

Know what you're going to have to do, and allow yourself plenty of time to do it in.

—WILLIAM STEINKRAUS, *RIDING AND JUMPING*

I haven't been able to ride very much since my hip operation several years ago. I think I would still be playing polo if I hadn't had that. If I ever got to where I couldn't ride, I don't think I'd live very long.

—CECIL SMITH, POLO PLAYER UNTIL AGE EIGHTY-THREE, AND LAST RODE AT NINETY-THREE

There was a rhythm to the canter. Up, forward, down; up, forward, down. It soon became pleasant. The broad warm rump felt good beneath her … The ridden horse was a marvel, diminishing space.

—MORGAN LLEWELYN, *THE HORSE GODDESS*

Whatever your purpose in riding, be sure that it includes the elements of fun and appreciation of your horse. Then you will be well on your way to becoming a true horseman.

—SHEILA WALL HUNDT, *INVITATION TO RIDING*

Experienced riders are not prone to brag. And usually newcomers, if they start out being boastful, end up modest.

—C. J. J. MULLEN

A perfect book on riding could be written only by a horse!

—VLADIMIR S. LITTAUER

When I can't ride anymore, I shall still keep horses as long as I can hobble about with a bucket and a wheelbarrow. When I can't hobble, I shall roll my wheelchair out to the fence of the field where my horses graze, and watch them.

—MONICA DICKENS

He was grateful and happy, even to the end ... Patience and endurance were his assets ... He ate slowly, spoke slowly, and moved slowly. But he could *ride*.

—ED HOTALING, *WINK: THE INCREDIBLE LIFE AND EPIC JOURNEY OF JIMMY WINKFIELD*

Moments spent on the back of a horse are ne'er counted against the hours of a man's life ...

—ANONYMOUS

Scared? The hell I'm scared of any horse ever wore a shoe! Come on, I'll show you! I'll show you!

—Wilbur Daniel Steele, *Blue Murder*

The knowledge of the nature of a horse is one of the first foundations of the art if riding it, and every horseman must make it his principal study.

—François Robichon de la Guérinière (1688–1751)

Those I have watched and marveled at from afar for all their grace and beauty. This is the stuff of a child's dream, the kind that doesn't die with time.

—Anonymous

His trot felt like riding in a jeep at full speed across a field of gopher holes.

—CHRISTA IACONO, *THE PERFECT HORSE*

The child who ran weeping to you with a cut finger is now brought home, smiling gamely, with a broken collarbone and incredible contusions—"it wasn't Jezebel's fault, Dad."

—PAM BROWN

I hear in my heart,
I hear in its ominous pulses,
All day, on the road, the hoofs of invisible horses.

—LOUISE IMOGEN GUINEY

No matter how fast the horse trots the damn cart still chases him.

—*Horse Illustrated*

———◆———

There are many forms of riding. The classical way, however, reaches back centuries and has proved to be the right one. When following it, one realizes that it is a very open way of schooling. It is a wide road that accommodates every horse.

—Arthur Kottas-Heldenberg

———◆———

I don't think the head makes the horse, and it's amazing how much better he's has gotten over the years … maybe because I see his heart now instead of his head.

—Anonymous

———◆———

On arriving somewhere in the approximate area of take-off, I let the horse take command and jump the fence. I try to be an un-interfering passenger from there to the other side, and then I take up command again.

—David Broome

A horse is the matter and subject whereupon the art worketh, and is a creature sensible, and therefore so far as he is moved to do any thing, he is thereunto moved by sense and feeling. ...

—Sir John Astley

A free horse running is a beautiful sight. The long tail high and proud. The mane rising and falling with his rolling step ... are a pleasure to behold. But a mustang herd running ... I have seen it countless times and it always stirs my heart.

—Monty Roberts, *Shy Boy: The Horse That Came In From The Wild*

When the rider is thrown or is unable to make his mount do what he wants, it is always the horse that is blamed. When a horseman takes a spill, he looks to himself for the cause.

—MARGARET CABELL SELF

━━◆◆◆━━

My first school horse was Pluto Kerka, who reminded me immediately and unmistakably that the reins were for the horse to be guided and not for the rider to hold on to.

—ALOIS PODHAJSKY, *MY HORSES, MY TEACHERS*

━━◆◆◆━━

No one can teach riding so well as a horse.

—C. S. LEWIS, *THE HORSE AND HIS BOY*

━━◆◆◆━━

A horse dealer and his son went to look at a horse for sale. The father asked his son to get on one of the horses. The son turned to his father and asked, "Shall I ride the horse as if I am selling it or as if I am buying it?"

—ANONYMOUS

It is better to ride for half a year on a good horse than to spend your entire life riding on a mule.

—DUTCH PROVERB

She was a flash of gold as she cantered around the ring. Ears pricked, neck arched, she moved like a movie star in the spotlight as she sailed over the last fence.

—ALISON HART, *SHADOW HORSE*

We are, after all, an unnatural encumbrance on the horse's back, and it behooves us as riders to make that burden as easy for the horse to carry as we are able.

—HEATHER MOFFETT, *ENLIGHTENED EQUITATION*

It may be a lifelong process, but if we can start with being mindful while we are riding and working with our horses, we may find a head start on being mindful in the rest of our lives and we certainly will find working with our horses greatly affected.

—CHERYL KIMBALL, *MINDFUL HORSEMANSHIP*

If riding were all blue ribbons and bright lights, I would have quit long ago.

—GEORGE MORRIS

Riding gives me tremendous pleasure. It's both a physical and a mental challenge. ... I'm fascinated by the intricacies of movement by the horse, the rider, and their interplay.

—SPRING SWINEHART

———⊰◆⊱———

She saw the hedge ahead of them, and the first stab of real fear contracted her stomach. She gathered her reins up tight, and pulled hard. It made no difference at all. 'Don't panic,' she thought, but the panic was in her whether she wanted it or not.

—K. M. PEYTON

———⊰◆⊱———

The riding of young horses is an excellent nerve tonic.

—GEOFFREY BROOKE

———⊰◆⊱———

[I]t's remarkable how threatening even the softest, grassiest turf suddenly begins to look when you realize you're about to hit it hard, head—or shoulder—first.

—MICHAEL KORDA, *HORSE PEOPLE*

The horse has such a docile nature, that he would always rather do right than wrong, if he can only be taught to distinguish one from the other.

—GEORGE MELVILLE

"The great art of riding ... is to keep your balance properly. ..." He let go the bridle and stretched out both arms to show Alice what he meant, and this time he fell flat on his back, right under the horse's feet. "Plenty of practice!" he went on repeating, all the time that Alice was getting him on his feet again.

—LEWIS CARROLL (1832–1898), *THROUGH THE LOOKING-GLASS*

Another behavior that is breed-specific is homing ability which, while present in other breeds, is legendary in Icelandic ponies. Why the equines of a northern island should have a refined talent for finding their way home is not clear.

—Paul McGreevy

Great riders are not great because of their talent; they are great because of their passion.

—Anonymous

"Dancing and riding, it's the same damn thing," he would say. "It's about trust and consent. You've gotten hold of one another. The man's leading but he's not dragging her, he's offering a feel and she feels it and goes with him. You're in harmony and moving to each other's own rhythm, just follow the feel."

—Nicholas Evans, *The Horse Whisperer*

A lot of people focus intently on riding mechanics. They develop into "perfect" riders and support the horse just by the mechanics of staying in their seat, good balance, and quiet legs and hands. ... But their masters of equitation often seem to be lacking something. That something is feel.

—CHERYL KIMBALL, *MINDFUL HORSEMANSHIP*

If he had a great horse, he would give him a great ride.

—WILLIAM FAIN, *HARMONY*

A good horse and a good rider are only so in mutual trust.

—ANONYMOUS

O the horseman's and horsewoman's joys!
The saddle, the gallop, the pressure upon the seat, the cool gurgling by
      the ears and hair.

    —WALT WHITMAN, *LEAVES OF GRASS*

When I'm approaching a water jump, with dozens of photographers
waiting for me to fall in, and hundreds of spectators wondering what's
going to happen next, the horse is just about the only one that doesn't
know I am Royal!

    —ANNE, PRINCESS ROYAL

The rider casts his heart over the fence, the horse jumps in pursuit of it.

    —H. H. ISENBART

Horse shows are the one form of competition where it really matters how you play the game, not if you win or lose.

—DANIEL LENEHAN

When the horse dies, dismount.

—ANONYMOUS

The rider, being the senior partner, has to make all efforts to learn the language of the horse, and to speak to him by means of that dialect.

—LT. COL. A. L. D'ENDRODY

Be it known … that I ride rather more than twelve stone—have a good seat—never was afraid of a horse in my life … being still under middle age, I am of course far from indifferent whether I am well mounted. Such I take to be the average pretensions … in search of a horse.

—GEORGE STEPHEN, *THE ADVENTURES OF A GENTLEMAN IN SEARCH OF A HORSE*

If a rider's heart is in the right place, his seat will be independent of his hands.

—PIERO SANTINI, *THE FORWARD IMPULSE*

Smoothness of execution in every detail is the sine qua non of good horsemanship; jumping in particular, in itself a violent effort, should be rendered as easy and as pleasant as possible for both horse and man by every means in our power.

—PIERO SANTINI

In these days when science is clearly in the saddle and when our knowledge of disease is advancing at a breathless pace, we are apt to forget that not all can ride and that he also serves who waits and who applies what the horseman discovers.

—HARVEY CUSHING (1869–1939), *CONSECRATIO MEDICI*

Each leg in its gallop seems to stream with a rush of speed as though from a bucket of water poured o'er the field.

—ARABIAN POET

He entered first and with a graceful pride,
His fiery Arab dextrously did glide,
Who, while his rider every stand surveyed,
Sprung loose, and flew into an escapade;
Not moving forward, yet, with every bound,
Pressing, and seeming still to quit his ground.

—JOHN DRYDEN (1631–1700)

Riding a horse is not a gentle hobby, to be picked up and laid down like a game of solitaire. It is a grand passion.

—RALPH WALDO EMERSON

Ride your horse as you feel him, provided you were born to, or over the years have learned to feel! It is the one thing no book can teach you, no teacher can give you, the one conquest of the laurels which will be entirely yours.

—JEAN FROISSARD, *CLASSICAL HORSEMANSHIP FOR OUR TIME*

The most important principle is to want to do it, to be committed before you start off to getting to the other side of every fence every time ... If you are not certain about whether you want to go or not, do yourself and your horse a favor—don't start.

—CAPTAIN MARK PHILLIPS, *THE HORSE AND HOUND BOOK OF EVENTING*

I was stealing a ride on a big bay horse named Sleepy, who, admittedly, was sometimes a little bit better at bucking than I was at riding. Sleepy had a way of coming awake as the least expected times …

—DAYTON O. HYDE, *ALL THE WILD HORSES*

One can get in a car and see what man has made. One must get on a horse to see what God has made.

—ANONYMOUS

A horse "held in shape" by his rider is only posturing in a seemingly correct form, usually for the benefit of inexperienced observers.

—CHARLES DE KUNFFY

I am back in my youth again, riding the finest darn horse a kid could ever dream of owning. Riding against some of the fastest horses and some of the best jockeys in our part of the country.

—JESSE COLT, *WHEN I DREAM I HEAR HOOFBEATS*

Riding allows me to distance myself from life's daily occurrences. When I am on a horse I forget everything else. I am absorbed by what I do. It is a certain escapism. When sitting on a horse my mind reaches a higher plane, especially when walking on a loose rein!

—JEAN-LOUIS GUNTZ

And of the wond'rous horse of brass, on which the Tartar king did ride ...

—JOHN MILTON

Don't hang on to his head going into the fences, or you'll get pulled off … This fellow knows it all. Let him have his head and hold on by the neck strap.

—JOHN WELCOME, *MY FIRST WINNER*

Give a man a horse he can ride… .

—JAMES THOMSON

Life is too short to ride bad horses.

—ANONYMOUS

Today, when most people ride for sport or pleasure, the horse's ability to move is his most essential trait. It is what makes him useful, able, and beautiful.

—SUSAN E. HARRIS, *HORSE GAITS, BALANCE AND MOVEMENT*

George Wyndham once told me that he had seen one of the first aeroplanes rise for the first time and it was very wonderful but not so wonderful as a horse allowing a man to ride on him.

—G. K. CHESTERTON, *THE EVERLASTING MAN*

What a delight to back the flying steed that challenges the wind for speed! … Whose soul is in his task, turns labour into sport!

—JOHN SHERIDAN KNOWLES (1784–1862)

[A]s I got on to the flat stretch of road outside the gate I tried what the pony could do. He went even better than I thought he could, very rough and uneven, of course, but still promising. I brought him home, and had him put into training at once, as carefully as if he was going for the Derby.

—SOMERVILLE AND ROSS

No one ever notices how you ride until you fall off.

—MURPHY'S HORSE LAW

Although a riding horse often weighs half a ton, and a big drafter a full ton, either can be led about by a piece of string if he has been wisely trained. This to me is a constant source of wonder, and challenge.

—MARGUERITE HENRY

Its strength, its speed, its vision, its hearing, its sense of smell, its reflexes—they are better than a human's. Its memory—a big factor in intelligence—is very good. It can learn the complex routine required of it in everything from circus acts to herding cattle on the range.

—MILTON MELTZER, *HOLD YOUR HORSES!*

I also believe that horses are the closest to God in the animal world.

—DOMINIQUE BARBIER, *DRESSAGE FOR THE NEW AGE*

No matter how good a man is, there's always some horse can pitch him. You just climb up again before he gets to feeling smart about it. Pretty soon, he won't throw you no more, and pretty soon he can't throw you no more.

—JOHN STEINBECK, *THE RED PONY*

As far as I'm concerned, a rider's fear is real—it's a non-negotiable issue. What it feels like to her is what it is. Period. It doesn't matter whether the trainer, buddy, college professor, mother, or grandfather thinks she is overreacting, overprotective, or overindulgent.

—JANET SASSON EDGETTE, PSY.D.

To ride you need to be moderately fit if you are going to get the best out of it, although riding itself is one of the best ways of solving the problem …

—JANE HOLDERNESS-RODDAM, *FITNESS FOR HORSE & RIDER*

The hardest thing to get in riding is feeling, but that's what riding is all about. After a certain point, our sport is 90 percent horse and how you can learn to adapt to that horse.

—NORMAN DELLO JOIO

When most people see others riding along on the trail, they get the urge to do it themselves.

—AUDREY PAVIA, *TRAIL RIDING: A COMPLETE GUIDE*

His hooves pound the beat, your heart sings the song.

—JERRY SHULMAN

Rider and horse—friend and foe—in one red burial blent!

—LORD BYRON

What is it that makes horses give their rider everything? It can only be a reaction based on mutual trust. Once a horse trusts his partner, he develops and grows ...

—ELIZABETH FURST

The horse knows how to be a horse if we will leave him alone … but the riders don't know how to ride. What we should be doing is creating riders and that takes care of the horse immediately.

—CHARLES DE KUNFFY

———◆———

By George! The pony went like a flash of lightning! I had him galloped next; same thing—fellow could hardly hold him. I opened my eyes, I can tell you, but no matter what way I looked at him I couldn't see where on earth he got his pace from. …

—SOMERVILLE AND ROSS

———◆———

Been there … jumped that!

—ANONYMOUS

———◆———

Grace is so great an adornment for a rider, and at the same time so important a means to the knowledge of all that which is necessary for persons aspiring to become riders, that such persons should willingly sped the time required to obtain that quality at the outside of their endeavors.

—FRANÇOIS ROBICHON DE LA GUÉRINIÈRE

It's the horse you are the most unwilling to ride that will take you the furthest.

—ANONYMOUS

"Kerrell's just bought a horse that could have been made for you. Even you won't be able to fall off him."
"I could fall off a gym horse standing still."

—JOHN WELCOME

Competitive riding should be classical riding at its best.

—CHARLES DE KUNFFY

———◆———

I was hesitant to get back on a horse, but the wranglers were very helpful, and after a while, I got in the groove of it.

—ROBERT DUVALL

———◆———

You can think your way out of many problems faster than you can ride your way out of them.

—WILLIAM STEINKRAUS, *RIDING AND JUMPING*

———◆———

Riding: The dialogue of two bodies and two souls aimed at establishing perfect harmony between them.

—WALDEMAR SEUNIG

———◆———

Talk to a dreamer and get caught up in the excitement. Sit on a fabulous horse and dream about having a horse of such quality to ride. Go to the big shows. Watch the great riders and dare to think … That could be me.

—JANE SAVOIE

Riding is mostly a kinesthetic experience. Yet it requires the ability to visualize what you want … so that you "see" the line you want to ride. Auditory skills other than simple voice commands and intonations aren't employed unless you are trying to teach riding to someone else.

—WENDY MURDOCH, *SIMPLIFY YOUR RIDING*

Get your tack and equipment just right, and then forget about it and concentrate on the horse and your ride.

—WILLIAM STEINKRAUS

Too much thinking was the enemy of instinct, and without instinct riders were nothing. ...

—BILL BARICH

—◆—

[A] quiet, well-trained, steady horse will help bring out the best in a timid rider.

—JUDITH DUTSON

—◆—

You only need two things to ride a horse. Confidence and balance. Everything else you can pick up as you go along.

—ALLAN D. KEATING

—◆—

As riders, our problem is that too often we try to provide all the upward activity ourselves instead of allowing our bodies to use the bounce provided by the ground. You can become aware of this upward energy. You cannot hold it in reserve; if you do, you'll lose it ...

—SALLY SWIFT, *CENTERED RIDING*

Horses, like babies, are there only to be admired.

—*THE HORSEMAN'S ETIQUETTE BOOK*

Riding turns "I wish" into "I can."

—PAM BROWN

The sight of riders mounted on quiet horses enjoying the beauty of nature is one that appeals to just about everyone who enjoys the outdoors.

—AUDREY PAVIA, *TRAIL RIDING: A COMPLETE GUIDE*

If the art were not so difficult we would have plenty of good riders and excellently ridden horses, but as it is the art requires, in addition to everything else, character traits that are not combined in everyone: inexhaustible patience, firm perseverance under stress, courage combined with quiet alertness.

—GUSTAV STEINBRECHT (1808–1885)

Being wholly in charge or another creature ... is quite an exhilarating sensation in itself, not to mention the tremendous feeling of power and motion which can only be experienced when actually on top of a horse.

—JANE HOLDERNESS-RODDAM, *FITNESS FOR HORSE & RIDER*

[A] good horseman can get anything he wants out of any horse, and I have never been able to figure out the logic that makes poor riders think that they can control a high-spirited horse when, by their own admission, they can't even make the quiet horse move forward!

—GORDON WRIGHT, *LEARNING TO RIDE, HUNT, AND SHOW*

—◈—

I love the disciplined panic of a horse flirting with a tantrum at every turn, the delicate voluptuous play of muscles, the grace-sprung power.

—DIANE ACKERMAN, *ASTRIDE THE TWILIGHT*

—◈—

If you love horses, you want to ride … I'll bet that horseback riding proves to be an immensely gratifying experience that enriches you life in ways you never thought possible.

—DIANA DELMAR, *TAKING UP RIDING AS AN ADULT*

—◈—

The ability to control an animal so much bigger than herself gave her a sense of awe and wonderful power. It was … not only gratifying in a physical sense; the caring for, riding, and showing of the horse also represented the mastery of a world … completely mysterious to the uninitiated.

—JOHN E. SCHOWALTER, *SOME MEANINGS OF BEING A HORSEWOMAN*

The right way to do almost anything with horses is mainly a matter of using your natural intelligence in an uncomplicated manner, and this holds true also for the rider's basic mounted position. Simplicity and economy of movement are the goals of classical technique.

—GEORGE H. MORRIS, *HUNTER SEAT EQUITATION*

The freedom of riding horseback has a place all its own; the companionship of a horse means you'll never be alone.

—HERMAN GEITHOOM

It is the seat on a horse that makes the difference between a groom and a gentleman.

—MIGUEL DE CERVANTES, *DON QUIXOTE*

Ride the horse in the direction it's going.

—WERNER ERHARD

Might my husband also ride him? Then he can see how lovely it is to sit on a well-trained horse.

—QUEEN ELIZABETH II

A good horseman trains his horses to go his way. A great horseman rides his horses the way they want to be ridden.

—BARBARA WORTH

Ride 'em and slide 'em.

—REINING IN A NUTSHELL

The main thing to remember about horsemanship is that is a physical art. If a man runs well, it is probably due to the fact that he was born with good legs and wind and has been able to keep himself fit. If a man rides well, it is probably due to the same reason.

—PAUL T. ALBERT

Your legs are a horse's courage.

—ANONYMOUS

Then we began to ride. My soul
Smoothed itself out, a long-cramped scroll
Freshening and fluttering in the wind …

       —ROBERT BROWNING

Most persons do not ride; they are conveyed.

       —M. F. MCTAGGART

One might as well try to ride two horses moving in different directions, as to try to maintain in equal force two opposing or contradictory sets of desires.

       —ROBERT COLLIER

Whatever your purpose in riding, be sure that it includes the elements of fun and appreciation of your horse. Then you will be well on your way to becoming a true horseman.

—SHEILA WALL HUNDT

There is only one place on a horse's back for a saddle … The shorter your leathers … the less you know about your mount. You are only aware whether or not he is winning. With the ordinary seat, you know whether he is lazy, and can make proper use of your spur.

—DONN BYRNE, *THE TALE OF THE GYPSY HORSE*

When a man is once well run away with, the first thing that occurs to him, I imagine, is how to stop his horse; but men by no means agree in the modes of bringing this matter about.

—GEOFFREY GAMBADO, *AN ACADEMY FOR GROWN HORSEMEN*

The wise horseman studies all he can regarding different methods of training, teaching, and riding, provided they are in accord with the fundamental principles followed by all good horsemen. Then he applies them according to the type of horse he is riding and the circumstances.

—Margaret Cabell Self

Oh, that ride! That first ride! Most truly it was an epoch in my existence; and I still look back to it with feelings of longing and regret. People may talk of their first love—it is a very agreeable event, I dare say—but give me the flush and triumph and glorious sweat of a first ride, like mine of the mighty cob.

—George Borrow

Riding is one of those pastimes which once experienced is never forgotten.

—Jane Holderness-Roddam, *Fitness for Horse & Rider*

You've got to control yourself before you kin control your horse.

—KEN ALSTAD

Ain't nuthin' like ridin' a fine horse in new country.

—ROBERT DUVALL AS AUGUSTUS MCCRAE IN *LONESOME DOVE*

Man has always attempted to become one with his horse when in the saddle, and he constantly seeks moments of perfect mutuality of movement, moments in which the skill becomes as art—if only for the duration of a heartbeat.

—H. H. ISENBART, *THE BEAUTY OF THE HORSE*

I never got hurt when I was in Morocco doing all the horse riding and my own stunts. But on the last day on the last shot I slid off my horse and landed on my bottom. I did not get hurt but it was very embarrassing.

—ODED FEHR

The great want in a man's seat is firmness, which would be still more difficult for a woman to acquire if she rode in a cross-saddle, because her thighs are rounder and weaker than those of a man. Discussion of this subject is, therefore, useless. Ladies who ride astride get such bad falls that they soon give up this practice.

—JAMES FILLIS, *BREAKING AND RIDING* (1890)

Riding provides a respite from the hassles of daily life. If you've had a bad day at the office or you've got a case of the blues, go ride a horse and see if it doesn't soothe your nerves, take your mind off your troubles, and raise your spirits.

—DIANA DELMAR, *TAKING UP RIDING AS AN ADULT*

When you ride a horse, balance comes, not from freezing your legs to the saddle, but from learning to float with the movement of the horse as you ride. Each step is a dance, the rider's dance as well as the dance of the horse.

—Chögyam Trungpa, *Shambala: The Sacred Path of the Warrior*

There are few gentleman, who, having moved much in society, have not at some time been called to assist a lady into her saddle; and I know nothing so mortifying to a gentleman as to stand by him.

—John Butler, *The Horse and How to Ride Him*

Many ... have been riding for twenty years or more and still cannot comfortably absorb the horse's movement.

—Heather Moffett, *Enlightened Equitation*

Horses move! It's what they do best, and it is why we ride, drive, train or just watch horses instead of eating them.

—SUSAN E. HARRIS, *HORSE GAITS, BALANCE AND MOVEMENT*

CHAPTER TEN

Horse Sense: On Training, Taming, Schooling, Breaking, Gentling, and the Like

Last weekend, a friend stopped by while Koda and I were in the middle of our ground exercises.

After watching for a few minutes, our visitor was kind enough to volunteer, "You really look tuned in to each other."

"Yeah, he's a very good boy," I replied—while as always adding to myself, *And thank God I didn't mess him up by training him.*

Here's what I mean:

Early on, I went at training with grim doggedness. Not surprisingly, I got grimly dogged results. My horse was a good horse, I could make him do stuff—big deal.

Then one day I saw the light. Who cared what I could *make* him do? The real magic happened when *he* wanted to do the stuff too. Thus the real training issue revealed itself to be: how could I develop and encourage in Koda the willingness, and maybe even the eagerness, to *want* to work with me?

From that point on, I think, a genuine partnership began to evolve.

This is why I admitted in a previous introduction that through working with Koda I've felt called upon to change in numerous ways and become a better person. In order for horse and man to work best together, training clearly needed to be a two-way street. As Monty Roberts says, "We can do little to teach the horse; we can only create an environment in which he can learn." And in attempting to create that environment, I've felt obliged to try to become more perceptive and more intuitive, more entertainingly creative and more adaptable, more confident as a leader, and so on—once you start down this road, there's really no end to it.

Tom Dorrance captured this unconventional aspect of horse training when he urged, "work on your horse by working on yourself." In its way, it's got to be the strangest saying in this book. What, horseless sessions out in the round pen? Afternoons spent standing with an unattached lead rope stretched in the dirt? Some training tip! But give those Zenlike words a chance to sink in and I bet you'll end up asking yourself some interesting questions. Such as: Am I holding up my end of the horse-man bargain? Am I striving to be the kind of person an equine partner would want to work with? Am I making that very particular effort? Dorrance lays down a challenge, all right.

Of course most horses get trained in a different school. Always have been, probably always will be. Call it the "kick 'em to go, pull 'em to stop" school. Works well enough for lots of folks, I'm told.

In any case, this chapter on training doesn't hew to a particular line on the subject. Nor will you find tips on how to make a horse do tricks or whatever. Instead, it's a wide-ranging anthology of training-related observations that, taken together, will probably convince you that there are as many ways to train a horse as there are horses.

Most conventionally started horses form an adversarial relationship with the humans who employ them. If they agree to perform, it is with a reluctant attitude. The first rule of starting a fresh horse, then, is *no pain*.

—MONTY ROBERTS

⟫⟪

We can do little to teach the horse; we can only create an environment in which he can learn.

—MONTY ROBERTS

⟫⟪

If a horse is capable of doing what you ask, it is up to you to ask in such a way that he will do it. Once you understand that the answer to your horse's problems is in finding your own mistakes, you are on your way to finding the correct solutions.

—MARY TWELVEPONIES

⟫⟪

A lot of people get along pretty well with their horses until they go to training those horses.

> —TOM DORRANCE, *TRUE UNITY: WILLING COMMUNICATION BETWEEN HORSE AND RIDER*

———◆———

Now I submit that the first thing a man who owns a horse should obtain is knowledge of the foot and the best method of protecting it. A horse without sound feet is no horse at all.

> —W. H. MURRAY

———◆———

The horse is a natural-born skeptic. He's a coward at heart. He's claustrophobic, and boy, when things get too close, too tight, he becomes a full-throttle-aholic. Instantly! He doesn't think. He reacts.

> —RONNIE WILLIS

———◆———

I do believe that things like education by and large serve to defraud humans of their own interests and sometimes thereby of their souls, and that crazy horses are one consequence of the "education" of horses.

—VICKI HEARNE, *ADAM'S TASK*

I have often noticed that good horsemen are like good sailors, meticulously and quietly tending to one detail after another, all to keep things running smoothly and safely.

—TOM MCGUANE

Work on your horse by working on yourself.

—TOM DORRANCE

They say that a person hasn't really learned a foreign language until he has learned to think in it. The same thing applies to training a horse. When he has learned to think in your language, then he is really trained.

—MARY TWELVEPONIES

If you're going to teach a horse something and have a good relationship, you don't make him learn it—you let him learn it.

—RAY HUNT

The better your horse backs up and goes sideways, the better he does everything else.

—PAT PARELLI

Remember that an easy hand is one of the principal aids we have; for it puts a horse upon its haunches, when he finds nothing else to learn upon; it pleases him, and prevents his being resty.

—WILLIAM CAVENDISH

The worst kick is from a trained horse.

—CORSICAN PROVERB

Our indirect methods have taught us a mountain of things about horses, but if you wished to learn even more, wouldn't you rather be Whirlaway in the stretch than interview Eddie Arcaro afterwards?

—STEPHEN JAY GOULD

When the spring round-up begins the horses should be as fat and sleek as possible. After running all winter free, even the most sober pony is apt to betray an inclination to buck; and, if possible, we like to ride every animal once or twice before we begin to do real work with him.

—THEODORE ROOSEVELT

[Horse] gentlers talk, not about people with horse problems, but horses with people problems. About the horse as teacher, about the slow way with horses as the quickest way. This is a horse-centered worldview that gentlers say offers a nice spinoff: It makes humans more humane.

—LAWRENCE SCANLAN

The educated horse is a thinking horse, and it seems that he understands that every now and then something happens that he must chalk up as a mistake and be done with it.

—DENNIS MURPHY

What you know for certain is that you don't know nothing for certain.

—ALLEN JERKENS

———⊱⊱⊰———

It was clear right away that horses had personalities and moods. Some became my friends and some stayed enemies until the day I left. Most interesting of all: They seemed more afraid of me than I was of them.

—CHRIS IRWIN, *HORSES DON'T LIE*

———⊱⊱⊰———

The school horse is a very important, almost indispensable assistant to the instructor. But he will be of full value only if the instructor is thoroughly acquainted with his movements and his temperament . . .

—ALOIS PODHAJSKY, *MY HORSES, MY TEACHERS*

———⊱⊱⊰———

You took care of your horse, and your horse took care of you.

—ELTON GALLEGLY

———⊱⊱⊰———

[H]e is not seeking companionship with horses, though his relationship with horses he likes . . . is equivalent to the consistent respect one accords an esteemed co-worker.

—Thomas McGuane

—⟨✦⟩—

A good grooming is equivalent to half a feed.

—Captain De Condenbove, French Army, World War I. This appeared in *Field Artillery Manual, Vol. 1*, by Arthur R. Wilson, Capt., Field Artillery, U.S. Army, 1926

—⟨✦⟩—

[T]here is no doubt that horse work was the roughest and most arduous part of our life.

—James Herriot, *All Things Bright and Beautiful*

—⟨✦⟩—

Positive horse training . . . defines the horse-human relationship as a team, with reasonable motivations and logical rewards for cooperation. Positive horse training uses well-timed rewards to build trust and respect between horse and human.

—SARAH BLANCHARD, *THE POWER OF POSITIVE HORSE TRAINING*

The books say never lead a Thoroughbred without that chain over his nose so you can pull him down sharply and really rap him, and I have heard Louise Meryman . . . tell her students they should never even lead a Thoroughbred across a courtyard without a metal chain on his nose.

—GENE SMITH, *THE CHAMPION*

The novice may want a trainer to work with a horse to correct deficiencies in its training or to help improve the novice's equitation or to prevent gross mistakes in training or riding.

—J. WARREN EVANS

A real horseman must not only be an expert—he must also be able to think and feel like a horse, that is, to realize that a horse is not equipped with human understanding.

—WALDEMAR SEUNIG

For, everything that we get [a horse] to do of his own accord, without force, must be accomplished by some means of conveying our ideas to his mind.

—JOHN RAREY (1827–1866)

[T]he horse has one factor which a machine does not have; it has a brain. Not a very large one, it is true, but large enough to introduce a random element of uncertainty into its operation.

—JACK COGGINS, *THE HORSEMAN'S BIBLE*

It can be set down in four words: the best of everything. The best hay, oats, and water.

—James E. "Sunny Jim" Fitzsimmons

It is also good to pet the beast while he eats so that he will relax.

—Marcus Aurelius

No instructor is capable of teaching this delicate language between rider and horse without the willing assistance of the horse.

—Alois Podhajsky

The first and most important basic is a good attitude toward the horse. I know that many of us were taught that we must "master" the horse. . . . I do feel that his kind of thinking is . . . outdated.

—Gincy Self Bucklin, *How Your Horse Wants You to Ride*

A horse cannot be expected to understand exactly what you want it to do the first time it is asked. It will, however, know when it has done something right if you will show that you are pleased.

—Colin Vogel, *Complete Horse Care Manual*

If a horse is no good, sell him for a dog.

—Ben Jones

When a horse is galloping, each leg in turn supports his entire weight.

—Preston M. Burch and Alex Bower, *Training Thoroughbred Horses*

He is my silent teacher . . . guiding me to understanding.

—Carole Hudgens

Horses are really high-maintenance creatures, and goats are low-maintenance creatures. I'm sorry I can't ride my goats, but I still love them just the same. I wish I had time for horses.

—KRIST NOVOSELIC

Horses are the same from the day they're born to the day they die. They are only changed by the people who train them.

—TOM SMITH

The greatest error in training horses lies in not showing up for work often enough and trying to accomplish too much when you do.

—TOM MCGUANE

If you have a problem getting along with neighbors or people in school, you might as well forget about training horses. Training horses is not fighting with them. And it's not a business for a person who is lazy. It takes a lot of drive.

—MARVIN MAYFIELD

The young rider, eager to learn, may rely on his four-legged teacher whose importance sometimes even rises above that of the two-legged one.

—ALOIS PODHAJSKY

[T]he majority of horses are willing and anxious to please and will give a great deal in exchange for a little praise and kind treatment.

—JACK COGGINS, *THE HORSEMAN'S BIBLE*

Pet me sometimes, be always gentle to me so that I may serve you more gladly and learn to love you.

—CAPTAIN DE CONDENBOVE, FRENCH ARMY, WORLD WAR I. THIS APPEARED IN *FIELD ARTILLERY MANUAL, VOL. 1*, BY ARTHUR R. WILSON, CAPT., FIELD ARTILLERY, U.S. ARMY, 1926

———

That moment of complete mutual respect and trust marks the beginning of a relationship between a horse and human that's one of the most special relationships you can have with an animal.

—BUCK BRANNAMAN

———

For me it is first and last about the relationship between a human being and a horse, nothing more. If a person . . . strives for integrity, humanity, truth and inner awareness and if he is prepared to question himself . . . it is . . . enough for the horses, because they seek mutuality, not differences.

—KLAUS FERDINAND HEMPFLING, *WHAT HORSES REVEAL: FROM FIRST ENCOUNTER TO FRIEND FOR LIFE*

———

Since the horse cannot speak the rider must endeavor to guess his thoughts and to interpret his reactions and draw conclusions from his behavior.

—ALOIS PODHAJSKY

I do know that I fell off just about every one of them. Even if I was hurt, as happened a couple of times, my father would always make me get right back on and ride some more.

—CAREY WINFREY

In its strict meaning, "dressage" is simply the training of the horse. In use, though, dressage has become the art and intensely competitive sport of training in the classical movements. Like figure skating, dressage emphasizes the power and beauty of motion.

—HOLLY MENINO, *THE PONIES ARE TALKING*

To properly train your horse, you have to be very patient.

—TWILA DIAN, *ALL ABOUT HORSES*

The secret to success with horses is knowledge, consistency, and time. You get consistency from understanding, which comes from knowledge—and you have to put in the time.

—STACY WESTFALL

A horse can be made to do almost anything if his master has intelligence enough to let him know what is required.

—ULYSSES S. GRANT (1822–1885)

It's what you learn after you know it all that's important.

—JIMMY WILLIAMS

I have a new horse. I get her to come to me from half a mile away. With just a simple call. That's because she knows that when she's with me, she's taken care of. She trusts me.

—RUSSELL CROWE

———⬥———

There are many types of bits for many different disciplines, but the severity of all bits lies in the hands holding them.

—MONTY ROBERTS

———⬥———

If training has not made a horse more beautiful, nobler in carriage, more attentive in his behavior, revealing pleasure in his own accomplishment . . . then he has not truly been schooled in dressage.

—COLONEL HANS HANDLER

———⬥———

No time spent in the saddle is wasted; as you learn to communicate with the horse and appreciate what he can do for you, it will add a fascinating dimension to your life.

—MARY GORDON-WATSON, *THE HANDBOOK OF RIDING*

Horses are not really intelligent; but they learn quickly . . . they learn what humans consider bad behavior just as easily as good behavior if they are allowed to. You must be careful not to allow a horse to learn that it can get what it wanted through undesirable behavior.

—COLIN VOGEL, *COMPLETE HORSE CARE MANUAL*

The way you start a colt is critical. Once [Tom Dorrance] taught us to be softer, kinder, gentler, our horses worked better. It actually makes a difference when a horse likes you.

—GREG WARD

Horses are much more adept at recognizing fear than we humans.

—KELLY MARKS

───◆───

A rider's total belief in an instructor is . . . essential.

—GEORGE H. MORRIS

───◆───

One longtime observer of horse sports remarked to me that a dressage rider could look at the horse standing in his stall and instantly detect a new fly bite on the animal.

—HOLLY MENINO, *THE PONIES ARE TALKING*

───◆───

The art of horsemanship assumes many forms . . .

—CHARLENE STRICKLAND, *WESTERN PRACTICE LESSONS*

───◆───

A ruthlessly condensed training only leads to a general superficiality, to travesties of the movements, and to a premature unsoundness of the horse. Nature cannot be violated.

—ALOIS PODHAJSKY

You need to get inside their head and understand them. If you use force on animals bred for hundreds of years to be war horses, they will wage war with you. You can't own them. You can befriend them. Loving these horses—if it's in your heart, you will never lose the passion.

—CHEN KEDAR

A true horseman demands respect from horses because he or she knows it's critical for safety. He or she also respects the horse: his size, instincts, and character. When you both feel safe and have mutual respect, you develop trust and confidence.

—BOB AVILA

Never . . . telegraph to your horse how you feel unless you want him to feel the same. No creature is more sensitive to mood than a horse. He will at once recognize fear or impatience on the part of his rider.

—MacGregor Jenkins

The horse does not execute down transitions by pulling the forehand backwards, but by stepping under his hind legs.

—E. F. Sedler

As a general rule ponies are considerably more intelligent than horses, are less easily frightened, and seldom panic. Their more phlegmatic disposition also enables them to tolerate the rough-housing and the excess of petting and attention which kids enjoy so much.

—Jack Coggins, *The Horseman's Bible*

Dressage, the art for art's sake school of horsemanship, does not involve the speed or danger of other horse sports, but many top riders have left fast times and big fences for the intellectual stimulation of manège and the rigor of its search for purity of movement.

—HOLLY MENINO, *THE PONIES ARE TALKING*

[I]f you ride, drive, or handle a horse at even the most basic level of interaction, you are contributing to the horse's training.

—SARAH BLANCHARD, *THE POWER OF POSITIVE HORSE TRAINING*

To practice equestrian art is to establish a conversation on a higher level with the horse; a dialogue of courtesy and finesse.

—NUNO OLIVEIRA

I've found that my most successful horses . . . all have certain traits in common. They're all very brave, good movers and solid individual jumping, with the boldness to attack the cross-country courses.

—MIKE HUBER

Movement is the basis of our communication with horses.

—HOLLY MENINO, *THE PONIES ARE TALKING*

If your horse says no, you either asked the wrong question, or asked the question wrong.

—PAT PARELLI

A variety of breeds can be mixed together to produce the show pony. Most often the mixture contains Thoroughbred and pony breeds.

—COLIN VOGEL, *COMPLETE HORSE CARE MANUAL*

If you act like you've only got fifteen minus, it'll take all day. Act like you've got all day and it'll take fifteen minutes.

—MONTY ROBERTS

Listen to what the horse is saying to you.

—ADELE McCORMICK AND MARLENA McCORMICK, *HORSE SENSE AND THE HUMAN HEART*

Neither should . . . the lessons be for too long a period; they fatigue and bore a horse, and it should be returned to the stable with the same good spirits it had upon leaving it.

—FRANÇOIS ROBICHON DE LA GUÉRINIÈRE

Care, and not fine stables, makes a good horse.

—DANISH PROVERB

When my horse is running good, I don't stop to give him sugar.

—WILLIAM FAULKNER

The human is supposed to be the teacher, but a lot of times maybe the owner of the horse can't ride a swinging gate in a windstorm. Yet, they are supposed to be this authoritative figure to the horse and it doesn't work.

—BUCK BRANNAMAN

Treat a horse like a woman and a woman like a horse. And they'll both win for you.

—ELIZABETH ARDEN (1878–1966)

Once the horse bites you, you never get over it.

—PAUL CLEVELAND

Sudden severe pain in the abdomen in the horse is referred to as colic.

—JAMES M. GIFFIN, TOM GORE, *HORSE OWNER'S VETERINARY HANDBOOK*

A trainer has to be observant. He has to watch the horses and figure out what they are thinking. This requires a feel for horses. This feel is directly connected to passion.

—DAVID COLLINS

You can often tell a horse's age by his teeth.

—DEBORAH BURNS, *STOREY'S HORSE-LOVER'S ENCYCLOPEDIA*

It's a funny thing, but we always seem to get the horse that teaches us the very thing we need to learn.

—PERRY WOOD, *REAL RIDING: HOW TO RIDE IN HARMONY WITH HORSES*

I didn't know anything about horses. But I got a job . . . mucking stalls.
I lived right with the horses. . . . I fell asleep listening to their nickering
and woke up with the smell in my nose.

—CHRIS IRWIN, *HORSES DON'T LIE*

Confidence is absolutely essential because without it the horse just
cannot make a sufficient surrender of himself, mentally and physically,
to learn and to absorb our teaching. Mental and physical processes are so
intimately connected, that they cannot be separated.

—HENRY WYNMALEN

During maximal physical exercise, the cardiac output of a racehorse
increases to seven times normal while the heart rate increases to 200 beats
per minute.

—JAMES M. GIFFIN, TOM GORE, *HORSE OWNER'S VETERINARY HANDBOOK*

Look again . . . instead of a fighting horse, you see a dancing horse.

—KLAUS FERDINAND HEMPFLING

———◆———

[W]hen your horse shies at an object and is unwilling to go up to it, he should be shown that there is nothing fearful in it, least of all to a courageous horse like him; but if this fails, touch the object yourself that seems so dreadful to him, and lead him up to it with gentleness.

—XENOPHON

———◆———

The name "horse whisperer" appears to be an ancient one from the British Isles, given to people whose rapport with horses seemed almost mystical.

—PAUL TRACHTMAN

———◆———

There is something noble about horses that makes us want to treat them well. When we treat horses with the respect they deserve, they provide us with many unique opportunities to find a type of nobility in ourselves as well.

—CHERRY HILL

━━◆━━

Time and patience are required of all good horsemen, so hurry when you are not around your horse.

—BOB DENHARDT

━━◆━━

The Imperial Spanish Riding School in Vienna existed for over two hundred years for the sole purpose of breeding and training their beautiful Leppizan horses and in developing that type of riding known as "Haute Ecole."

—CARL RASWAN, *DRINKERS OF THE WIND*

━━◆━━

A horse can see behind him, up to a point. There's a blind spot directly to the rear and out to about ten feet. If a horse doesn't really trust his rider or is bothered by him, he'll become very insecure every time the rider passes through that blind spot . . .

—BUCK BRANNAMAN

[B]onding is profoundly physical. We learn our horses' body language and they learn to respond to a body language we use—body pressures and positions called aids—to ask for changes in gait and direction.

—MAXINE KUMIN

Intimate acquaintance with the horse's knowledge and leading the kind of life that entails the continual reimaginings of horsemanship mark the faces of some older riders with the look that I have also seen on the faces of a few poets and thinkers, the incandescent gaze of unmediated awareness that one might be tempted to call innocence . . .

—VICKI HEARNE, *ADAM'S TASK*

I know the horse too well. I have known the horse in war and in peace, and there is no place where a horse is comfortable. A horse thinks of too many things to do which you do not expect. He is apt to bite you in the leg when you think he is half asleep.

—MARK TWAIN

Encephalomyelitis is a disease . . . that is spread by blood-sucking insects that transmit the disease from one horse to another; this explains why it is a late summer and fall disease, for it is then that the transporting hosts are most prevalent. It is . . . referred to among horsemen as "sleeping sickness."

—BEN K. GREEN, *SLEEPING SICKNESS*

A view of the ancestry of the horse provides us a foundation to understand the behavioral biology of the domestic horse . . .

—GEORGE WARING

For a horse with a solid head, don't try to break it through with a mallet, try to melt it with sugar!

—ANONYMOUS

When training his horse, the rider must repeat over and over again, "I have time."

—ANONYMOUS

When selecting your first horse, there is one absolute rule that you should consider sacred. Don't break it under any circumstances, no matter how tempting: Inexperienced riders must not work with inexperienced horses.

—JUDITH DUTSON

In training there is always the tendency to proceed too rapidly; go slowly with careful, cautious steps. Make frequent demands; be content with little; be lavish in rewards.

—General Faverot de Kerbrech

An extra pressure, a silent rebuke, an unseen praising, a firm correction: all these passed between is as through telegraph wires.

—Christilot Hanson Boylen

When you own a horse, you must give a part of your life to the horse. There will be occasions when you must give up other things you like—suck as sleep, warmth, and comfort—to ensure that your horse receives proper care.

—Cherry Hill

A good horse trainer can get a horse to do what he wants him to do. A great trainer can get a horse to want to do it.

—MONTY ROBERTS

⟞⟡⟞

A horse is the . . . subject whereupon the art worketh, and is a creature sensible, and . . . so far as he is moved to do anything, he is thereunto moved by sense and feeling . . . this is common to all sensible creatures, to shun all things as annoy them, and to like all such things as do delight them.

—JOHN ASTLEY

⟞⟡⟞

You want to do as little as possible but as much as it takes.

—BUCK BRANNAMAN, ON TRAINING

⟞⟡⟞

Nothing on four legs is quicker than a horse heading back to the barn

—ANONYMOUS

⟞⟡⟞

[A]ctions of dominance by horses in the herd are always "just." Through body language there is always a warning . . . before an actual strike or bite occurs. That is why . . . recognizing "what happened before what happened happened" is the critical part of the equation in teaching horses.

—PETER FULLER

They have different personalities . . . much like people do. . . . Until you learn to communicate in their language, you are not likely to effectively deal with their individual needs. When you do . . . horses will work as willingly with man as they do with one another.

—MONTY ROBERTS

Any horse being treated for a disease that is accompanied by high fever and severe dehydration might get over the disease but die from the exhaustion and malnutrition that had occurred during the time of the most severe part of the sickness.

—BEN K. GREEN, *SLEEPING SICKNESS*

Burt taught me how to rub down a horse and put the bandages on after a race and steam a horse out and a lot of valuable things for any man to know. He could wrap a bandage on a horse's leg so smooth that if it had been the same color you would think it was his skin . . .

—SHERWOOD ANDERSON

⇒◆⇐

To learn all that a horse could teach, was a world of knowledge, but only a beginning.

—MARY O'HARA

⇒◆⇐

When the horse understands what you want, he will do what that is, right up to the limit of his physical capacity and sometimes well beyond it.

—BILL DORRANCE AND LESLIE DESMOND, *TRUE HORSEMANSHIP THROUGH FEEL*

⇒◆⇐

Frank Whiteley Jr. is one of the deadliest trainers of first-time starters in the history of racing—a man who wins upward of 40 percent of all such attempts, a man who trains horses like they are put together with Swiss-clockwork efficiency.

—STEVE DAVIDOWITZ

Almost any sick animal with a raging fever will have the presence of mind or enough instinct to drink, but few if any will eat feed.

—BEN K. GREEN, *SLEEPING SICKNESS*

The wildest colts make the best horses.

—PLUTARCH

Hemlock is a deadly poison for humans, but is consumed without ill effect by mice, sheep, goats, and horses. PCP, or angel dust, which drives humans into a frenzy, is used as a sedative for horses.

—DEBORAH GOLDSMITH

There never was a rider so smart that some horse could not teach him a new trick. Because of this, horsemanship and horse training is a lifelong study.

—PAUL T. ALBERT

Don't catch your horse, let your horse catch you.

—MONTY ROBERTS

You can't train a horse with shouts, and expect it to obey a whisper.

—ANONYMOUS

Horses are predictably unpredictable.

—GAGE LORETTA

Ninety-nine percent of all horses have quite a number of bad habits which are commonly put down to disobedience. And 99 percent of all riders do not understand how to break their horses of such habits.

—WILHELM MUSLER, *RIDING LOGIC*

Thou must learn the thoughts of the noble horse.

—JOHANN WOLFGANG VON GOETHE (1749–1832)

It is the difficult horses that have the most to give you.

—LENDON GRAY

You never get the pleasure of owning a horse, you only have the pleasure of being its slave.

—ANONYMOUS

———◆———

We follow the book. If we have a disagreement, we open the book. . . . We have nothing to invent. Everything in this sport has been written down already.

—NELSON PESSOA

———◆———

In attempting to develop a satisfactory relationship with a horse, it is enormously useful to understand the animal's vocabulary of pantomime and sound. But truly effective communications depends on matters more fundamental than language.

—TOM AINSLIE, *THE BODY LANGUAGE OF HORSES*

———◆———

A horse doesn't care how much you know until he knows how much you care.

—PAT PARELLI

It takes no more time and effort to train and finish out a good looking horse than a poor looking one.

—DICK SPENCER III

Horses need care when they are idle as well as when they are actively being trained or ridden. Their needs do not diminish if your interest does.

—CHERRY HILL

The two outstanding memories in the animal kingdom are the elephant and the horse. In the case of the horse, you have to remember when to run in order to stay alive.

—DR. ROBERT MILLER

Nanticoke [a show jumper of the 1960s] reinforced a lesson I'd already started to learn from other horses: never try to muscle your way with a horse.

—RODNEY JENKINS

In training horses, one trains himself.

—ANTOINE DE PLUVINET

One key to getting along well with a horse is to view him as a fellow creature rather than as for entertainment.

—PATRICIA JACOBSON AND MARCIA HAYES

A horse's memory outweighs his reasoning ability. It is therefore important not to allow him to develop any bad habits because he is likely to remember him forever.

—TWILA DIAN, *ALL ABOUT HORSES*

Closeness, friendship, affection: keeping your own horse means all these things.

—BERTRAND LECLAIR

We dominate a horse by mind over matter. We could never do it by brute strength.

—MONICA DICKENS

You can't control a young horse unless you can control yourself.

—LINCOLN STEFFENS

Horses are not tamed by whips or blows. The strength of ten men is not so strong as a single strike of the hoof; the experience of ten men is not enough, for this is the unexpected, the unpredictable.

—BERYL MARKHAM (1902–1986)

Horses reflect the emotions of their herd mates, thus the emotion of fear can run rampant through the herd like wildfire.

—KELLY MARKS

In training there is always the tendency to proceed too rapidly, go slowly with careful, cautious steps. Make frequent demands; be content with little; be lavish in rewards.

—GENERAL FAVEROT DE KERBRECH

Breed the best to the best and hope for the best.

—JOHN MADDEN

I have thought that to breed a noble horse is to share with God in one of His mysteries.

—TOM LEA, *THE HANDS OF CANTU*

The horse will leap over trenches, will jump out of them, will do anything else, provided one grants him praise and respite after his accomplishment.

—Xenophon

[T]here is a potential for danger when working with large animals.

—Shawna Karrasch

Dressage's magic formula is the overpowering force of a combination of gentleness and repetition.

—Princess de la Tour D'Auvergne

Thou must learn the thoughts of the noble horse whom thou wouldst ride. Be not indiscreet in thy demands, nor require him to perform indiscreetly.

—Johann Wolfgang von Goethe

Patience is equally necessary in order not to grow immoderately demanding, which always happens when we do not reward an initial compliance by immediate cessation of the demand, but try to enjoy a victory until the horse becomes cross or confused.

—WALDEMAR SEUNIG

God, grant me the serenity to take in as many horses as possible, the courage to convince my partner this is a good thing, and, the wisdom to know how to accomplish this task.

—HORSE SERENITY PRAYER

Dressage lessons in the mange, by reason of their constraints on the horse, must be of short duration and the horse must return to the stable in as happy a frame of mind as when he left it.

—GENERAL ALEXIS L'HOTTE

The Arabs have found out that which the English breeder should never forget, that the female is more concerned than the male in the excellence and value of produce; and the genealogies of their horses are always reckoned from the mothers.

—WILLIAM YOUATT (1776–1847)

Some people claim that any damn fool can train a racehorse.

—CARL A. NAFZGER, *TRAITS OF A WINNER*

Those who claim it is "unethical" to ask a horse to do something it would not do of its own inclination are being naive and foolish; but equally naive are those who expect to teach a horse to do their bidding without taking into account its natural inclinations.

—STEPHEN BUDIANSKY, *THE NATURE OF HORSE*

If your horse doesn't care, you shouldn't either.

—LINSY LEE

⇒◆⇐

Understanding the instinctive behavior of the wild horse is crucial to our understanding of his domesticated relatives.

—CHERYL KIMBALL, *THE EVERYTHING HORSE BOOK*

⇒◆⇐

Horses do think. Not very deeply, perhaps, but enough to get you into a lot of trouble.

—PATRICIA JACOBSON AND MARCIA HAYES

⇒◆⇐

In order to make a horse, one must first create a rider.

—STEPHANIE LILE

⇒◆⇐

[H]orses have a phenomenal memory and there's no time lapse. They memorize something that impresses them, good or bad, and ten years go by, it's still there.

—Dr. Robert Miller

It takes all the dignity out of a horse to make him do tricks. Why, a trick horse is kind of like an actor—no dignity, no character of his own.

—John Steinbeck

Lew wondered if it was true that at the training gallops Charlie always carried two stopwatches, one for other people, showing whatever time he wanted them to see, and one he looked at later on, all by himself. Of course ... it's true. I wish he was training my horse.

—Maurice Gee, *The Losers*

I've spent so many years living and working with them that at times I still feel I understand horses better than humans.

—CHRIS IRWIN AND BOB WEBER, *DANCING WITH YOUR DARK HORSE*

In order to excel at an art it is not enough to know the principles and to have practiced them for a long time. It is also necessary to be able to choose wisely the subjects that are capable of executing these principles.

—GASPARD DE SAUNIER

Anticipate problems and correct them before they happen. Controlling the horse's thinking is much easier than trying to control 1,000 pounds. This holds true whether you're on or off the horse, and may be the most important concept you can learn.

—MIKE SMITH, *GETTING THE MOST FROM RIDING LESSONS*

Disappointment usually awaits beginners who expect to become accomplished horsepeople without experienced horses and without the aid of a professional trainer.

—J. WARREN EVANS

In a few generations you can breed a racehorse.

—PIERRE-AUGUSTE RENOIR (1841–1919)

It's a funny thing—the better you get at training, the cleverer your horses become!

—KELLY MARKS

Sometimes you have to put your foot down to get a leg up.

—DAVE WEINBAUM

It is the best of lessons if the horse gets a season of repose whenever he has behaved to his rider's satisfaction.

—Xenophon

———⟫•⟪———

A horse's conformation is its overall body shape or form. Conformation has also been described as the relationship between form and function. It ultimately determines how a horse moves and withstands impact-related stress.

—Equine Research, *Horse Conformation: Structure, Soundness, and Performance*

———⟫•⟪———

The hardest horses to train are received by those who are the most apathetic of the training process and personal progression with their animal.

—The 6W Ranch

———⟫•⟪———

The one best precept—the golden rule in dealing with a horse—is never to approach him angrily. Anger is so devoid of forethought that it will often drive a man to do things which in a calmer mood he will regret.

—XENOPHON

I'm often asked ... "How smart are horses?" I tell them that it's usually people who are a bit insecure about their own level of intellect who ask that question.

—BUCK BRANNAMAN

A good rider can feel his way into a horse very quickly. He knows what a horse needs. He must establish harmony between horse and rider. He must not wait for the horse to do this. ... The good rider quickly gains the trust and confidence of the horse, because the horse understands his aids.

—DAVID COLLINS

The switch is rarely used as a means of punishment, though it has manifold uses as an acid. It is more often an ornament than a necessity. If you choose to depend upon it in the training of the horse, your understanding may be said to be as ephemeral as the swish of the switch itself.

—WILLIAM CAVENDISH

Anyone can train a racehorse—but they will only become successful if they really learn to understand horses.

—CARL A. NAFZGER, *TRAITS OF A WINNER*

You don't break these animals, you come to an understanding with them.

—PHIL WEST

To make a perfect horseman, three things are requisite. First, to know how and when to help your horse. Secondly, how and when to correct him. And thirdly, how and when to praise him and to make much of him.

—THOMAS BLUNDEVILLE

When you can direct a horse's movement through feel, then there's understanding taking place between the person and the horse. That is the sign of true horsemanship.

—BILL DORRANCE AND LESLIE DESMOND, *TRUE HORSEMANSHIP THROUGH FEEL*

If there is one rule to follow when it comes to training horses, it is this: there are no hard and fast rules!

—DAVE KELLEY

What you must always remember, no matter how angry you are, is that rewards teach the horse, not the consequences.

—ANONYMOUS

I learned how to read and listen to the body language of horses to such a degree that I fully understood where they were coming from, and I vowed to be their voice.

—CHRIS IRWIN AND BOB WEBER, *DANCING WITH YOUR DARK HORSE*

To the mistress who thoroughly understands the art of managing [horses], the horse gives his entire affection and obedience, becomes her most willing slave, submits to all her whims, and is proud and happy under her rule.

—ELIZABETH PLATT KARR, *THE AMERICAN HORSEWOMAN*

Hard is to teach an old horse amble true.

—EDMUND SPENSER (1552–1599)

Only when a horse is physically and mentally comfortable in his work can he give you his maximum potential of the moment.

—SALLY SWIFT

All … horses … are a bit difficult. … They're like John McEnroe of tennis: while they may be difficult, this strong character is what it takes to be an event horse.

—MIKE HUBER

Success in your primary business or profession does not automatically translate into success as a horse owner. You could say that this business is "a horse of a different color."

—PAUL D. SIEGEL, *HOW TO OWN WINNING STANDARDBRED RACEHORSES*

Always finish the lesson with something the horse is able to do easily and that he will thus perform happily, so that there is cause for praise and display of affection.

—PETER SPOHR (1828–1921)

Above all, a horse should never be chastised out of foul mood or anger, but always with complete dispassion.

—FRANÇOIS ROBICHON DE LA GUÉRINIÈRE

I have been writing a little book, its special aim being to induce kindness, sympathy, and an understanding treatment of horses.

—ANNA SEWELL

My horses look to me for guidance and support rather than wondering what's going on with the crazy woman riding them.

—BUCK BRANNAMAN

When learning new information it is sometimes useful to have helpers. Having someone lead your horse gives you a moment to concentrate on yourself.

—WENDY MURDOCH, *SIMPLIFY YOUR RIDING*

The revolution in horsemanship that occurred at the end of the twentieth century had, at its heart, a simple theme: that horses can be controlled more effectively *without* the use of force.

—ROBERT MILLER AND RICK LAMB

A horse is an individual.

—Gaydell M. Collier and Eleanor F. Prince

———⊷◆⊶———

When your horse has reached his potential, leave it. It's such a nice feeling when you and your horses are still friends.

—Dr. Reiner Klimke

———⊷◆⊶———

Rider and horse must meet with joy and part as friends. The friendly greeting, the patting hand should never be absent when mounting and dismounting.

—F. V. Krane

———⊷◆⊶———

The punishment is directed only at the disobedience, never at the horse; as soon as the disobedience is over, it is our good horse.

—E. F. Seidler

———⊰•⊱———

The horse doesn't understand the difference between right and wrong.
… If I kick and he does a behavior after that, whatever that behavior is,
he thinks that's what he's supposed to do. He doesn't think in terms of
this is right behavior and this is wrong behavior.

—JOHN LYONS

———⊰•⊱———

A firm hand is one which holds the horse in full contact.

—FRANÇOIS ROBICHON DE LA GUÉRINIÈRE

———⊰•⊱———

European horses are used to a soft turf while American horses prefer a
more solid turf surface.

—C. N. RICHARDSON

———⊰•⊱———

Ask often, be content of little, reward always.

—CAPTAIN ETIENNE BEUDANT (1861–1949)

Mrs. Betham laughed. … "Haven't we been well trained?" Connie said: "Yeah, but not as well as the horses."

—MAURICE GEE

In fifty years James Rowe trained thirty-two champions. Nobody else in the history of the American Turf can make such a claim or have it made on their behalf.

—EDWARD L. BOWEN

But if a rider teach his horse to go with the bridle loose . . . he would thus lead him to do everything in . . . pleasure and pride.

—JOHN ASTLEY

We found that the best use for his candy was lurin' your horse in the morning.

—BILL CRAIG

⸺◈⸺

The scariest moment in filming, with the horse, was the scene where they had the horse laying down because that is not natural for a horse to do.

—JULIE BENZ

⸺◈⸺

We can't lie to each other, my horses and I. We know the price of such deceits, and the time it takes to regain a balance.

—SHELLEY R. ROSENBERG, *MY HORSES, MY HEALERS*

⸺◈⸺

[T]here's the carrot attitude, used by a person who sweet-talks the horse into doing something. Such a person is usually ineffective and begs the horse instead of asking for and getting respect from the horse.

—PAT PARELLI

⸺◈⸺

Perfect harmony between the rider and his horse, i.e. beauty, is the ultimate goal of all dressage. The horse must be visibly at ease, and nothing in the rider's demeanor should betray how hard the road is.

—WILHELM MUSLER, *RIDING LOGIC*

Working with horses . . . is best done without time limits. Once you start something, you should plan to finish it. If you can't finish it, at the very least end on a positive, learning note, not a sour note where you and your horse came to an impasse . . .

—CHERYL KIMBALL, *MINDFUL HORSEMANSHIP*

Horse training becomes horseplay as we compete with horses to earn their respect, focus, trust, and willingness by having the right stuff to be seen by them as "the better horse."

—CHRIS IRWIN AND BOB WEBER, *DANCING WITH YOUR DARK HORSE*

I don't help people with horse problems, I help horses with people problems.

—NICHOLAS EVANS, *THE HORSE WHISPERER*

What does it take to train a horse? More time than the horse has.

—LARRY MAHAN

For what the horse does under compulsion . . . is done without understanding; and there is no beauty in it either, any more than if one should whip and spur a dancer.

—XENOPHON

[E]very riding school where ladies are to be taught, there should be at least one lady assistant . . . in giving the idea of a correct seat and the proper disposal of limbs . . . in these matters she can instruct her own sex much better than a man can.

—ELIZABETH KARR

The results of allowing the horse to tell you when you are wrong (as long as he doesn't tell you in an aggressive way) are astounding and rewarding for everyone.

—GINCY SELF BUCKLIN

Almost anything humans have demanded of it, the horse has done.

—MILTON MELTZER, *HOLD YOUR HORSES!*

A horse is like a violin, first it must be tuned, and when tuned it must be accurately played.

—ANONYMOUS

[W]e ought to consider the natural form and shape of a horse, that we may work him according to nature.

—WILLIAM CAVENDISH

If novices want to break and train their own horses, they need a professional to watch and direct their efforts. Failure to do so usually results in injury to the novice or in an improperly trained horse.

—J. WARREN EVANS

Progression in the schooling of horses must, quite definitely, be graduated, because gradual progress is the main road to success.

—GENERAL ALEXIS L'HOTTE

If a horse becomes more beautiful in the course of his work, it is a sign that the training principles are correct.

—ALOIS PODHAJSKY

Horse-Man-Ship is three words linked together. It's a horse and a human going willingly together. Horse-Man-Ship is for horses as well as humans, and the horse comes first.

—PAT PARELLI

Horses size humans up pretty quickly. If you ask for something and don't mean it, the horse knows and trouble will surely follow. If you are acting in a way that you do not truly feel, the horse knows it. ...With pure thoughts and pure actions, good horsemanship is yours.

—CHERYL KIMBALL, *MINDFUL HORSEMANSHIP*

What an excellent horse do they lose, for want of address and boldness to manage him! ... I could manage this horse better than others do.

—ALEXANDER THE GREAT (356–323 BC)

The horse puts the human's wishes after his own, and with that comes a multitude of problems.

—BUCK BRANNAMAN

A horse can't be bribed with treats. Not even with love.

—RUSSELL A. VASSALLO

Horsemanship is the one art for which it seems one needs only practice. However, practice without true principles is nothing other than routine ... a false diamond which dazzles semi-connoisseurs often more impressed by the accomplishments of the horse than the merit of the horseman.

—FRANÇOIS ROBICHON DE LA GUÉRINIÈRE

A horse should be treated like a gentleman.

—LELAND STANFORD (1824–1893)

———

A horse's dark eyes speak to me only in a language that I hear.

—NORA MAHAN

———

With his willing-to-please nature, his "user-friendly" shape, his strength, his speed and his stamina, the horse might have been specifically designed for the service of mankind.

—CHERYL KIMBALL

———

Barclay knew firsthand how hard the game was, how quickly good fortune could go bad. Even when he was training good horses, apprehension always lurked nearby.

—GEORGE ROWAND, *DIARY OF A DREAM*

———

For some people, working with the horse is just a way of stroking their own egos. Sometimes they have a lot of emotional baggage. Sometimes they lack awareness of their surroundings. That's why horses have so many problems with humans.

—BUCK BRANNAMAN

A teacher will be successful with his teaching when he is understood and respected by his pupils. In much the same way a horseman will be able to learn from his horse only when he respects him as a creature and has affection for him.

—ALOIS PODHAJSKY

When you reason with a horse, he'll participate because he wants to. Not because he's forced to.

—MONTY ROBERTS

Training a horse is like drawing a picture. The better I draw the picture, the better the communication.

—JOHN LYONS, *LYONS ON HORSES*

———◆———

A good man will take care of his horses and dogs, not only while they are young, but also when they are old and past service.

—PLUTARCH

———◆———

All horses are wild and skittish when unsure hands touch them.

—CLARICE LISPECTOR, *DRY POINT OF HORSES*

———◆———

It takes time to get close to horses, get to know them. They're strange creatures—utterly individual, unpredictable, and powerful. And yet they allow us to get close, to care for them, groom them, and ride on their backs.

—BARBARA E. COHEN

———◆———

A herd instinct: that's the horse's strongest basic urge. Understandable when you realize that before horses were domesticated, their survival depended on sticking together. A group of horses had a better chance against predatory animals than one horse alone.

—MILTON MELTZER

—◆—

There are bad days in training when everything is a struggle, and moments when the connection is so complete that the flow of muscle and motion beneath you feels internal.

—BARBARA E. COHEN

—◆—

Remember, a horse can tell you a lot of things, if you watch, and expect it to be sensible and intelligent.

—MARY O'HARA

—◆—

A good head means a pretty head and nothing more. Of course, vital functions go on inside of it. Eating, drinking, breathing, seeing, hearing, and housing of the brain are life-and-death responsibilities. But structure, in this case, does not reflect usefulness.

—ALEXANDER MACKAY-SMITH

Taking one breath after another with my horses—and you must breathe with them if you want to understand their rhythms and emotions—I can settle myself, become calm, take stock of my surroundings.

—SHELLEY R. ROSENBERG

When the instructor has not trained the horse himself, he should ride the horse before starting to train his pupil in order to get to know his capabilities.

—ALOIS PODHAJSKY

We shall take great care not to annoy the horse and spoil his friendly charm, for it is like the scent of a blossom—once lost it will never return.

—ANTOINE DE PLUVINEL

Some people . . . fancy that by beating and spurring they will make his a dress'd horse in one morning only. I would fain ask such stupid people, whether, by beating a boy, they could teach him to read, without first showing him his alphabet.

—WILLIAM CAVENDISH

Be considerate of your horse. He is not a machine—and even machines run better with good driving.

—SHEILA WALL HUNDT

Sire, it has been close to sixty years that I have been working towards learning what you have given me the honor of telling me. And here you want me to teach him all that I hope to accomplish myself.

—GASPARD DE SAUNIER (1663–1748), RETELLING A STORY OF HOW ONE OF THE FOREMOST PRINCES OF FRANCE TOOK HIS SON TO M. DUPLESSIS TO HAVE HIM TRAINED

Learning to manage a fear of horses is an attainable goal for anyone, by following this systematic process of intellectualizing the fear, developing a plan for recovery, learning acting skills for physical and mental control, and improving horsemanship and safety skills.

—JULIE GOODNIGHT

Anything forced and misunderstood can never be beautiful.

—XENOPHON

Learning about our horses is learning about ourselves as well, seeing how our personalities mesh or clash with the horses we choose to ride or train.

—LINDA TELLINGON-JONES

A rider that uses his horse like a tool has no respect for horses and no love. He is not a friend of the horse. This rider will never learn to dance with horses.

—DAVID COLLINS

When students doubt me a little, I suggest other teachers they should go to. Without belief, discipline is a mockery, if not downright impossible.

—GEORGE H. MORRIS

In order to obtain the greatest amount of usefulness from horses, through endurance, speed, and physical strength, it behooves us to look closely to all things pertaining to their health, for without this they become useless … it is nothing more than humane to look after their welfare.

—J. R. COLE, *THE HORSE'S FOOT AND HOW TO SHOE IT*

Creating a partnership with my horses and keeping them healthy, fit, and safe is a way of life. A kind of trust comes into it that takes hold of you. It's hard-won and a gift at the same time.

—BARBARA E. COHEN

If I had to pick one thing that I had to hang my hat on, I would want the horse I was going to buy to have a face that I would enjoy seeing poked over the stall webbing every morning, waiting for breakfast.

—JAMES C. WOFFORD

A good horse should be seldom spurred.

—THOMAS FULLER, M.D.

———⊰⋄⊱———

I purchased some classics on horse care ... I gradually came to understand that they were like nineteenth-century religious tomes on how to save your soul: objective, good; instructions, extremely detailed; practical application, impossible.

—C. J. J. MULLEN

———⊰⋄⊱———

DRESSAGE, n.: the passionate pursuit of perfection by the obsessively imperfect.

—ANONYMOUS

———⊰⋄⊱———

A rider has to be able to judge whether a horse is physically and mentally strong enough to carry out what has been asked for. In this way a horse will never get into a stressful situation.

—ARTHUR KOTTAS-HELDENBERG

———⊰⋄⊱———

Practice sharpens, but over-schooling blunts the edge. If your horse isn't doing right, the first place to look is yourself.

—JOE HEIM

The only approbation a rider should covet is that of his horse.

—E. BEUDANT

The horse is an incredible animal that is willing to interact with the likes of humans. I believe those of us who choose to interact with horses . . . are obligated to treat them with respect—which includes them to treat us with respect.

—CHERYL KIMBALL

I never worked with a Northern horse before. They are very different from Western horses.

—JULIE BENZ

While another profession has coveted the title of "the world's oldest," horse training is certainly the world's oldest honorable profession.

—C. N. RICHARDSON, *SMALL TRACK BETTING*

There is something very special about building up a relationship with a horse, to the point where you are so in tune with each other that the aids become mere thought communication.

—HEATHER MOFFETT

CHAPTER ELEVEN

"Boot, Saddle, to Horse, and Away!": Some Closing Observations

Horses are an inexhaustible subject. I knew this before starting work on this book, and now that I'm done I'm more convinced of it than ever.

And it's not just that there are countless additional quotations out there to fill up other, even *more* gigantic *Gigantic Books*. What I mean is that the horse has been a singular presence in human history and his traces remain throughout our language and culture.

No single book, in other words, could hope to do justice to what "horse wisdom" has been to us—and can continue to be.

So in closing, let me just say what a pleasure it's been to be your guide through these pages.

Now what do you say we finish up and go spend some time with our horses?

God made a perfect world but he would like one chance to redesign the horse.

—ATTRIBUTED BY TOM MCGUANE TO "A FRIEND OF MINE IN OKLAHOMA"

———

A pony is a childhood dream. A horse is an adulthood treasure.

—REBECCA CARROLL

———

There will always be stock horses. When all our needs can finally be fulfilled by merely pressing a button, there will still be men who ride horses to bring the cows to market.

—PAUL T. ALBERT

———

Never thank yourself; always thank the horses for the happiness and joy we experience through them.

—H. H. ISENBART

———

Let a horse whisper in your ear and breathe on your heart. You will never regret it.

—ANONYMOUS

———◆———

He serves without servility;
He has fought without enmity.
There is nothing so powerful,
Nothing less violent; there is nothing
So quick, nothing more patient.

—RONALD DUNCAN

———◆———

Give a horse what he needs and he will give you his heart in return.

—ANONYMOUS

———◆———

[T]here's nothin' in life worth doin', if it cain't be done from a horse.

—RED STEAGALL, *BORN TO THIS LAND*

———◆———

When your horse follows you without being asked, when he rubs his head on yours, and when you look at him and feel a tingle down your spine ... you know you are loved.

—JOHN LYONS

———⬖———

Horses make a landscape look beautiful.

—ALICE WALKER

———⬖———

The horse through all its trials has preserved the sweetness of paradise in its blood.

—JOHANNES VILHELM JENSEN (1873–1950)

———⬖———

When we associate with horses, we claim back something of our lost wilderness. With horses, we are back in touch with our fellow animals. With horses, we become more truly human.

—SIMON BARNES

———⬖———

My horses understand me tolerably well; I converse with them at least four hours every day. They are strangers to bridle or saddle; they live in great amity with me, and friendship of each other.

—JONATHAN SWIFT (1667–1745), *GULLIVER'S TRAVELS*

———•———

You and your horse … What can heaven offer any better than what I have here on earth?

—MONICA DICKENS

———•———

The connection between people and horses is both ancient and timeless. Even as equestrian sports and disciplines change and grow, the tie remains secure.

—ELIZA MCGRAW

———•———

Boot, saddle, to horse, and away!

—ROBERT BROWNING

———•———

The substitution of the internal combustion engine for the horse marked a very gloomy milestone in the progress of mankind.

—Sir Winston Churchill (1874–1965)

⟹⟸

We may fly or sail or glide over the roads on pneumatic tires with more comfort, but the love of good horseflesh will never be stamped out of humans while they still have red blood in their veins. This is not a prophecy, but a fact.

—Paul T. Albert

⟹⟸

"He makes me feel happier than anything else does." Others have tried to explain the effect that horses have on our lives, but has anyone said it any better?

—Steven D. Price

⟹⟸

Those Quoted

THOSE QUOTED

A

Aadland, Dan
Abbey, Edward
Abd-El-Kader, Emir
Ackerman, Diane
Adams, Cindy
Adams, Douglas
Adams, Joey
Adams, John
Adams, Ramon
Ade, George
Adler, C. S.
Aesop,
Agate, James
Ainslie, Tom
Albert, Paul T.
Alexander the Great,
Allen, Marty
Allen, Richie
Alstad, Ken
Andalusian
Anderson, Allen
Anderson, Chic
Anderson, C.W.
Andrews, Lynn V.
Anderson, M. Paul
Anderson, Sherwood
Anonymous
Ansell, Colonel Sir Mike
Anthony, Piers
Apperly, C. J.
Aragon, Vicky
Arcaro, Eddie
Arden, Elizabeth
Arendt, Hannah

Armstrong, Louis
Armstrong, Samantha
Arnold, Matthew
Arundale, George S.
Ashbery, John
Asmussen, Steve
Asquith, Margot
Assante, Armand
Astaire, Fred
Astley, John
Auden, W. H.
Auel, Jean M.
Auf der Maur, Melissa
Aurelius, Marcus
Austen, Jane
Avicenna,
Axthelm, Pete

B

Babel, Isaac
Baer, Arthur
Bagnold, Enid
Bailey, Tom
Balding, Clare
Baldwin, James
Balkenhol, Klaus
Barbier, Dominique
Barich, Bill
Barnes, Simon
Barry, Dave
Bartok, Bela
Baruch, Bernard
Bauken, Manuel
Bean, Alan
Becker, Teresa

Beddoes, Dick
Behan, Brendan
Belloc, Hilaire
Bench, Johnny
Benet, Stephen Vincent
Benson, Gary J.
Benz, Julie
Berenger, Richard
Beresford, Bruce
Berio, Luciano
Berkman, Ted
Bernard, Jeffrey
Beston, Harry
Beudant, Etienne
Beyer, Andrew
Bierce, Ambrose
Billings, Josh
Binding, Rudolf C.
Bixby, Lawrence
Bjelke- Petersen, John
Blackmore, Richard
Blake, William
Blanchard, Sarah
Blazer, Don
Blinks, Sue
Bloom, Harold
Blunderville, Thomas
Blunt, Wilfrid Scawen
Bohn, H.G.
Bonaparte, Napoleon
Bonheur, Rosa
Boone, Daniel
Borgmann, Albert
Borrow, George
Bowen, Edward L.

Hughes, Hollie
Hughes, Karen
Hugo-Vidal, Victor
Hundt, Sheila Wall
Hundt Ventrone, Ashley
Hunt, Ray
Hunter, Avalyn
Husher, Helen
Huxley, T. H.
Hyde, Dayton O.

I

Iacono, Christa
Inge, W.R.
Irving, Washington
Irwin, Chris
Isenbart, H. H.
Ishoy, Cindy
Issigoris, Alec
Ives, Charles

J

Jackson, Charles Tenney
Jacobson, Jacob
Jahiel, Jessica
James, Charmayne
James, Melissa
James, Will
James, W. S.
Jeffries, Lambert
Jenkins, MacGregor
Jenkins, Rodney
Jenkins, Sally
Jensen, Johannes
Jerkens, Allen
John Randolph of Roanoke
Johnson, Boris
Johnson, Dirk
Johnson, Marjorie
Johnson, P. G.
Johnson, Samuel
Joiner Jr., Eric J.

Joio, Norman Dello
Jones, Ben
Jonson, Ben
Jorrocks
Josey, Walter
Jovius, Paulus
Joyce, James
Juhasz, Ferenc

K

Kahn, Roger
Kant, Immanual
Karr, Elizabeth
Karr, Mary
Karrasch, Shawna
Keane, Molly
Keating, Allan D.
Keats, John
Kedar, Chen
Keegan, Kevin
Keehn, Sally
Kees, Walter T.
Keith, Toby
Kelleher, Betsy Talcott
Kelley, Dave
Kelly, Carol Wade
Kelly, James
Kennedy Onassis, Jackie
Kennedy, Yates
Kerr, Connie
Ketchum, Hank
Khan, Genghis
Khrushchev, Nikita
Kimball, Cheryl
Kindred, Dave
King, Alan
King Charles V
Kinsey-Warnock, Natalie
Kipling, Rudyard
Klimke, Reiner
Klinkenborg, Verlyn
Knebel, Fletcher
Knibbs, Henry Herbert

Knowles, John Sheridan
Kohanov, Linda
Kopfle, Rolf
Korda, Michael
Kottas-Heldenberg, Arthur
Krane, F. V.
Krantz, Judith
Krone, Julie
Kubrick, Stanley
Kumin, Maxine
Kurtz, Scott
Kyd, Thomas

L

Lamb, Rick
Lame Deer,
Lange, David
Lardner, Ring
Larson, Ann
Lauber, Patricia
Laurel, Stan
Lawler, Jerry
Lawrence, D. H.
Layden, Tim
Lea, Tom
Leacock, Stephen
Lear, Edward
Leclair, Bertrand
Leclerc, George Louis
LeDoux, Chris
Lee, Linsy
Lee, Robert E.
Lefcourt, Blossom
Lehman, Robert
Lemon, Sharon Ralls
Lenehan, Daniel
Lester, Geoff
Lewis, Bonnie
Lewis, C. S.
Lewis, Joe E.
L'Hotte, Alexis
Licart, Commandant Jean

Mortensen, Ky
Morton, Kim
Morton, J.B.
Moser, Barry
Moss, Jerry
Mott, Bill
Mozart, Wolfgang Amadeus
Mullen, C. J. J.
Munchkin, R. W.
Munro, H. H.
Murdoch, Wendy
Murphy, Dennis
Muschamp, Herbert
Musler, Wilhelm
Mutannabi, Al
Myers, David J.
Myles, Alannah

N

Nack, William
Nafzger, Carl A.
Naisbitt, John
Nash, Raymond
Nelson, Willie
Newell, J. Philip
Newton-John, Olivia
Niemus, O Anna
Nietzsche, Friedrich
Noel, George Gordon
Norman
Norton, Caroline Sheridan
Novoselic, Krist
Nusser, Susan

O

O'Hara, John
O'Rourke, P. J.
Oaksey, John
O'Brien, Vincent
O'Connor, Sally
O'Doherty, Ian
O'Flaherty, Liam

Ogilvie, Will H.
O'Hara, Mary
Okakura, Kakuzo
Oliveira, Nuno
Oliver, Alan
Orwell, George
Ours, Dorothy
Overmeyer, Eric
Ovid
Owens, Jesse

P

Packard, Vance
Palmer, Joe
Palmer, Lucinda Prior
Pared
Parelli, Pat
Parker, Dorothy
Parker, Marjorie Hodgson
Parkman, Francis
Pascal, Blaise
Patel, Maya
Paterson, A. B.
Patsolic, Kris
Patterson, Robert
Patton Jr., George S.
Pavia, Audrey
Paxman, Jeremy
Peele, George
Peers, John
Peluso, Theresa
Penn, William
Peoples, David Webb
Pessoa, Nelson
Peyton, KM
Phaeton,
Phayer, Ellie
Phillips, Captain Mark
Philips, Wendell
Pierson, Melissa
Pike, Jimmy
Pinch, Dorothy Henderson

Pittsburgh Phil,
Plantagenet, Edward
Plato
Plutarch
Pluvinel
Podhajsky, Alois
Polo, Marco
Pomerantz, Rich
Pomme Clayton, Sally
Pool, Chris
Pope, Alexander
Porter, Peter
Praed, Winthrop Macworth
Price, Steven D.
Prince, Eleanor F.
Prince Philip
Princess Anne
Prochnow, Herbert V.
Prudent, Katie Monahan

Q

Queen Elizabeth
Queen Elizabeth II
Quigley, Philip
Quinn, Mick

R

Rabelais, François
Rachlis, Eric
Raffi
Ramey, M. Adelia
Randolph, John
Rarey, James
Raswan, Carl
Ray, John
Read, Thomas Buchanan
Reagan, Ronald
Red
Redford, Robert
Reed, Billy
Reekie, Jocelyn
Rees, Lucy

Sterne, Laurence
Stevens, James
Stevenson, Adlai E.
Stewart, Kelly
Stewart, Lindsey
Stewart, Mary
Stone, Christopher
Stone, Sharon
Stout, Nancy
Strickland, Charlene
Sugar, Bert
Summers, Charles
Summers, Rita
Surtees, Robert Smith
Sutherland, Joan
Sweczek, Dr. Thomas
Sweet, Ronnie
Swenson, May
Swift, Jonathan
Swift, Sally
Swinehart, Spring
Synge, John Millington
Syrus, Publicus

T

Tadlock, Annamaria
Tafford, Tyler
Tagg, Barclay
Tagore, Rabindranath
Taylor, Elizabeth
Taylor, Henry
Tellingon-Jones, Linda
Tennyson, Lord Alfred
Tesio
Theodorescu, George
Theroux, Phillis
Thomas, Dylan
Thompson, Helen
Thompson, Jim
Thomson, James
Thoreau, Henry David
Thorn, Stephanie M

Thornicroft, Lady
Thornton, T. D.
Tolkien, J.R.R.
Tolstoy, Leo
Topsel, Edward
Trachtman, Paul
Trollope, Anthony
Trotsky, Leon
Truman, H. S.
Truscot, Jr., Lt. Gen. L.K.
T'sai, Yeh-lu T'su
Tse-Tung, Mao
Tubervil, Tre
Tuchman, Barbara
Turcotte, Lindsay
Turgenv, Ivan
Twain, Mark
Tyler, John

U

Ulph, Owen
Underwood, Tom R.

V

Van Gogh, Vincent
Vanderbilt, Victoria
Vassallo, Russell A.
Vaughn-Thomas, Wynford
Venner, Elsie
Villa, Jose Garcia
Virgil
Vogel, Colin
Von Bismarck, Otto

W

Wadsworth, William P.
Walker, Alice
Walker, Clay
Wall, Maryjean
Wallace, Edgar
Walpole, Horace

Walsh, M. Emmet
Walsh, Ruby
Walsh, Ted
Wanless, Mary
Ward, Greg
Waring, George
Warner, Gertrude Chandler
Watkens, Vernon
Watkins, Eileen
Watman, Max
Wayne, John
Weaver, Jason
Weber, Bob
Weil, Simone
Weinbaum, Dave
Welch, Buster
Welcome, John
Wellseley, Arthur
West, Deputy
West, Jessamyn
West, Karen
West, Phil
West, Rebecca
Westmark, Jan
Whitbread, Bill
White, T. H.
White, William Allen
Whitlam, Gough
Whitman, Walt
Whyte-Melville, George John
Wiescamp, Harry
Wilcox, Ella
Wilhelm II
Williams, Jimmy
Wilson, Diane Lee
Wilson, Earl
Winfrey, Carey
Winn, Matt
Wittgenstein, Ludwig
Wodehouse, P. G.
Wordsworth, William
Wofford, James C.